# The Sailing Adventures

## Of

## La Boatique

### From Lake Erie to New Zealand

*To Karen,*

*Get Started !*

*Susan Foote Wagner*

## Susan Foote Wagner

La Boatique Press

The Sailing Adventures of La Boatique: From Lake Erie to New Zealand

Web site: www.kellnet.com/LaBoatique

Published by La Boatique Press, 47 Kentucky Road, Vermilion, Ohio 44089

Typesetting and composition by the publisher.

Printed in the United States by BookMasters, Inc. Mansfield, Ohio
Book design by the author. Maps by the author.

Publisher's Cataloging-in-Publication
*(Provided by Quality Books, Inc.)*

Wagner, Susan Foote.
    The sailing adventures of La Boatique : from Lake Erie to New Zealand / Susan Foote Wagner. -- 1st ed.
    p.cm.
    ISBN 0-9721580-0-6

    1. Wagner, Susan Foote--Journeys. 2. Wagner, Peter M.--Journeys. 3. La Boatique (Ketch). 4. Voyages and travels. I. Title.

G477.W34 2002                      910.4'5
                                   QBI02-200482

Dedicated to our cruising friend, Barry Dobbs

1942 – 2002

"It doesn't get any better than this."

# World Map

## 1998 — 2002

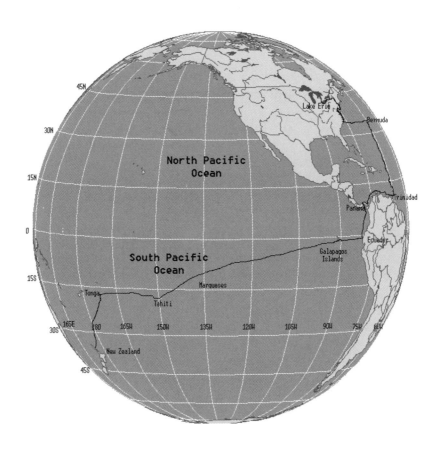

The Sailing Adventures of *La Boatique* from Lake Erie to New Zealand

# Contents

# Tables

# 1998

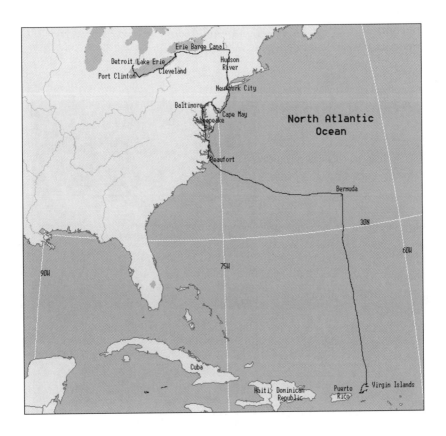

*La Boatique's* travels during 1998 from Lake Erie to the Virgin Islands

1

# The Eastern United States

## Getting Ready to Cruise

In the 1990's less than a dozen people lived year round on their boats along the shoreline of Lake Erie. Pete Wagner was one of those few. Winters were harsh. The ice on the lake became thick enough to drive vehicles out to the islands in the center of the lake. Through the effort of underwater bubblers, the water around Pete's boat was kept nearly ice free.

I spent the 1990's living in a comfortable condo on the shoreline of an inland lake near Toledo,

Pete at the helm of *La Boatique* in Port Clinton, Ohio

Ohio. I met Pete at a Western Lake Erie Sailing Club meeting.

Pete Wagner had dreams of South Sea Islands. He needed more than just the perfect cruising boat and his dreams. He needed a partner. He needed crew. He needed a person with passion for adventure. I was that person. And his dreams were about to come true. We were married in September of 1997 and spent that winter ashore.

*La Boatique*, the elegant burgundy and white 41-foot classic ketch spent the frosty winter of 1998 resting in her teak cradle at

Brands Marina in Port Clinton, Ohio. The blue-water ketch was designed for ocean trade wind sailing but had never even touched a drop of salt water. Instead, for 19 years *La Boatique* sailed the fresh water of the Great Lakes playing the part of a cosmopolitan lady in a small town. After all, Port Clinton was known as the walleye capital. A classic sailing ketch was a rarity in this town known for sport fishing. On May 8th, 1998 *La Boatique* was lifted off the sturdy teak cradle and gently lowered into muddy brown Portage river water. It was time for us to move aboard. Most of our possessions were in the process of being sold. Soon we would no longer have a house or cars. We carefully sorted through our stuff and stowed the items we wanted to take aboard. We had to be picky because compared to a house there was precious little room on the boat. I loved to windsurf and kayak but finding room for both was impractical. So instead of the windsurfer I chose sit-on-top rigid kayaks, one for Pete and one for me.

We were certainly taking a big gamble. We knew we would head for the ocean and then south for the winter. But we weren't sure where we were going or how long we would be gone. Maybe we would not like ocean cruising and would only make our way to Florida. The Caribbean seemed inviting as a destination if we could only cope with the open ocean for days. And then there were Pete's thoughts of far off exotic Tahiti, his ultimate destination. We had lived a frugal life style and put aside a nice cruising kitty, but we did not know how long our kitty would last. We did not know if we would like wandering, a lifestyle of never staying in one place for long.

We went for our first test ride on May 17th. We motored out onto Lake Erie and found we had a loose alternator belt. After our short ride Pete tightened the belt. We weren't cruising, but at least the boat moved.

We had our first trip Memorial weekend. We covered about 175 miles. The weather was windy, cloudy, and cold the entire weekend. For Pete, this was a shakedown cruise. For me, this was practice, practice, practice. On Friday, May 22nd, we sailed from Port Clinton to Middle Bass Island. I was anxious and excited as we raised our sails for the first time since last fall. I had little experience sailing *La Boatique*. My sailing experience was with boats less than half her size. We spent the night anchored off Middle Bass Island.

Saturday morning we wove our way between Middle Bass and North Bass Islands and then raised the sails. A strong east wind on our beam pushed us north to Canada. The boat performed well as we sailed along between 6 and 7 knots. I found that I did not have sea legs. The boat was heeling 15 to 25 degrees along with my stomach. I wasn't seasick, but I did not feel in top shape. I was glad to see the skyline of Leamington, Ontario Canada. Once we got settled at the dock we had dinner with friends, Manfred and Barbara from Amherstburg, Ontario. Manfred and Barbara were also planning a cruise similar to ours. We hoped that someday we might even sail with them over some salty water.

Our Sunday sail back across Lake Erie toward Huron provided us with a lot of practice in sail manipulation when we ran into a storm system. First the mainsail had to be lowered with a south wind, but an hour later it has to be raised as the wind shifted again. We were fortunate the accompanying thunderstorm didn't bother us much, so we were able to stay on course for Huron. Closer to port, we were even able to raise the jib and mizzen, for a nice colorful show prior to docking.

The next day the wind was out of the west. Since that is the direction we wanted to go, toward our home port of Port Clinton, we decided to just go on engine power that day. We felt we were in too much of a hurry to afford all the time it would take for the tacking necessary to make headway.

Back in Port Clinton we noticed that we had a few leaks coming through the deck. The worst ones were right over the navigation station. Worse yet, the leaks were right where I wanted our new fancy computer installed. The leaks had to be plugged. Pete figured that the leaks were coming through the teak deck. Pete had just finished sanding the teak and was getting ready to seal it. Now we had a big decision to make. *La Boatique* is a classic boat with much of its character coming from the teak decks. Do we remove the beautiful teak decks or do we try to repair our problem? Pete studied various resources. Teak decks are hot in the summer. Teak requires much more maintenance than fiberglass. Teak decks often leak. Teak is very heavy and adds nearly 300 pounds to the boat. We needed to make a decision soon. The leaks could ruin the boat.

But we had an even bigger problem. Our condo had been sold. We had to move out in two days.

By early June we were out of the condo and living on the boat. The oven broke, so Pete ordered a part to fix it. We often had a hard time finding our "stuff." Some of it was at my parents, some things found hiding places on the boat, and a few things we may have thrown away by mistake. Our decision was made to remove the teak.

4

Pete and I tore the teak off all by ourselves during the last weekend in May. That was some backbreaking work. The leaks seemed to be gone. What a messy job! The fiberglass deck that was below the teak deck was streaked with green 3M Marine Repair Filler and gray West Systems Epoxy Resin. The deck looked wider without the teak.

For a month *La Boatique* was tied to the dock — no sailing for us. I have read that only 10% of cruising time is spent actually sailing. The remainder of the time is spent with daily living tasks and working on the boat. We hoped that there would come a time soon when we could do nothing and just enjoy life. We had been too busy trying to get ready to cruise.

As the month of June slipped by *La Boatique* began falling apart about as fast as we could fix her. First, the fresh water pump rusted out and began to leak our fresh water from our tanks into the bilge. Pete tried to repair the pump, but the pump was a lost cause. He ended up installing a new more powerful pump. Not even 24 hours after cleaning out all the water Pete found a new leak. This time the leak was diesel fuel. Pete found that the leak was coming from our new fuel purification system. Pete had to take the system apart and add Teflon tape to all the connections. While Pete was checking out his corrections to the fuel cleaning system, he heard a strange noise coming from the engine room. He quickly shut down the engine and found that the alternator belt was loose again. Pete had just tightened the belt only a few weeks ago.

Something more was wrong. Something critical and dangerous was wrong.

The nut that holds the crankshaft pulley backed off the crankshaft. If the pulley had fallen off, our engine could have been ruined. We were very lucky that Pete found and corrected that loose nut.

We still had not painted the deck where we had removed the teak. We were now into the season of the lake bugs, known as mayflies. We could not paint with these 2-inch long bugs covering everything. As fast as we could wash them off they returned.

The end of June came and with it came a hot summer. It was hot, very hot, 98 degrees one day. It was stormy; a tornado one-mile from our slip ripped condos in half and threw boats in the air. It was windy. Somehow with sheer determination we got the boat painted and back together. We were finally able to go sailing. We had a wonderful time on our latest shakedown cruise. Once again we crossed Lake Erie to Canada. This time we sailed northwest near Detroit to LaSalle, Ontario. The round trip was about 100 miles.

The Fourth of July holiday weekend is the highlight of summer on Lake Erie. We untied our lines around noon July 3$^{rd}$. As we motored out the end of the Portage River in Port Clinton we raised the main, the mizzen and then the jib. Alongside were our friends Phil and Sue on *Whitehawk*, a shiny new Passport 41 sailboat. Up went their main, followed by their colorful spinnaker. What a beautiful day! What a beautiful sight! The wind slowly died off. But that didn't bother us because now we were going slow enough to troll for Lake Erie walleye. I reeled in a medium size walleye and then filleted it on the back deck. We enjoyed fresh walleye for dinner anchored off Middle Bass Island.

The next morning we motored southeast to Huron. There was very little wind and what wind we had was on our bow. My Mom and Dad drove four miles to the yacht club to greet us and take me back to their home. While picking raspberries with my Mom in her yard I got stung by a wasp. I swell up a lot whenever I get stung, so I was miserable Saturday night.

Sunday was my family's reunion picnic on the lakeshore. My Uncle Glen and his daughter Renee decided to sail back from Huron to Port Clinton with us. I hadn't seen my Uncle Glen in at least 10 years. I really enjoyed visiting while we cruised back to our homeport. Uncle Glen took the helm for much of the trip home and said that this was the best July 4$^{th}$ holiday weekend he ever had. But poor Renee couldn't keep our big picnic lunch down. We got to see the whole lunch again come out of her mouth. Lunch didn't look as delicious the second time around. It had to be one of her worst holidays.

So much for fun holiday weekend trips... Our focus needed to be on our big trip to the ocean. We ordered a new transmission. We could not get our RPMs up to a high enough speed while in gear. Our exhaust contained black smoke when we tried to motor at the correct speed. Pete had tried 8 different variations of propellers. Finally he decided to investigate the transmission. Our Borg Warner transmission is 2.1 to 1 but it should be 2.57 to 1. We found through talking to other boaters and through the use of an equation that the transmission installed on our boat was designed for a shallow drafting trawler, not a deep-keeled sailboat. We decided to go to 2.91 to 1 so that we could spin our big feathering propeller.

The first item on Monday, July 6th, for Pete was to remove our old transmission. Pete found the removal to be a much easier job than anticipated — maybe too easy. Once the transmission was out, we wished we still had it installed. Now we were stuck at the dock until the new transmission showed up. Instead of sailing, we spent a beautiful summer weekend stowing gear and cleaning the boat. We installed the new transmission on Monday, July 13th. The ratio on the new transmission was 2.9 to 1. Since our old transmission was 2.1 to 1, the new transmission caused the drive shaft and the propeller to spin slower at a given RPM. Now our "big" feathering propeller was not big enough. We could not get enough speed with our current 17-inch diameter 10 1/2-inch pitch propeller.

We lifted the boat on Tuesday to install our spare propeller, which we had pitched to 18-inch diameter 14-inch pitch. Pete still was not satisfied with the results. We decided to order a new 20-inch diameter 15-inch pitch propeller to replace our 17 - 10 ½. The bigger the propeller should be more efficient.

We motored out to South Bass Island on July 17th for the weekend. South Bass Island is Ohio's version of Key West. Instead of Jimmy Buffet, we have Pat Dailey, the "Great Lakes Troubadour." There are no panhandlers on South Bass Island as there are in Key West. The island is beautifully landscaped. Inland there are quaint cottages, vineyards, forests, and a few bed and breakfast hotels. At the bay there is a small town geared up for the tourists. Perry's Monument, standing 352 feet high, the third tallest monument in the United States, dominates the island and the bay. Along the shore are rugged limestone cliffs. We spent hours kayaking along the jagged cliffs squeezing between the giant boulders. We listened to the "varoom" sound as waves washed deep into limestone caves along the shore. After kayaking we walked a mile and a half inland to attend Gary Milson's 50th birthday party. I played sandy, dusty volleyball while Pete visited with friends. Gary had a great party, our kind of fun. Back at the boat that evening *La Boatique* bobbed quietly attached to our mooring ball in the bay. The sun set as we relaxed on the bow of our boat.

Our last of three going away parties was at Brands Marina. The party was potluck on the picnic tables. We reminisced with friends.

Some at the party were planning cruising trips of their own. Gary read a poem that Lori wrote to Pete:

| Poem by Lori Milson |
| --- |
| *You were the first one to greet us when we arrived at Brands.* |
| *From then on we relaxed — Tessa was safe in your hands.* |
| *We've known many sides of you —* |
| *Especially the "feminine" one* |
| *When you wore my bra and pantyhose —* |
| *Without RESERVATION ONE!* |
| *You've been a great help, an advisor, a friend.* |
| *It's hard to accept that our party must end.* |
| *But your ship came in, when Susan stole your heart* |
| *And now you're going cruising and we must be apart.* |
| *We love you — We'll miss you — We hate to see you go.* |
| *The good part is, you'll do everything FIRST* |
| *And tell the rest of us what WE need to know!* |
| Love Gary & Lori & Ches & Jon |

# We are Cruisers

Sunday, July 26th at 3:40 p.m. we cast off our lines from our dock. We both fought back tears as we waved goodbye to our friends on the dock. We were both anxious. We didn't raise the sails because neither of us could think clearly. Were we beginning a great adventure or a great mistake? Lucky for us, we had an easy 2-hour trip to Put-in-Bay on South Bass Island. We had pizza for dinner on shore and then I enjoyed an evening kayak ride.

Monday, July 26th, was a day of superlatives. We had our first sail as cruisers and our first foreign country (Canada) as cruisers. I had the fastest ride ever on *La Boatique*. At 570 feet above sea level, the boat was the highest it would ever be on this ocean bound trip. Maybe we were embarking on a great adventure after all.

*La Boatique* departs Port Clinton on a busy Sunday afternoon

We departed Put-in-Bay with an easy 10-knot wind on our beam. The wind steadily increased. We expected the wind to let up as we approached the Detroit River. But instead, the wind turned to our back and funneled up the river. We were not prepared for the 20 to 25 knot wind since we had all three sails up. We pulled in over half of our roller-furling jib and then later pulled all of it in as we entered the channel. Sailing in these turbulent waters was more like white water rafting with sails instead of paddles. The strong Detroit River current was heading toward us while the 4-foot choppy waves were coming from behind us. Pete was at the helm. Steering was not easy. We were often above our hull speed of 7.7 knots. Once as we surfed down a wave we hit a surprising 8.8 knots! The "white water raft" ride was a thrill, but I was relieved when Pete suggested we take the sails down and motor the rest of the way to La Salle, Ontario.

At La Salle Mariners Yacht Club we met a Danish couple (Tove and Bjorn Dolby) who had sailed all the way from Denmark. Pete was fascinated with the tales of their experiences. We purchased about 30 charts from them covering many places throughout the world (South America, New Zealand, Australia, Cuba, and the U.S.) We worked on the boat and relaxed for a few days.

From La Salle Mariners Yacht Club we sailed southeast to Huron, Ohio for one last visit with my family. While in Huron, Pete learned a lot about refrigeration. He replaced the large front load Norcold with a more efficient Grunert top load refrigerator. This was a big do-it-yourself job and kept Pete very busy for all of the hot muggy days. I spent a lot of time designing and updating my web page. I wanted to be able to share our adventure with anyone who might be interested. I believed that writing a web page was the best way to do it. We also reviewed our supplies. We added some items and removed others.

Gregg Boehler, sailing alone in *Atlantic High* met us in Huron. Gregg was headed for the ocean. *Atlantic High* and *La Boatique* would sail side by side for how long we could not know. Gregg would be our friendly neighbor in a lifestyle that would require a new neighborhood nearly every night.

## Lake Erie

*La Boatique* and *Atlantic High* motor-sailed east to Cleveland on August 11th. This was the city where I was born and spent my early childhood. The busy city was full of old memories. Our new anchor was called The Cleveland Anchor because a man from Cleveland invented it. We used it for the first time in, of all places, Cleveland. We anchored in front of Burke Lakefront Airport. I wanted to use the phone to call some Cleveland friends, so Gregg, Pete, and I used Gregg's dinghy to go ashore. The only place we found to tie up was by the Coast Guard station. I was told that the pay phone was at the Coast Guard dining hall. While I was on

Gregg sails *Atlantic High* on Lake Erie

the phone, Gregg noticed a $1.25 dinner special. We decided to try our luck and see if we would be allowed to eat Coast Guard food. The three of us had a great meal of potato skins and one pound of crab legs for under $12. Our waitress then gave us 2 free passes to the Rock and Roll Hall of Fame across the street.

The next day we had lunch with Kathy and Ed (from NCR where I used to work). We walked the downtown streets. We toured an old submarine on display a short walk from our boat. We had an easy day until a passing boat notified us that the Coast Guard was trying to reach us. We wondered if their call had something to do with our Coast Guard dinner the previous night. When we called the Coast Guard we were told that a package was waiting for us. We could not figure out why the Coast Guard would have anything for us. The only package we were waiting for was a lid for our refrigerator. Mom and Dad had received it and had decided to surprise us by delivering the lid to us in person. I enjoyed visiting with them again. But darkness was closing in and we had to dinghy back to the sailboats.

Pete on the bow of *La Boatique* in Cleveland

Pete woke up about 3:30 a.m. to calm water. The forecast was for a northeast wind. Since we needed to head northeast, we did not want a northeast wind. The best thing for us to do was to get going before the northeast wind came. We woke Gregg and got ready to leave. We found our brand new chain and new Cleveland anchor covered with slimy Cleveland muck. As the electric windless raised the chain and the anchor, Pete poured buckets of water over them. Pete and the deck got spattered with mud. I stayed clear of that mess. The skyline of Cleveland twinkled behind us as we motored away in the quiet of predawn. Hours later, the dark night slowly gave way to pink colors to the east. Soon the sun rose over the Northeast Ohio coastline. We were cruising along at least a knot faster than Gregg. Gregg got even more behind when he changed his fuel filter. At 1 p.m. *La Boatique* was outside Ashtabula with Gregg so far behind that he was out of sight. We all agreed to push on to Erie, Pennsylvania. The northeast wind came and slowed us down. Pete and I took naps. Pete sanded the teak while I polished the bronze. As the shoreline passed by, so did the hours. We dropped anchor at Presque Isle State Park in Erie, Pennsylvania in a small cattail and tree-lined bay. Yesterday we had city lights, planes and trains. Tonight was quiet except for the frogs and crickets. We covered 91 miles in 17 hours. We were tired. We were worried about Gregg and no longer even had radio contact. But we quickly fell asleep.

On August 14th, we were still worried about Gregg, but I could not resist the lure of distant meandering channels that connected with our bay. In the morning while I was having a wonderful kayaking adventure through the wooded swamps of the State Park, the Coast Guard called Pete and told him that Gregg was in Ashtabula with engine trouble. Gregg told the Coast Guard to tell us not to wait for him. Was Gregg giving up on his dream already — after only 4 days? Pete and I felt terrible. We moped about. Pete said that none of the seven sailboat friends planning to cruise south would make it to Buffalo to meet us. Would they have to give up too? We kept an ear to the radio with the hope of hearing something. Pete decided to call the Coast Guard. The Coast Guard tracked Gregg down and found that he was on his way to Erie. Gregg wasn't going to give up. Gregg finally dropped anchor at 10:30 p.m. He had lost all his fuel into the bilge. He replaced his fuel pump because of bad fuel. The threads were stripped and fuel sprayed all over Gregg and the boat. Poor Gregg got sick from the fumes and the fuel.

The next day there was very little rest for Gregg. We took off at 5:30 a.m. for Buffalo. I don't know yet about Gregg, but we sure had a good time. The wind was at our back. We flew the spinnaker. We took sun showers on deck. We enjoyed the last of summer on Lake Erie. What a nice goodbye! Nevertheless I had tears in my eyes because Lake Erie was home and maybe I was not ready to leave home just yet.

Behind us were Lake Erie and our past. In front of us beckoned the city of Buffalo and the state of New York.

# The Erie Canal

On August 16th, my Mom and Dad (Joyce and Harvey Foote) joined us in Buffalo. We spent three days on the job of taking the masts down. The next leg of our adventure was a 338-mile passage on the Erie Canal. The Erie Canal cuts through New York State. We had to take the masts down because this canal contains many fixed bridges with some only 15 feet above the water. Just before the first bridge is a crane at a timeworn place called Wardell's. The crane is used to lift the masts and then set them on the boat. Mom and Dad brought wood, which we used to make tripods to hold the masts.

Mom and Dad headed back home as we looked forward to our first lock in the canal.

The Erie Canal was the nation's first major transportation system. Construction of the Erie Canal began in 1817 and was completed in 1825. It allowed goods to be shipped to and from New York City and the Upper Midwest, starting the migration that created the USA as we know it today. The Erie Canal connects the Great Lakes to the Hudson River. The Hudson River then flows south to the Atlantic Ocean. The canal is 524 miles long and drops nearly 500 feet. The Erie Canal is no longer used to ship goods. Instead, it is used for recreation. There are 57 locks and 16 lift bridges on the Canal System. The lift bridges only lift to 15.5 feet above the level of the canal greatly limiting the size of the boats that can traverse the entire canal system. Canal System locks and lift bridges operate from early May to November. During the winter the canal is drained. The Canal System is operated and maintained by the New York State Canal Corporation, a subsidiary of the New York State Thruway Authority.

On August 18th *La Boatique* and *Atlantic High* began the journey along the Erie Canal. The first day would take us from Buffalo to Middleport, New York. The morning was rainy and cool, but the rest of the day was beautiful. Our first lock was a surprise. Instead of one lock, we went right from the first lock into the second lock. We dropped a long way down — about 65 feet. The canal was narrow and often we were above the surrounding landscape. Pete noticed a man running on a trail beside us. He was running as fast as we were motoring along. We were worried about our new refrigerator. *It* was running *all* the time and using way too much power.

We liked Middleport with its soft green grass and towering trees. We had all of this for free — nice dock, electricity, water, shower, and bathroom. The small town more than met our needs. The laundry was inexpensive and right by the dock. A near-by produce stand had the best sweet corn of the summer. We also enjoyed Hershey's ice cream cones. We worked on the radar and cleaned up the boat. Waiting for the refrigerator repairman to come was a welcome break. The repairman found that our system had too much refrigerant and must have been overcharged at the factory.

*La Boatique* in the Erie Canal waiting for a lock to open

August 20$^{th}$ was a long day (and night). We went through Rochester and finally stopped at Fairport at 9:45 p.m. Fairport had signs reporting a charge of $5 to dock, but we didn't see anyone collecting money nor any place to pay. We left Fairport and headed east at 9:30 a.m. the next morning. We had another beautiful day with perfect weather. Not much was left of civilization. We were deep in the woods. We stopped for the day at a lock east of Clyde at 4:15 p.m. This was the place to be to get away from everyone. There was the forest, the lock, the canal and our two boats.

August 22$^{nd}$ was a winding scenic cruise on a narrow river. Gregg said he was hungry for pizza, so I got out some yeast and flour and made pizza dough as we traveled along. The refrigerator was working so well that we were freezing all our food. We kept setting the gauge warmer and warmer. We had pizza for dinner at the lock before Brewerton. We were ahead of our schedule.

In Brewerton, New York, we stopped at Ess-Kay Yards for fuel — $1.15 for diesel. Then we crossed the open expanse of Oneida Lake. Small boats were sailing in the gentle breeze. But not us, our mast was still down and strapped to the wooden tripods. Sunday afternoon we spent at Sylvan Beach. Sylvan Beach has a long sandy beach and an old-time amusement park. The only things we found worthwhile at the park were chicken wings and "fried dough." The dock next to the park was free which is, of course, where we moored.

We left Sylvan Beach early — 7:20 a.m. While I steered the boat through the canal, Pete trimmed out the top of our new refrigerator with black and white marbleized tile.

Little Falls was another great stopping place — free dock, showers, pavilion, and electricity. The river running next to the canal splashes over large boulders making the "little falls." The grocery was well stocked, but most stores closed at 5 p.m. We were tracking the hurricanes heading toward the East Coast with some concern. Each day along the canal brought us closer to the Atlantic Ocean.

On August 25$^{th}$ we motored on from Little Falls to Amsterdam, New York. We enjoyed the views of rocky rugged cliffs and old towns. We glided along listening to tranquil piano solos by Jim Schroeder from Toledo, Ohio, on our CD. I sewed a pouch for my computer parts while Pete steered the boat. I also steered and was able to practice docking through many of the locks.

We had been on the canal for over one week. I was finally comfortable – well, almost, managing the boat through the locks. I steered the boat through all 10 locks in one day with very little screaming from Pete. Often the canal joined various rivers. One portion of the river had rock cliff walls. We wove through rock boulders large enough to be islands. The depth dropped 30 feet. This was rugged terrain, similar to the North Channel in Northern Lake Huron. I noticed Gregg wander just outside the channel. I blew our horn to warn him, but he didn't hear it. He saw the channel marker and turned hard, too late!

Crash! *Atlantic High* was high all right!

The boat bounced up on a rock and then dropped back into deep water. Gregg could not find any major damage, so we carefully continued.

Greg worked from aloft while Pete worked from below to step the mizzenmast. The hand-operated crane used to raise the mast is in the foreground.

The locks dropped us over 250 feet on this day. The last five locks were one after the other and took us two hours of hot sweaty work. The Erie Canal had become the familiar. Now just as I was used to the canal and the locks, they were gone. We tied up near Albany in Waterford, New York where Ray and Dari Munger (from Albany) delivered our mail that had been sent to them from Ohio.

# The Hudson River

August 27th was a big day for *La Boatique* and *Atlantic High*. We entered the Hudson River. We logged 1000 miles since leaving Port Clinton, Ohio.

Most important of all, we raised the masts!

Gregg, Pete and I used a hand-operated crane at Castleton Boat Club. The crane was very easy to operate because it had a low gear ratio. I operated the crane while Pete and Gregg set the masts in place.

The next day we got *La Boatique* ready to sail.

*La Boatique* was ready for sailing, but on August 29th, there was no wind. So, we motored down the Hudson. We anchored for the night at Kingston, NY with 36 swans, 2 great blue herons, ducks, and a sunset view of the Catskill Mountains.

We anchored next to the Statue of Liberty

The next day we stopped early in the afternoon. Pete, Gregg, and I crowded into our dinghy and motored across the busy Hudson River to visit West Point Academy. We were just three more Sunday afternoon tourists. But we were the only ones that had arrived by boat.

On August 31$^{st}$ the DOW dropped over 500 points, and where were we? We were in New York watching Wall Street from the Hudson River. It was a terrible day for our investments, but a wonderful day to be out on the water. We anchored for the night next to the Statue of Liberty. The anchorage was shallow and the boat rocked from the ferryboats going by, but the view of the New York skyline was fabulous.

# The Atlantic Ocean

We motored to the mouth of the Hudson on September 1$^{st}$ and anchored for the night at Sandy Hook (Atlantic Highlands, New Jersey). While there, Gregg met another single-handed sailor, Carol Kingsmore, on a 31-foot boat named *Marna*. Carol was planning to sail to Atlantic City and so were we. So now we had three boats heading south. Gregg checked the weather forecast. The forecast called for great conditions early in the day, but the weather was supposed to deteriorate later in the day. We decided to leave at 4 a.m. in order to go out with the tide and get the best weather.

We departed on schedule using the radar to help us through the jumble of channel markers, tugs, barges, and fishing boats. One tug pushing a barge was heading right toward us. The tug was moving fast, we were moving slow, and we had some confusion figuring out how to get out of his way. Pete turned hard to port about the time the tug blinded us with its huge spotlight. The tug and barge plowed through our little flotilla, behind *La Boatique* and in front of our companion boats, *Atlantic High* and *Marna*. At least the water was calm, except for the tug wake. We headed out into the Atlantic with easy conditions. The wind could have been more on the beam, but we were still able to sail. I was not used to the big swells. For a few hours, I felt a little bit of motion sickness. Pete sanded and oiled the teak cap rail while I polished a bronze port. Our first day in the Atlantic was starting out easy. In the afternoon the wind went from 10 to 15 to 20 knots. Compared to *Atlantic High* and *Marna*, *La Boatique* was big and fast and could easily handle the wind. We went from trailing the other two boats to passing them up. Soon they were out of sight behind us. The rollers went away and were replaced by 5-

foot choppy seas. *La Boatique* easily cut through the waves, but the salt spray picked up by the wind was making everything sticky. This was a new annoyance for us. The fresh water spray of Lake Erie never did that. We dropped anchor in Atlantic City about 5 p.m. The anchorage was difficult because the current and the wind were both strong. *La Boatique* was turning around in circles. We were concerned that we would bump another boat. The wind got stronger. Carol and Gregg, in much smaller boats, were not having any fun out in the Atlantic. We pulled up anchor and decided to spend the night securely docked at Harrah's Casino. Gregg and then finally Carol arrived. Both had a rough time at the end of their trips. Entering the Atlantic City Harbor was difficult for them since the tide was going out and the wind was blowing surf in.

We walked the Boardwalk in Atlantic City and rode the Jitney bus. We wandered through a few casinos but we did not play any games.

On September 4th we had our first nice sail since home on Lake Erie. We sailed from Atlantic City to Cape May, New Jersey. We had steady wind above 20 knots with 8-foot choppy seas. We hit a speed of 8.2 knots in a 25-knot gust. The Sailing may have been fun but getting the sails down was not. The bowsprit was crashing in the waves while Pete pulled the sails down. Rarely would we see big waves like these in Ohio. We realized that we would need to make lowering the sails an easier process.

Cape May was a tourist town and here we were on one of their busiest days of the year. We saw the Victorian fishing town the way it should be seen, from a bicycle. Pete, Carol, Gregg, and I biked from 10 a.m. until 5 p.m. with a break for lunch and a few walks along various beaches. We stopped by a farm and bought some produce. We watched families catch flounder from the beach. We bought flounder for dinner from the fish market. Pete grilled the fresh caught flounder while I prepared the butternut squash I bought from a local farmer's garden. We watched the full moon rise while we ate our delicious dinner.

# The Chesapeake Bay Area

We seemed to be on a circle tour of New Jersey. On September 6th we completed our New Jersey visit and ended the day in Chesapeake City, Delaware. We started the day at 5:30 a.m. going through the Cape May Canal. Then we sailed around the southern end of New Jersey up through the Delaware Bay. We saw our first dolphins. We then turned west across Northern Delaware through the Chesapeake and Delaware Canal. We dropped anchor in a bay filled with other boaters enjoying the holiday weekend. I kayaked into a quiet tidal marsh inhabited by wildlife. What a great day!

September 7th was an adrenaline day. We started the day with a fuel dock crash and ended the day with stormy nasty weather on Chesapeake Bay. The day started out with heavy winds. The tidal current was strong in the C&D Canal. We were tied to the fuel dock at Schaefer's Marina. Pete and I were both at the stern of the boat when an inexperienced gas dock attendant tried to loosen up the bowline so that we could leave the gas dock. Once the line was loose, he could not hold on and the wind blew the bow of *La Boatique* toward the channel. Since two stern lines were still firmly attached, we were in big trouble. By the time Pete got to the helm, *La Boatique* had already turned around. In another second our dinghy and davits were wedged against the dock while the port side of our boat was rubbing hard against a large houseboat that was moored behind us. The tide would not turn for another two hours. I wondered how we were going to get out of this mess. Pete found a way. He cut our favorite mooring line and fended off the other boat while I powered out into the channel. The damage was slight.

# A Month in Baltimore

*La Boatique* needed tender loving care after 1387 miles. We decided to get a slip at Anchorage Marina in Baltimore for a month. We were very satisfied with Anchorage Marina. It was a great place to wait out the hurricane season. The floating slips were sturdy and wide. Nice laundry facilities were available at the Marina. The grocery store was across the street. West Marine was only a block away. Many restaurants were close by. Mom and Dad (Harvey and Joyce Foote) drove from Ohio and visited with us for a week. One of our favorite activities with Mom and Dad was riding the water taxis. For $3.50 we traveled all over Baltimore harbor. We were thankful that cruisers like Frank and Joanne Finney recommended this location. On the other hand, Baltimore had its drawbacks. We had never seen so much trash floating in the water. The water was often covered with an oily film. The air was heavy with pollution. When we got rain the boat got dirty. The black soot left on the boat was difficult to remove. Sirens blared day and night. One thing nice about living on a boat, when we got tired of the neighborhood we could easily move on.

Gregg on *Atlantic High* also stayed at Anchorage Marina. Gregg planned to be in the Virgin Islands by November but at this time we did not know that he would have to turn back and not venture to the Caribbean Islands. Barb and Manfred Albrecht from the boat *St. Pauli* had finally caught up with us. (We had left them in La Salle, Ontario in July.) Bob and Viviane Fleury from Laval, Quebec on the boat *Varuna* also had a chance to find us. We had been friends with Bob and Viviane over e-mail but had never met in person. Carol Kingsmore from the boat *Marna* also decided to stay there. We were beginning to have an assortment of cruising friends. We were beginning to feel a part of the cruising neighborhood. Many friends from Ohio drove by car to the Annapolis Boat Show. This show was one of the largest boat shows in the world. Old friends from Ohio, Eric and Susan Kirker, stayed with us on *La Boatique* during the time the boat show was running.

Is it possible to take a vacation from a major vacation? We certainly were taking a break from our travels, but not from being busy. Here is a list of some of our work involved with continuing the cruising lifestyle:

---

**Cruising Tasks**

1. Washed the salt spay off the boat

2. Fixed the damage caused by the boat accident at Schaefer's Marina

3. Sanded the teak trim

4. Layered 4 to 6 coats of Deks Olje on the teak trim

5. Polished the stainless steel trim

6. Polished bronze

7. Reversed the back stay for better reception on the single side band

8. Practiced receiving weather and other information using the single side band

9. Replaced a worn-out exhaust hose

10. Replaced a worn-out head hose

---

11. Replaced the jib sheet lines

12. Replaced the 12 volt house batteries

13. Had the life raft repackaged in Annapolis at Air Works

14. Had a tear in the mainsail repaired by North Sails in Annapolis

15. Took unneeded items to a consignment shop

16. Visited John Hopkins World Travel Clinic to get our inoculations

17. Had a dodger made by Atlantic Custom Canvas

18. Painted the golden dragons on the bow of the boat

19. Installed a boat alarm

20. Cleaned the dinghy

21. Replenished supplies

22. Re-stowed and reviewed gear

23. Studied charts and cruising guides in order to define the next portion of our trip

24. Added a salt water wash-down (for washing off the anchor)

25. Replaced the gas tank in the dinghy motor because it leaked and was recalled

On October 12th *La Boatique* finally moved, but she might have been better off staying where she was. Pete often gets the well-deserved reputation of being highly competent. On this day, however, he was anxious and incompetent. When he gets hyper, I get bothered and then I also start making mistakes. We had the boat lifted out of the water at Tidewater Marine. The Tidewater people were real professionals. We weren't. I jammed my finger while trying to catch a line. Pete drilled four holes in the bottom of the boat for the Dynaplate, but the holes were in the wrong place. Then Pete removed two of the batteries to make more room to work and spilled battery acid. To top off our rotten day, we installed an expensive Prowell Feathering Sailprop that performed worse than our old inexpensive fixed prop. Now we have got to get the propeller pitch changed. The boat will have to be pulled out again October 14th at Holiday Point Marina in Selby Bay, Maryland.

We had not cruised for over a month. Would we remember how? We started off easily. After an uneventful motor trip to Selby Bay, we dropped the hook on October 13th. Adventure and excitement seemed to come when we least expected it. The evening was so boring that Pete fell asleep on the couch soon after 7 p.m. At 8:30, I was reading in bed and Pete was snoring next to me. The wind began to whistle through the rigging. Where did this come from? It wasn't supposed to be windy. The lights on the shoreline were moving by outside the porthole. Were we moving or were we just swinging around in the wind? I watched the shoreline carefully. We didn't seem to be dragging our anchor. I laid down and closed my eyes. I was tired.

"Tick." That sounded like the kayak hitting the stern of the boat. I looked out the porthole. I touched Pete and said, "I don't remember that boat next to us."

Pete said "What?" and flew out of bed leaving his glasses behind.

We were sliding toward the boat I saw. We ran to the cockpit in our pajamas. We were filled with nervous tension.

Pete shouted, "Turn on the engine. Turn on the windless so that we can raise the anchor."

I turned the key and the engine started right up.

Pete was on the bow. Pete said, "Get going, we are going to hit that boat!"

I was confused. What boat? Go where? I could not see a thing outside the cockpit. The anchor light was on in the cockpit and shining right in my eyes. The light was reflecting off the plastic windows surrounding me. I wondered if I should put the engine in gear or try to find out how to stop the light from blinding me? There was not enough time. I put the engine in forward idle. I then unplugged the light. My eyes adjusted. Oh, that boat was close! I drove a little faster.

Pete said, "Watch out for *St. Pauli*."

I didn't want to hit that boat either. I soon saw *St. Pauli*. I found a good spot to idle between the two boats. I finally could see the surroundings clearly. I was shaking. I was cold.

Pete said, "I can't see a thing. My glasses are down below."

Thank goodness he saw those two boats. We re-anchored as the rain started followed by the lightening.

I thought how could our great Cleveland Anchor let us down.

Just then Pete said, "We can't fault our Cleveland Anchor. I should have let out more scope. We never backed down to set the hook. I was stupid. " We promised to be more careful anchoring from now on.

On October 14th, we lifted *La Boatique* twice out of the water to adjust the Prowell feathering propeller. We found that the prop performed well under sail, but slowed us down nearly a knot under motor. The propeller was a disappointment.

The morning of October 15th we set sail for Solomons Island, Maryland. We had a broad reach with the main, mizzen, and jib all up. There were over 20 boats behind us and not a single one was able to pass us while under sail. Wow, were we fast! What a fun day!

We set out a crab trap on October 16th and caught two crabs for dinner.

Pete catches his first crab

On October 17$^{th}$ we motor-sailed from Solomons Island to Irvington Marina in Irvington, Virginia. Irvington Marina is where our masts were made two years ago. We were having our rigging carefully reviewed. Barb and Manfred were with us. Barb and I enjoyed a kayak ride up the river tributaries. We saw widely spaced large beautiful homes that were nestled in the forests with expensive yachts moored near each home.

Pete and I caught lots of crabs in our crab trap for dinner on October 18$^{th}$. After having a great time, we left Irvington Marina and sailed on to Norfolk, Virginia, on October 20$^{th}$. The wind at times was over 20 knots and the waves were rough. We made a bad jibe and broke our main traveler. Thank goodness we had our rigid boom vang so that no other damage was done. Pete fixed the traveler the next day.

On October 21$^{st}$, both *La Boatique* and *St. Pauli* made it to the Intracoastal Waterway (ICW), but bridge repairs caused us to sit in Norfolk. Those bridge repairs caused a big backlog of boats. We wanted to beat the crowd, so on October 22$^{nd}$ we left the anchorage at 5:45 a.m. to get through the first bridge before it closed at 6:30 a.m. The next scheduled opening for that bridge was after 8 a.m. Then a bridge further south held us up from 7:50 until 9 a.m. The crowd of boats caught up with us while we waited for the 9 a.m. opening. The day was cold and nasty. We anchored along the ICW in North Carolina. On October 23$^{rd}$ we continued on the ICW. What a crowd of boats going south! We saw large motor yachts and all kinds of sailboats. We shared the great bridge lock with 21 other boats. We were packed in as tight as could be.

On October 24$^{th}$ and 25$^{th}$ we anchored in a bay in the town of Belhaven, North Carolina. We had a short dinghy ride to River Forest Manor, a lovely southern mansion. It is used as an old south country inn and marina. The Sunday brunch was a great southern meal. Barb and I used the mansion's laundry building to wash our clothes after the inn's staff finished with the laundry from the inn.

Barb and Sue get the laundry done at River Forest Manor in Belhaven, North Carolina.

On October 26th we arrived in Oriental, North Carolina. We preferred the convenience of the city dock. But the limit at the city dock was two consecutive days. When we weren't at the city dock, we were at anchor near by. While in Oriental we prepared the boat for a trip to the Virgin Islands.

*St. Pauli* and *La Boatique* at the city dock in Oriental, North Carolina

# The Atlantic Ocean and Bermuda

It seemed to me that our last twelve hours in Oriental were an omen. Not since we left home in Ohio did we have so many people make a special effort to say goodbye. Ohio friends Ted and Kathy Algren cooked us a delicious chili dinner at their vacation condo. As we strolled back to the boat I commented to Pete that the dinner would probably be our last meal in a home on the U.S mainland for a long time. The next morning former Ohioans, Gary and Alice Johnston, along with a collection of others waved goodbye as we cast our lines off the city dock. We then motored along the ICW to Beaufort, North Carolina.

We had planned to wait at Beaufort for a few days for a good off-shore sailing weather window. We found that the weather window was now and the sooner we left the better. But were we ready and prepared for possibly twelve days at sea? Could we convince Manfred, Barbara, and their extra passenger, Ron, to leave tomorrow? When we presented the weather forecast to them, they also realized that our ocean trip was now or never. One predicted cold front after another would force us to continue on the ICW if we didn't leave in the next 24 hours. The weather window for a trip like this is critical. For example, the boats only a few days ahead of us got caught in tropical storm Mitch. At least one boat had to be abandoned in the near hurricane force conditions. We scrambled to prepare for this major adventure.

### The Gulf Stream

On the morning of November 8th, we left the crowded ICW and entered the wide-open Atlantic Ocean. We were heading for the Gulf Stream and needed to cross it as soon and as fast as possible. I really wanted to enter the Gulf Stream during the daylight because I had been told that I might actually see the difference in the water. However, we entered the Gulf Stream right after dark. *La Boatique* rocked and rolled. We crossed the Gulf Stream with a light north wind. We had been told not to cross the Gulf Stream with a north wind because opposing wind and current cause nasty waves. Since the wind was light, we didn't have walls of water, but the ride was very uncomfortable. I considered taking some Dramamine. Instead, I concentrated on not throwing up. I wasn't much help for Pete.

Monday arrived with very little wind from our stern. We motored nearly the entire day. The boat rocked and rolled along with my stomach. I was not throwing up, but I could eat very little food. We were using too much fuel. Instead of sailing on to the Virgin Islands, we decided to head to Bermuda.

### Deep Sea Fishing

Tuesday was a totally different day. The weather could not have been nicer. *La Boatique* was sailing along and providing a comfortable ride. I was even getting hungry. Pete got out a Lake Erie deep diving lure that my Mom had found on the beach in front of her home in Vermilion, Ohio. Zing! Minutes later we had a strike. We were deep-sea fishing and fighting our fish. While I ran below to get the camera, the colorful fish jumped four feet out of the water. Pete thought he won the battle when he got the fish on board the aft deck. The large fish got loose and flipped all over trying to get away. Pete was chasing after it with the gaff hook. The fish found a hiding place under the kayak (tied to the fife rail). The fish was winning. One more flip and it would be over the rail and back in the ocean. Pete tried a new tactic. Forget the gaff, he reached for the fish with his bare hands. He caught the fish by the tail. But the fish still was fighting. Blood from the fish was sprayed all over Pete and the stern of the boat. As I tried to snap some pictures, the fish finally gave up. We caught a 32-inch long dolphin fish (mahi-mahi fish). I got out our knives and sliced into the fish. Soon the fresh meat was sizzling in our cast iron pan. We enjoyed our meal on deck in the sunshine.

Tuesday night Pete was becoming exhausted from lack of sleep. By Wednesday morning, he was exhausted and I was not much better. We both decided to sleep as much as possible for the next 24 hours. Pete had just read, "Bermuda is like a paradise but one has to go through purgatory to get there." Even though the weather was great, we were too tired to have fun. We let autopilot sail the boat as we tried to get rest. This was a "purgatory" day.

Pete holds our first ocean fish.

We had covered over 2000 miles since leaving home.

By Thursday, November 12th, we were both rested and the weather was still perfect. I made a large omelet for breakfast. I then took a refreshing shower. I was feeling good. A school of dolphins swam beside us. It seemed to me that once they knew we were watching, they decided to put on a show. They danced around the boat and one even jumped straight up in the air clear out of the water. Wow, our own private dolphin show! Then, we watched the flying fish show.

Soon after dark we could see the lights of Bermuda on the horizon. The bright lights deceived us into believing that a safe harbor was a few hours away. During the night, far behind us, lightning flashed illuminating storm clouds. In front of us were dangerous reefs. We did not want to be near the reefs during a storm. We were hoping to enter Bermuda at dawn but with the storms behind us we decided to negotiate the reefs and enter the harbor during the dark night. We had been unable to find a good Bermuda chart before we left the East Coast, so for five tense hours we mostly used our cruising guide and got in late that night. Even with the professional help of Bermuda Harbor Radio we had a very hard time finding the correct channel through the coral reefs.

# Bermuda

We decided to treat the boat and ourselves by staying at St. George's Dinghy and Sports Club in Bermuda for 6 or 7 days. The temperature was in the 70's and 80's.

We found Bermuda to have perfect weather. The island and bays were beautiful, colorful and very clean. I was so glad we were able to spend time there. I was able to take two walks to some of Bermuda's most beautiful beaches. One walk was with Barbara from *St. Pauli* while the other walk was with Marge from *Dream Weaver*. Joe and Marge on *Dream Weaver* were tied next to us at the dock. We did not know that we would see *Dream Weaver* again and again in the Eastern Caribbean. While Pete installed a fuel purification system on *Dream Weaver* I paddled along on a kayak trip through the bay. I was surprised to find Bermuda to be not one round island but many small slender islands linked by bridges. Between the islands are bright blue bays filled with tropical fish and corals. The only problem I could find with Bermuda was extremely expensive food.

Winter was coming. We had to move soon. As we contemplated our departure, Julius and Sally on *Argonauta* arrived. We barely said a word to this unfamiliar couple from New York. We had no way of knowing we would depend on them when Pete got a hernia followed by kidney stones. They had no way of knowing they would depend on Pete to keep their diesel engine running. None of us knew that this chance meeting would blossom into a lasting friendship.

# Seven days and nights alone on the Atlantic Ocean

On November 18th a cold front arrived bringing north winds. It was time for us to head south. We sailed away with three other boats — *St. Pauli, Glide*, and *Mecca*.

This adventure brought the unexpected.

I expected that we would be close to at least one of these boats for the trip. But out in the ocean we never saw any of them again. We were alone — no television, no radio, no phone, no mail, no land, and no other people. I expected to be a little sea sick at the beginning and then be fine. However, I felt great the first day, pretty good the second day and awful the third day.

I did find a routine. If I could, every two or three hours I would use our GPS (Global Positioning System) and our Yeoman Sport (electronic chart plotter) to mark our progress. I felt as if we were accomplishing something as my pencil line traveled down the chart.

Our first two days out had good conditions with *La Boatique* sailing along on a beam reach, a very comfortable ride. But dark clouds were on the horizon. Our third day, November 21st, was tough on me. Squalls, large waves, and strong gusty winds came during the night. Neither of us got much sleep. Imagine trying to sleep on a roller coaster – not an easy task.

As the sun rose among even more dark clouds, I felt weak and tired. I had no appetite, but I was very thirsty. Simple tasks were a great effort. For example, I needed to lie down and rest after using the bathroom. As the boat was on its roller coaster ride, I climbed down the companionway steps grabbing handholds to get through the galley and the master stateroom. Then came the toughest part, the head (bathroom). I could not get my clothes on and off without falling into something. Afterward, as I lie down in the cockpit, a flying fish trapped in the scupper died. If the fish had been somewhat smaller he could have ridden out through the scupper along with the salt water flowing off the deck. I did not have the energy to push him off the boat. I could barely lift my head high enough out of the cockpit to see the sun set.

Night came. Pete needed sleep. I needed to force myself to be on watch. As Pete tried to sleep, I tried to stay on a routine. I would go below and study the radar screen. I tried to see if I could find the other three sailboats. I couldn't. Sometimes I saw squalls on the screen. Sometimes I saw merchant ships. Usually the screen was blank for 24 miles around us. Then I climbed the companionway stairs and studied the horizon for storms or ships. The sky was mostly clear of clouds. Next I watched the stars. There are so many more stars to be seen in such a dark place. I saw lots of shooting stars. One night I saw two stars that seemed to explode and then disappear. After stargazing I checked the instruments — oil pressure, RPMs, water temperature, boat speed, wind speed, and wind direction. Our Navico 8000 Autopilot (Clyde) was steering. Sometimes I would adjust the course a little. Once in a while I would adjust the mainsail or the jib. Next I would lie back and rest for ten minutes. Then I would start the routine again. I counted the hours as they slowly passed by. I tried to give Pete three hours of undisturbed sleep. Rarely did he get it.

The hours passed by. The days passed by. The weather got better. I got better.

About sunset every evening we would listen to Herb Hilgenberg provide each and every boat with a weather forecast for that boat's location. We both were excited when he would mention *St. Pauli* or *La Boatique*. We would provide our latitude, longitude, and current weather. Then, like a fortuneteller, Herb would tell us whether tomorrow would be stormy, windy, or nice. Form Herb's single side band radio show we realized that every day our distance from *St. Pauli* grew. *St. Pauli* headed way east of the rhumb line while we decided to stay on course. We were getting way ahead of them.

On Monday, November 23$^{rd}$, we seemed to have a charmed day. There were squalls all around, but we stayed in sunshine and nice wind. The waves began to build as the sun set on enormous thunderheads. We assumed the storms would not bother us. They would dissipate. Wouldn't they? We double reefed the main as usual for nighttime conditions.

# The Rogue Wave

The first storm arrived soon after dark. There was little time between the first and the second. The wind blew and the waves built but *La Boatique* cut through the waves at speeds above 7 knots. We were making great progress south. Pete and Clyde (autopilot) took turns steering. Near midnight I was at the helm adjusting Clyde when necessary. The wind was at gale force with gusts coming from various directions. We no longer were cutting through the waves. The confused seas were tossing us about. Salt water sprayed from stem to stern but we stayed dry under the dodger, bimini, and side curtains. We wore life jackets and harnesses. We were tethered to the boat so that we couldn't be washed overboard.

Pete looked up to see a wall of water towering above us. I saw him put his head between his knees. Why? I did not see the rogue wave. Pete figured there would be little left on deck after this wave.

Whoom!

*La Boatique* seemed to be under water. First to take the water was the mainsail. Water shot through every crack and crevice of the dodger and bimini. The water tumbled off the back of the bimini and right on my head and down my back. I immediately began to shiver more from fear than from being doused. Water was filling the cockpit and running down the stairs into the cabin. But by now we were back on top of the water and out of the rogue wave. *La Boatique* seemed as concerned and surprised as we were. She about slowed to a stop as she tried to rid herself of the water. Minutes seemed to go by as the water flowed out of everything and then out the scuppers. We were not going as fast as before. We seemed low in the water. Pete checked the bilge — no water. We inserted the hatch boards to protect the cabin from further giant waves. A few other big waves came that splashed on the bimini top. The storm continued off and on through the night. However, there were no more rogue waves.

# The Caribbean

On Tuesday, November 24th, we sailed on toward the Virgin Islands. The islands glittered in front of us at night. We were filled with anxious anticipation. We were six miles off the island of Anegada when the depth sounder repeatedly went off. Anegada has a notorious reputation for claiming more ships than any other Caribbean Island. It was supposed to be deep where we were. The water was strangely calm — no ocean swell.

"Beep beep." The alarm went off again and again. Twenty feet. Five feet. Two feet! We shined a spotlight on the water and all we saw was bright turquoise, not deep blue. Enough of this, we wanted to get back to the deep ocean. But how? We called the coast guard. They reported that we were in deep water. We headed north back out into the ocean.

We had enough of Anegada and headed toward Jost Van Dyke. The approach was easy once daylight arrived.

We dropped anchor at Jost Van Dyke, British Virgin Islands, at 10:30 a.m. November 25th. We had made it to paradise but all we wanted was sleep.

*La Boatique* anchored in the bay at Jost Van Dyke, British Virgin Islands. *La Boatique* is the boat with two masts in the foreground.

On Thanksgiving Day while Pete was caulking the chain plates, a dolphin came next to the boat. It sure would be neat to swim with the dolphins. But was it safe? There was a guy swimming from boat to boat in the anchorage. Soon he and the dolphin were swimming together. Once other boaters saw this, they jumped into the water. I thought the dolphin would leave, but he stayed and swam with all the people. We wished then that we'd jumped in to swim with the dolphin while he was near our boat.

Later, we savored a gourmet turkey dinner on a picnic table under a palm tree at a great place called Foxy's.

# U.S. Virgin Islands

On Saturday we went to St. Thomas in the U.S. Virgin Islands. We needed stuff for future adventures. St. Thomas was supposed to be a good place to re-supply. We also needed to get our mail that had been forwarded to us.

We took a break from high seas adventures for a month. We spent weeks anchored next to the cruise ships in Charlotte Amalie, St. Thomas. There was plenty of action to see in the harbor — the cruise ships, seaplanes, charter boats, party boats, luxury yachts, and frigate birds diving for fish. However, the dinghy dock was in an unsafe neighborhood. Many people warned us that we should not walk the neighborhood at night. But, during the daylight hours, I felt fairly safe walking the streets alone.

We relaxed. I read <u>Five against the Sea</u> given to me by my cousin Harry Bratton before we left Ohio. Our mail finally showed up December 16th. We had not seen mail for about 2 months. We were thankful for all the news and I especially enjoyed comments I received concerning the website I was writing.

We found out that Gregg from *Atlantic High* was in Norfolk, Virginia. He had started out into the Pacific but then headed back to the safety of the coastline. We located Barb and Manfred by using Virgin Islands Radio. The VI Radio tower was atop the highest peak and reached all over the Virgin Islands. Once Barb and Manfred knew where we were they decided to anchor next to us.

J Boats racing in St. Thomas, U.S. Virgin Islands

We became tourists enjoying the island. We took a gypsy bus ride for $1 to Red Hook where we visited with John Hayes on *Stardust II* from our home port of Port Clinton, Ohio. The gypsy busses were pickup trucks with benches and a canopy. We shopped at various stores and markets. We ate out every few days, but nothing fancy. We watched the top-ranking sailboat racers in the world compete on J boats. What a show!

We worked on the boat. We re-bedded the stanchions to try to stop some leaks. We polished the stainless steel. Pete oiled the teak. Pete finished installing the water maker and we used it nearly every day to add fresh water to our tanks. We got our power from our solar panels, wind generator, and the diesel engine.

# Lost in Red Hook

On December 14th Pete, Barb, Manfred, and I took the gypsy bus to Red Hook. *La Boatique's* mainsail was at the sail maker's shop there and we wanted to review the progress so far. After meeting with the sail maker we walked across the street to Duffy's Love Shack for some fun coconut tropical drinks. Barb and Manfred then headed toward the hardware store. Pete decided to follow them while I mentioned to Pete that I would meet him at the grocery store. I shopped slowly looking over items in every isle. I wondered what could be taking them so long at the hardware store. I decided to buy some sesame oil.

I started to worry. Maybe they decided to go to a different store. The hardware store and the grocery store were at opposite ends of the same strip shopping center. I decided to walk back to the hardware store looking in each of the other stores along the way. When I got to the hardware store I described Pete to the store clerk. Yes he was there, but he left long ago. I walked the strip mall again. They weren't in any of the stores in the mall.

Where were they?

I walked down the street. There was another grocery store. They had to walk right past the grocery where I was to get to this second store. They weren't there either. Where could they be? I asked around town.

The guard at the shopping center…No.

The marine supply store…No.

The bus stop…No.

Duffy's Love Shack…No.

The other end of town…No.

The strip mall again…No.

The second grocery again…No.

I know. They must have gone to John Hayes' boat.

There was John. No, he had not seen Pete.

Pete should certainly have been looking for me by now. I looked up to see the tropical sun set behind a dark cloud. The volcanic peaks were not much below the cloud. It would be dark in about an hour.

Should I get a taxi and return to the boat alone? No. I would look some more.

It started to get dark.

"Taxi?"… "Want a ride?" Why is it that the only taxis out now are lone black guys in dark vans? What happened to the open gypsy busses full of people?

I began to feel like easy prey for any local hunter. I wanted to get off the street.

I returned again to the marina. I saw John. I felt much safer. John and I looked everywhere. They were not in Red Hook.

Did they leave me and go back to the boat?

The streets were too dangerous now for me to get back alone. John decided to accompany me all the way back to the boat. We walked to the marina office. John got on their powerful radio, but it was not powerful enough to carry over the volcanic peaks. He then called Virgin Islands Radio. In seconds the "*La Boatique*" call was beamed to all radios throughout the U.S. and British Virgin Islands. Barbara answered the call and told us that Pete was waiting for me at the dinghy dock. John and his sister accompanied me back to the boat in John's car. I sure was thankful for John Hayes and his help. I was angry with Pete for leaving me and he was angry with me for not being in the grocery store where he expected to find me. Pete did not realize that there were two grocery stores and that I was at the other store. There was no point in staying angry so we got over it the next day.

On December 21$^{st}$ we motored east into the wind to Maho Bay, St. John. St. John is only nine miles long and five miles wide. The U.S. Park System owns two-thirds of this rugged hilly island. St. John is the most densely wooded of all the Virgin Islands and with all the rain we were getting every day, the vegetation was more lush than normal. Colorful flowers were in abundance. Wild orchids containing white flowers with purple centers wound their way around small branches while bromeliads clung to the crevices in rocks and trees. I enjoyed the sound of the waves as they rolled ashore. Tropical birds sang during the day while tree frogs serenaded us at night. The pelicans worked in teams diving for fish and often stood in the trees on the edge of the bay. We found brown termite nests nearly three feet in diameter sometimes on the ground and other times as much as 15 feet up in the trees. These soft musty nests must be a tasty treat for the wild donkey we saw munching away at one.

In the hills above our anchorage was a privately maintained ecological camp designed for the eco-tourists and open to us yachties. I enjoyed strolling along the miles of elevated boardwalks linking together the small airy cabins in the lush tropical forest.

**Christmas in Paradise**

We belong to a club called Seven Seas Cruising Association. The club had various Christmas activities planned. We were becoming part of a new community, a community of travelers living on their boats cruising the oceans. The first activity was a "dinghy drift." We all piled into dinghies and then tied them all together. Then, we drifted through the bay. We munched appetizers that we passed from boat to boat. There were 22 dinghies in the group having a great time when a squall arrived bringing wind, cold rain, and putting an end to our party.

*La Boatique* anchored in Maho Bay, St. John, U.S. Virgin Islands

On Christmas day we decided to make a present for us and the boat. We decided to make sunshades. Pete and I had fun working together designing, cutting, pinning, and sewing. We attached the two sunshades (kind of like awnings) to the sides of our bimini top. Our cockpit is now well shaded.

Christmas dinner was a potluck lunch with over 100 others from Seven Seas Cruising Association. Christmas day was one of the few days we did not have rain.

Sue sews the sun shades.

# Swimming with the Dolphin

On the morning of December 26th Pete saw a dolphin's dorsal fin coming toward the bow of our boat. Pete whistled a few times. The dolphin turned toward *La Boatique*. Pete, wearing his white underwear, then jumped in the water next to the boat. The dolphin swam over to Pete. Pete reached out and petted the dolphin. The skin was soft like vinyl. The dolphin swam over to other boats and made a large circle around our boat. The dolphin came near but never close enough for us to swim with him again.

Late in the day we decided to clean the bottom of the boat with a brush and a scraper. While we scraped off barnacles and scum, six-inch long skinny silver fish eagerly gobbled the items we removed. The fish then nibbled away at the things still clinging to our hull. Watching the fish eat made cleaning the hull a fun job.

We motored back to St. Thomas for a few days to get our mail, the clothes washed and buy some supplies. Then we motored back to Maho Bay, St. John. We enjoyed New Years Eve on *La Boatique* with Barbara and Manfred. We played a dice game. We watched our favorite movie, Captain Ron. We toasted in the New Year with ice-cold Champagne under the full moon. The temperature was in the low 70's.

# 1999

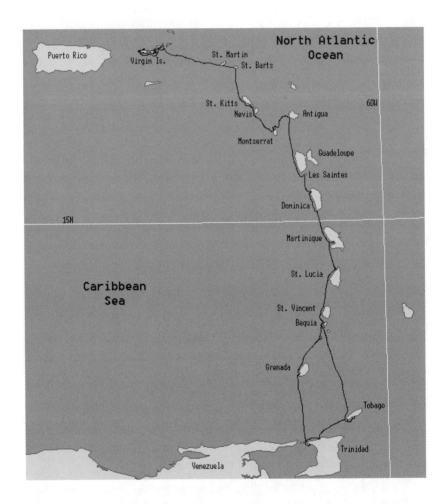

*La Boatique's* travels during 1999 from the Virgin Islands to Trinidad and then north to Bequia.

There always seemed to be something to see and do at Maho Bay, St. John U.S. Virgin Islands.

The water was very clear so we could see all the fish, and there were lots of them. Pete used one of the Lake Erie lures to try to catch a jack. The jacks were all around the lure ready to strike, then the jacks jumped out of the water. Next, from nowhere a huge five-foot long barracuda hit the lure. Pete and I had just switched from a heavy line to light 10-pound line. Of course, the barracuda cut the line and was off with our lure. Pete couldn't wait to start fishing again. But he wished that he had kept more of our fishing tackle that we'd left behind in Ohio.

I was kayaking every day. I often combined a kayak trip with a walk along a park trail through the tropical forest. Barbara often joined me.

There were boats of every kind anchored here in the bay. We saw world-class mega-yachts, large charter boats, cruising sailors, trawlers, power boaters from Puerto Rico and even small day sailors. Many boats we saw were home made and unique.

The Afrigan Queen IV

The *Afrigan Queen IV* was one of the unique boats. (The name was <u>Afrigan</u>, not <u>African</u>.) I could not resist kayaking over and meeting the captain of this 32-foot long gaff rigged schooner. This boat also intrigued Pete. We found out that the captain, David Wegman, built the fiberglass boat himself 20 years ago in Coral Bay, St. John. David's family was from Pemberville, Ohio, but David grew up in Fort Wayne, Indiana. Both of these towns were places where we had spent time before we started cruising. David sailed the *Afrigan Queen IV* all the way around the world sailing the trade winds. Pete and I were full of questions for David.

Had he ever had anything stolen? No.

Where would he like to go now that he had been around the world? Ireland and Cuba.

Did he have any words of wisdom? Don't worry. If you have a concern, act on it now. Take care of it. Don't sit and worry about what ever it is.

Two other interesting characters we met were 61-year-old Jim Homes and his 8-year-old son Mike. Jim and Mike flew to the Virgin Islands from Williamsville, New York. They stayed at the Maho Bay Camp Grounds. I met Jim and Mike while they were out paddling in a bright red inflatable kayak that they had brought with them on the plane. Since Pete had been trying to convince me that we should have easily stowed inflatable kayaks rather than bulky rigid kayaks, I decided to check out their kayak. While Jim and Mike toured *La Boatique*, I tried out the red inflatable. I was pleased with its performance. We decided to sell the rigid kayaks and buy inflatables.

On January 9th, we sailed to St. Thomas, with two passengers, Jim and Mike. We had a great sail using the jib and mizzen but anchoring was another story. For the first time ever we had towed 3 boats, the dinghy and both kayaks. While maneuvering in the tight anchorage, one of the kayak painters got wedged tightly around the propeller. The strong "floating" painter line pulled the shaft out of the engine coupling. No damage was done except for the loss of the kayak painter. Pete was able to get the shaft back into its proper position.

While at Charlotte Amalie St. Thomas we replaced our large 155% genoa with our small 100% genoa. We made this change so that we would be better able to point into the strong trade winds.

We ordered an inflatable kayak from West Marine and had it shipped to Light House Marine in St. Thomas. We did not use general delivery at the U.S. Post Office because previously we had one general delivery package returned to my mom, one package never showed up, and two Christmas cards had been opened. We heard that other cruisers had similar problems.

On January 17th we motor-sailed from Charlotte Amalie, St. Thomas to Maho Bay, St. John. During the trip we caught a three-foot long fish. Was it a barracuda? We threw it back with only a little cut on its lip. Oops! It wasn't a barracuda, but a great eating kingfish. During the trip we thought we were making fresh water with our Pur 80 water maker. Oops! The intake water valve was closed so no water was made.

Once we got to Maho Bay I tried out the new kayak. It did not track as well as the old rigid kayak but it had nice seats with backrests and we stayed much dryer.

On January 18th we had a nice sail from Maho Bay, St. John USVI, to Jost Van Dyke, BVI. We did not have to check out of the USVI because we were US Citizens. We did have to check into the BVI. Pete went fishing with Manfred (from *St. Pauli*) and caught a blackfin tuna. Pete cleaned the fish, but lost a lot of meat because he was not sure how to clean it. Barbara and Manfred suggested lobster for dinner at *Rudy's* restaurant. Rudy sure is one hard worker. He heads out into the Atlantic in his small boat and brings up lobster from 200 feet down. Then he and his wife prepare the dinner. Rudy then serves the food. This is a small operation. There were only three tables to serve for dinner that night. The large fresh caught Caribbean lobster was delicious but expensive at $30 per plate. We could not afford to continue cruising and eating like that.

The next day we received the following fish cleaning lessons from another local fisherman, Mr. Goodwin. Don't filet the fish. Don't even gut the fish. Remove the scales and hard pieces near the gills. Then cut the fish into steaks. Then remove the guts from each steak. He then gave us four tuna steaks to grill for dinner.

# The American Versus British Virgin Islands

In the American Virgin Islands people on boats were usually living year round on the boats. In the British Virgin Islands, the boaters tended to be on weekly rentals — bareboat charters. The U.S. Virgins were less crowded with boats then the British Virgins. Many of the anchorages in the British Virgins were nearly filled with $20 per night mooring balls. When we anchored, we had trouble with bareboat charter boaters trying to use our anchor ball as a mooring ball. To try to stop the confusion, Pete painted an anchor and "*La Boatique*" on the ball. Charter boats still sped to the ball, but then they gave it a look of frustration and moved on.

# The British Virgin Islands

On January 21st, we sailed from Great Harbour, Jost Van Dyke to The Bight, Norman Island. We entered a deep channel with steep banks. At the end of the channel, we dropped our anchor. The kayaking was great and so was the snorkeling. While snorkeling near our boat, I watched a group of maroon, black, and white squid. Some squid swam forward while others swam backward. While I was busy in the water, Pete was relaxing in the hammock on the bow of *La Boatique*.

We both relaxed as the days passed by. Pete thought that maybe we were turning into "mush pumpkins." What are "mush pumpkins"? After big fat orange pumpkins sit around awhile, they get soft. We liked to relax once in a while, but we didn't want to turn into "mush pumpkins."

From our anchorage at Norman Island we dinghied to The Caves, Pelican Island, and The Indians. While snorkeling at The Caves Pete had a great time feeding fish. He fed the fish an orange cut in half and left by a previous snorkeling group. I could barely see Pete through all the fish. I enjoyed snorkeling into a dark cave until I could no longer see. The Indians and nearby Pelican Island were very popular dive sites. We enjoyed watching the divers even more than the snorkeling.

On January 25th, we sailed from The Bight, Norman Island, to Road Town, Tortola, and then onto Little Harbour, Peter Island. We had a hard time finding a place to anchor at Road Town (the capital of the BVI). There were lots of boats and the holding was not good. Road Town was far from being a nice clean place to stay. The anchorage was polluted and the town looked shabby. The place we finally chose had oily fuel on top of the water. The reason we came was because our refrigerator pump had stopped working. But by the time we anchored, the pump worked fine. We decided to purchase a few groceries and fuel and then left for Peter Island.

Little Harbour at Peter Island was a small nearly round but deep bay. The water was so clear that we could easily see 30 feet down. The anchorage was not crowded like the others in the BVI. However, nearly all the boats in the anchorage had to use an anchor off the bow with a line from the stern tied to rocks ashore. Our line slipped off the first rock Pete tried, but the second larger rock worked fine. In the evening, we played a dice game with Barbara and Manfred.

The wind was blowing more than 20 knots in the anchorage at Peter Island on the morning of January 27th. The steep slopes around the anchorage caused the wind gusts to veer nearly 180 degrees. *La Boatique* had moved close to the rocks near shore on the starboard side of the boat. We either needed to tighten up on our anchor chain or leave. We decided to leave the anchorage.

There were two difficult jobs to be done before we could get going. One person needed to be at the helm to keep *La Boatique* out of danger while the other person needed to remove the stern line from the rocks.

The stern line handler would have to row the dinghy ashore. Then he would have to pull the dinghy far enough up onto the jagged rocks so the dinghy would not drift out into the anchorage. Then he would have to climb the rocks. Once the helmsman got *La Boatique* as far as possible from the rocks jutting out near our starboard side, then the line handler would pull hard on the stern line and slip the line off the rocks.

Now the really tricky part begins. Once the tension is off the stern line, *La Boatique* will start drifting toward rocks jutting out from shore. But putting the engine in gear may suck the stern line into the propeller.

The line handler would have to hold onto the line as the dinghy is pushed back into the choppy water. Then the line handler would need to pull the line into the dinghy as hard and as fast as possible. Once the line is tight, the helmsman could put the propeller in motion to get us out of danger. As the line handler would pull the line into the dinghy, the dinghy would be brought closer to *La Boatique*. Then the helmsman would need to get the line aboard *La Boatique* and get back to the helm as soon as possible. Finally, the line handler would secure the dinghy and climb aboard.

So what job did I choose? I chose to be the line handler. By the time I scrambled back aboard *La Boatique*, I was breathless.

The strong wind was right on our nose as we motored to Trellis Bay, Tortola. We found the anchorage nearly full of mooring balls. Because of the weather forecast we decided to pay $20 per night for a ball. We were glad we did since the wind during the night reached gale force.

While in Tortola, we decided to sign up for the Caribbean Weather Net with David Jones. David talked on the single side band frequency 8104.0 at 6:30 a.m. EST.

# St. Maarten/St. Martin

Bruce Van Saint in the book <u>Passages South</u> wrote that the passage from the Virgin Islands to St. Maarten is a hard motorsail. The ninety-six mile passage was certainly hard on us. We needed to head southeast right into the prevailing wind and current. The weather forecast was for northeast to east wind 15 to 20 knots. But what we got were east and even a little bit southeast winds at 20 to 30 knots. The waves were about five to nine feet. We both got seasick. We made the passage even longer and harder to weather by departing from Tortola instead of the more recommended departure point of Virgin Gorda.

We raised the mainsail and unfurled the small genoa at 3 p.m. on January 30th. We used up our remaining daylight hours crossing the Sir Francis Drake Channel to get out of the Virgin Islands. As the red sun set on the Virgin Islands the bright white blue moon rose in front of us.

Once darkness arrived the moon lit the black waves before us like a spotlight. The light would go on and off as clouds passed by.

As the night wore on, we wore down. Up the waves and sometimes crashing down the waves, on we motor-sailed. Annoying salt spray was everywhere. I took a couple of two-hour naps. But instead of feeling refreshed, I felt seasick. I could revive myself by concentrating on the waves and then taking the helm.

We arrived at St. Martin at sunrise on January 31st. Pete believed that our passage to St. Martin was worse than the passage from Bermuda to the Virgin Islands because we had to beat into the wind and waves.

We checked in through customs at the French side at Marigot even though we were anchored in the Dutch side because the French side was free and once you were checked in, you could go anywhere on the island. So we were told by the friendly French customs agent. After the Coast Guard boarded us and searched the boat, we found out that we needed to check into the Dutch side.

When rain arrived on February 1st, Pete put on his bathing suit and I put on my rain suit. We then washed the sticky salt off *La Boatique*.

I had not been able to call home in over two weeks. When I did get through to home in early February, my parents were full of frustration over our income tax documents. When I suggested that I fly home, they thought that was a great idea. So did I, until I got caught up in the American Airlines pilot strike.

My flight out of St. Martin on February 9th was cancelled because the pilots did not show up. I was to fly out on February 10th instead. On February 10th, I found out the flight was cancelled again. American had no idea when they would have a flight available. I had to wait in line for over 2 hours at the airport. I was becoming annoyed. I suggested that they transfer me to another carrier and put me up for a night in a hotel. So American put me on a TWA flight on the afternoon of February 11th. They paid for a night at the Maho Bay Beach Resort Hotel near the airport and provided me with $90 worth of meal vouchers.

I had more than a day to wait for the TWA flight so I went back to the boat and got Pete. The two of us had a great time at the resort hotel. I played in the surf on the beach while Pete watched the planes land overhead. I enjoyed long showers. Pete enjoyed soaking in a hot bath. What a change from the boat!

On February 11th, the TWA flight was late and I missed the connection in New York. American Airlines then put me up for a night in New York. I finally arrived in Cleveland around noon on February 12th. The American Airlines staff bent over backwards to please me as best they could during a difficult situation.

While I was in Ohio, Pete kept busy on the boat.

**Boat Maintenance Jobs**

1. Rewired the solar panels so that they would perform better.

2. Worked on the single side band to get it performing better.

3. Painted and varnished the front head.

4. Cleaned the bilge.

5. Painted the decks.

6. Layered many coats of Deks Olje on the teak.

7. Cleaned out some cabinets.

8. Changed the engine oil.

9. Cleaned the water maker.

10. Ran new battery cable to the windless battery.

11. Cleaned the bottom of the dinghy.

12. Polished stainless steel.

13. Checked the turnbuckles for wear.

14. Cleaned the roller furler.

I flew back to St. Maarten on March 1st without any delays. Pete was waiting with open arms and a big kiss. Our month at the Yacht Club would be up on March 5th, so we needed to decide whether to sail on or to stay. We tried not to stay at any one place more than a month because the longer we stay at any one place, the harder it is to get back into sailing. Mistakes are much more easily made when we are away from the sailing routine. However, our next island destination was less than a day sail away. So, we decided to stay another month at Simpson Bay Yacht Club Marina.

We tended to spend half the day working on boat chores and half the day being tourists. Barbara and Manfred Albrecht from *St. Pauli* had sailed south. They planned to fly home to Canada from Trinidad soon. We would not see Barbara and Manfred until August when we would also fly to Lake Erie from Trinidad. Jay and Sandy Wright from the boat *Nokandolah* just stopped by for a visit. We had seen them off and on since Bermuda.

Another couple that we met in Bermuda was Joe and Marge Scrowcroft from the boat *Dream Weaver*. Joe and Marge are from Rhode Island. Joe and Marge decided to upgrade from a Yamaha 8 hp to a Yamaha 15 hp outboard dinghy motor. Since our 5 hp Nissan had been running roughly, we decided to purchase their 8 hp dinghy motor. Our dinghy performed much better and faster with the 8 hp motor.

Sue at Dawn Beach

Joe and Marge rented a car and asked us if we would like to see the island. Saint Martin / Sint Maarten is the only island to bear the flags of two major world powers. One half of the island is Dutch while the other half is French. The island has only 36 square miles. It is only 7 miles long. But it seems much larger because of the hilly volcanic terrain. Between the rugged cliffs plunging to the sea, there are 26 beaches. We drove the car to many of them. I liked the white sand and palm trees at Dawn Beach. Orient Beach is where the nudists hang out. And hang out they did since they were mostly old fat people. Our favorite beach was at Maho Bay. This beach was often called jet blast beach because of its location at the end of the airport runway.

March 5$^{th}$ — 7$^{th}$ was the Heineken Regatta. Over 250 sailboats from 60 different countries raced around the island. We used the car to get to great locations to watch the race. The big boats were over sixty feet long. These very fast boats gracefully cut though the waves with barely a splash. The smallest boats to race were the beach catamarans with lengths of 18 to about 22 feet. These boats were also very fast, but they did not gracefully cut through the waves. The little cats bounced along over the waves throwing salt-water spray high and wide. The vast majority of the boats were the charter boats ranging in length from 35 to 50 feet. The race has become an event of international stature.

On March 15$^{th}$ we sailed for seven hours, but not aboard *La Boatique*. While *La Boatique* sat moored to the dock, we sailed around St. Martin with Jay Wright on *Nokandolah*. Jay's wife, Sandy, had flown home to Connecticut because of an illness in her family. Jay asked us to accompany him as he circumnavigated the island.

During the evening before our departure the soft gentle wind turned strong. During the night the wind howled. The mooring lines groaned against the push of the wind on *La Boatique's* hull. What kind of wind would we have at dawn? Would the waves be huge?

When I opened my eyes to the light of dawn, the wind was down. I showered and put on my bathing suit and shorts. Pete poured cereal in our bowls while I made peanut butter and jelly sandwiches for lunch. At 9 a.m. the lift bridge rose. The three of us on *Nokandulah* motored out of the narrow channel under the bridge. The quiet lagoon waters gave way to the ocean swell. Jay raised the main and jib. *Nokandolah* pitched 15 degrees as the 18-knot wind filled the sails. We soon sailed past three cruise ships at anchor in Philipsburg. The first leg of the trip involved beating into the wind. My stomach did not like the ride over the swells and waves. I gave my breakfast to the fish. I took the helm and began to feel better. Ahead of us was the mile long island of Tintamarre.

Jay suggested we anchor near a few other boats on the west side of the island. Jay tried to start the engine, but it would not start. Salt water had flowed through the exhaust pipe into the engine. Jay hit the decompression switch while Pete pushed the starter button and I steered the boat. The starter motor was getting very hot. Maybe we would not stop after all. Finally, the motor started. I turned into the wind while Jay and Pete dropped the sails. After Jay and I swam to the beach and back, we all enjoyed our lunch.

Thank goodness we were done with beating into the wind. We raised the sails and soon rounded the northern tip of St. Martin. There wasn't anything here except for the burning dump on shore. The wind became very light as we sailed along the western coast past the French towns of Anse Marcel, Grand Case, and Marigot.

When we were near the western tip of the island, we were sailing close to the shore. Big rollers crashed against cliff walls sending spray high in the air. Jay saw the bright blue water ahead turn yellowish. Was there shallow water ahead? Jay steered us out farther from shore. The smell of sewage was in the air. The yellowish water must have been sewage. I could see what looked like a sewage treatment plant near shore. We sailed on and were across from St. Maarten, the Dutch side of the island. Soon we were at anchor and our day's adventure was over.

The next morning when Jay went to start his engine, he found that the starter had burned up. He dinghied over to *La Boatique* and separated his shoulder when he lost his balance while climbing from his dinghy to our boat. Pete walked him to a nearby clinic where his shoulder was reset. Jay was not having a good day.

St. Martin is known as the gourmet capital of the Caribbean. The cuisine is reported to be equal to the best of Paris or New York. So Joe, Marge, Pete and I decided to get dressed up and have at least one fancy meal while there. We chose the restaurant called Rainbow because I met the owner during my flight to Ohio. The beachfront restaurant was bright, airy and eloquent. We ordered wine followed by escargot in a puff pastry. We then had elegant full course meals. Joe and I had duck with raspberry sauce. I was too full for dessert but I did eat part of Pete's dessert. He had ice cream in puff pastries with warm chocolate sauce topped with slivered almonds. His dessert was like cream puffs. We thought the meal was great, until the bill came. Our dinners averaged $50 apiece. That was the last expensive meal for us.

# Digital Cameras and Communications

We used a digital camera. When we started cruising, we had a digital camera made by Minolta called a "Dimage V." The camera was conveniently small, 2 inches by 4 inches by 1 inch. The picture was supposed to display on a small LCD screen. However, in bright sunlight the screen washed out and looked black. We had no idea what the picture would look like until we got the camera in dark or dim light. Also, the double A batteries seemed to last for only a few pictures.

The cameras in St. Maarten were very inexpensive, so we decided to get a new digital camera. We settled on a Sony Digital Mavica with Mpeg Movie capability. This camera was bigger, 4 inches by 4 inches by 2 inches. However, we could see the image displayed on the LCD in bright sunlight. We now had a 3X zoom lens. The battery lasted a long time and was easy to recharge. We could take better quality pictures. However, for the web page I tried to keep the picture size small so that the pictures downloaded fast.

I used our computer on the boat to insert the pictures into our web page. Then I e-mailed the HTML web page files along with the pictures to my mom. My mom with the help of my sister transferred the files to Kellnet, her ISP. My e-mail server was Excite.com because it was free and available wherever the Internet was available. We did not have a phone on the boat and did not feel that we needed one. Locations to do e-mail were very easy to find. The cost for Internet time was about $10 per hour. On the other hand, phone time was very expensive. The least expensive phone location charged 90 cents a minute, when the business was open. A pay phone on the street was at least $3 a minute. Phone cards only worked on certain phones and cost about $1 a minute.

## Pete's Cruising Recommendations

Pete writes:

My first topic is ocean currents. We only had strong currents coming down from the BVI. They seem to be no problem if you use your GPS. Most currents are set to the west in the Caribbean. I figure for every knot of current, figure one-degree course change for every 10 miles.

My second topic is fixes and repairs. You must carry spare engine parts, injectors, impellers, zincs, hose, filters and wire. Carry as much oil as you can carry because oil here is expensive. If you have a unique item on the boat, be sure to carry spare parts because you probably won't be able to get the parts here. The hardware is priced better than West Marine, but not all items that West Marine carries are available.

We have made a nice kitty repairing things for people. I have worked on BMW engines and Yanmars. I have rewired some boats and repaired winches. The help down here is so-so. If they show up to work, they are not cheap. If you dive you can make money cleaning bottoms, and props. I think the biggest things I see are bad maintenance habits from the people themselves. I see engine rooms a mess, wiring a nightmare, and major fuel problems, even on the big boats. Everyone who looks at my engine room says you can eat off it. But looking at an engine room tells a lot about the boat and the owner.

The things we have put on the boat have all paid off. The engine rebuild, Airsep system, and the fuel purification system have helped us keep our engine running great.

I think you have to make a "what to check" list that includes time intervals. So when you hit that time, you know what has to be checked or changed. Be sure to change the oil and filters regularly. Also check the bolts and clamps. Check your zincs every 6 months. If the zincs disappear then any metal parts on the boat will be next to go. Do not forget to clean your strainers often. You don't want your water intakes to become clogged.

Have a good windlass that works and a cover for it. If you are at a dock or at anchor run it every other day. Keep it greased.

I believe that watermakers are a must. We have had great success with ours. The PUR 80 runs about 7—8 amps. It makes about 4 gallons an hour of good water. We add Clorox bleach to our water tanks. We add a capful for 30 gallons to keep the tanks clean. While at the dock we have put the watermaker to sleep because the marina water is very dirty. But we will wake it up soon. We depend very much on it. We like our showers and hot water for dishes. We have had no breakdowns with the watermaker. But you must grease the pump shaft. We grease ours when we clean the pre-filter. Try to install the unit below the water line and close to the through-haul fitting so that it will run more efficiently.

Make sure you have screens for your hatches and ports. There are biting bugs here also.

Have a good dinghy and motor. I have found that here in St. Marrten dinghies and outboards are much less expensive than in the United States.

For overnight passages you should have a marine single side band radio in good working order. We have ours working pretty good.

Install big ground plates. The ones we added in Baltimore have helped greatly.

Now for my thoughts about propellers: our Prowell Sailprop feathering propeller may not justify the extra cost. We like our feathering prop for sailing, but we lose some performance when motoring. We motored better with our fixed prop. But the reverse performance is better when we use the feathering prop. It's a 50/50 deal.

Our refrigeration works super. The time we spent redoing it was well worth every penny we put into it. Insulate as much as possible. Our vacuum lid is great. I have found that stainless liners look great but don't hold the cold and sweat a lot. Also, I believe that water-cooling is a must down here. Our refrigeration system draws about 5.5 amps. It runs about 15 minutes per hour if the door is kept closed.

Our solar panels work fantastic. I believe that we are getting about 60 amp hours a day from the panels. We have two 80-watt Kyocera panels.

I think that one of the most important things you can do is to keep salt water out of the boat. We found that keeping salt water out of the boat is much easier said than done. Your things will stay cleaner and last longer if you can keep them out of salt water. I like to use WD 40 for wiping down parts.

We are always going through lockers, moving around things and getting rid of things. You really don't need a lot. However, I found that tools are a must. I use pullers and special tools. You will need to push, pry and bang at times. I suggest having a vise with at least a 3-inch opening.

As far as steering is concerned, we see windvanes. We found that most cruisers who have windvanes never use them and they look ugly on the back of the boat. Windvanes are also a maintenance headache. Windvane parts are hard to find. Most cruisers have good autopilots or even two autopilots. You will use the autopilot a lot. Get the biggest you can use and it will pay for itself.

Our Yeoman electronic chart plotter has been a great help, fast easy and accurate. Often, we use it up in the cockpit instead of the navigation station.

So the main things I have loved: good fuel causing less problems, good anchor windlass, heavy anchor, clean engine, good cold drinks with ice, lots of tools and my great helper, my wife. We learn everyday.

*La Boatique* at Simpson Bay Yacht Club Marina

# St. Barts

Sue continues:

After two months in Simpson Bay, the anchor was buried deep in mud and the chain was turning into a spiky coral reef. Pete handled that spiky slimy mess while I took the helm. At 11 a.m. March 5th we were under the Simpson Bay Bridge and out in the ocean. *La Boatique* was like a butterfly coming out of her cocoon. The first wing of the butterfly opened as I slowly raised the mainsail. The next wing opened quickly as we unfurled the jib. The air filling the sails was light and gentle. The waves were tiny. The island of St. Maarten blocked the ocean swell. Surprisingly, just as Pete raised the mizzen sail a lone white butterfly fluttered through the cockpit. The water was turquoise blue. The tiny waves gently splashed along side of the

*La Boatique* at La Salle Mariners Yacht Club in Canada

Harvey, Sue, Joyce and Pete prepare *La Boatique* for the Erie Canal near Buffalo, New York

Sue kayaks past New York City

Pete finds time to relax in the Eastern Caribbean.

Sue finds time to relax in the Eastern Caribbean.

*La Boatique* sails on to Antigua.

Fresh fruit delivery in St. Lucia

Sue in the yellow shirt climbs Trafalgar Falls, Dominica

Bequia Carnival

Pete helps this fishermen remove fish from the net in Tobago

Argyle Falls in Tobago was our favorite waterfall because there were three pools of cool clean water for relaxing and swimming shaded by a canopy of exotic rain forest trees.

*La Boatique* gets launched in Trinidad

Pete on the beach in Bequia

*La Boatique* in Marigot Bay

Pete and Sue smile for the camera during a lull in the race, St. Lucia

Diamond Waterfall, St. Lucia    Julius and Sally in St. Maarten

*Argonauta* sails south toward St. Kitts

Pete cleans barnacles off the bottom off *La Boatique*

Abandoned leper colony home, Trinidad

Sue has a smile for the camera because this is the first time we flew the spinnaker since Lake Erie. We are sailing north of Venezuela in superb conditions.

*Maritime Express* seems to be suspended, Tortuga

Sue holds live lobsters, Tortuga Island, Venezuela

*La Boatique* sails on to Bonaire.

The capital of the Dutch West Indies, Willemstad, Curacao

Sue looks up toward Pete at the top of the mast.

The children at Isla De Pinos, Panama, posed with Pete and Sue.

*La Boatique* at anchor at Isla De Pinos

Sue holds up the sailfish mola she purchased in the village.

Kuna Indian saleswomen arriving in canoes try to sell molas to Barry and Julie on Cherokee.

Our favorite anchorage, Snug Harbor in Panama

Local officials from the Indian village of San Iganacio De Tupile asked us if we would like to visit their community. They picked us up in the chief's large canoe. Once ashore three small parrots toured the island on Pete's back.

hull. Pete tossed our big fish lure into the Caribbean Ocean. An hour later we had a huge fish running with the lure. Pete started the fight, but he was the loser. The fish cut through our 90 pound test line and took off with our lure. As the island disappeared behind us, the wind picked up to 15 knots. *La Boatique* heeled about 12 degrees and sped up to 6 ½ knots for the remainder of our trip. We arrived in Columbier Bay, St. Barthelemy (St. Barts) at 2 p.m.

Columbier Bay is secluded from the rest of St. Barts because it can only be reached by boat or by a mile long trek over the hills. I inflated the kayak and paddled over to *Dream Weaver*. Joe and Marge from *Dream Weaver* had arrived just before we did. Marge and I kayaked to shore. We then snorkeled off the beach. The water around St. Barts is much cleaner than the water around St. Maarten. In fact, the entire island of St. Barts is much cleaner than the island of St. Maarten.

The next day, we dinghied over to Gustavia to check in through customs. The dinghy ride meant a trip out into the Caribbean Ocean and included a ride over rollers and choppy seas. I was on the bow and the ride was fun. However, a few of the waves were big enough to hurt our backs. Soon after we returned to our boats and motored both *La Boatique* and *Dream Weaver* over to Gustavia and anchored in a bay called Anse Du Corossol.

Marge and I dinghied into the town of Gustavia and then went swimming at the nearby Shell Beach.

## St. Kitts and Nevis

On April 9th Pete raised the mainsail and the jib at 7:15 a.m. We sailed 42 miles south from St. Barthelemy to St. Christopher (St. Kitts). I had not seen such a gray dreary day since a mid winter day in Ohio. There were high light gray clouds and low dark clouds. The ocean was blue gray. The islands of St. Barts, St. Eusatatius and St. Kitts were charcoal gray. Dark gray clouds often concealed most of the islands. *La Boatique* easily cut through the three-foot waves and rode over the five to eight foot swells while the 15-knot wind filled the sails. We checked in at Basseteere Bay and not downtown as our guide book recommended. We were told we would have to wait until Monday to go downtown to the immigration office because the office was closed already for the weekend. We should not have arrived late on Friday afternoon. Before dark we motored 5 miles to White House Bay, St. Kitts. White House Bay is the most protected bay on St.

Kitts. We shared the large anchorage with only 6 other cruising boats. The hilly shoreline was desolate except for a few cows. The cow manure brought flies and the wind carried the flies out to the boat. We swatted over 100 flies. No wonder the anchorage was not crowded.

Early in the morning of April 10th a local fisherman in a colorful bright blue and yellow open boat sold us two live lobsters for $12. For lunch we dipped the succulent lobster in butter and had side dishes of corn and sweet potatoes. The meal was great but there were still too many flies.

On April 11th we motored a few miles from bay to bay. We started in White House Bay and then spent most of the day at Ballast Bay. Late in the day we went from Ballast Bay to Majors Bay. When we arrived at Majors Bay, we had the bay all to ourselves except for a small red tug, 4 barges with 2 bright red 200-foot Manitowa cranes, and a red and white push boat. We never found out what they were doing there. Ocean swells rolled in making the anchorage uncomfortable. However, we decided to stay a while. We had a great time snorkeling. The seabed was nearly covered in sea grass. Huge conch shells were everywhere. Pete brought one live conch up to the boat for us to temporarily inspect. It made squeaky noises. Then Pete fought a live lobster but let it go because he was concerned that it might cut his bare hand. At least the spiky Caribbean lobster does not have large claws. The lobster was much stronger than Pete expected it to be.

On April 12th we motored from Ballast Bay to Basseterre Bay. We took an island tour with Joe and Marge from *Dream Weaver*. The lowlands of St. Kitts were covered in sugar cane. The rain forest was the most fun for us. Basseterre Bay was dusty, sooty, and oily. It was also not well protected from the ocean swells. It was not a good anchorage. As soon as we could, we headed to Majors Bay after the island tour. Jay and Sandy from *Nokandolah* were already in Majors Bay. Jay had caught four conchs. Jay made us delicious conch fritters for dinner. The wind died down to nothing and the ocean was like glass the entire night.

On April 13th the wind was calm. We motored to Nevis. We had lunch at Muriel's Cuisine with Joe, Marge, Jay and Sandy. We visited the Barclays Bank where we found a brand new NCR ATM. We withdrew our first Eastern Caribbean money. (I used to work for NCR programming ATMs, so ATMs always interest me.) We also bought some locally grown and processed sugar at the grocery. While in

Nevis we got a boat pass so that we could visit the dangerous island of Montserrat with its active volcano.

# Montserrat and the Active Volcano

The wind was nearly on our nose for most of our motor sail to Montserrat. The sky was clear except for the clouds building over the volcano ahead of us. The clouds were dirty. They were heading toward us. We could not see that under the clouds the volcano was erupting and spilling out a stream of 3000-degree mud and rocks down the far side of the mountain. When we were about 12 miles away from the island, we were under the dirty cloud. The air smelled hot and somewhat sulfuric. My throat felt scratchy. We changed our tack from southeast to northeast. We were soon in clean air.

We anchored in Rendezvous Bay on the northwest coast of the 12-mile long island with four other boats. We were maybe 6 miles from the dangerous volcano. No place on this island was really safe from the volcanic activity. Before 7 a.m. all the boats were gone except for us. We would be the only boaters to visit the island that day.

Smiling Thomas Lee was our guide for our Montserrat tour. The fertile island was lush and green. At the start of our tour we saw mahogany, bamboo, cashew, papaya, mango, banana, breadfruit, citrus, and coconut trees. We saw large homes with beautiful gardens. But as we drove on everything we saw was covered with volcanic dust. Soon the air was thick with the volcanic ash. Some of the people we saw outside were wearing masks to try to keep the ash out of their lungs. Even though inside the van was hot, we were often forced to close the windows to keep the volcanic dust out.

Thomas Lee stopped the van and we walked on what seemed to be a large fresh mudslide. The area looked like a nearly dry river of mud. Thomas Lee explained that we were walking on a volcanic eruption that occurred only four days ago. He pointed out what was left of a restaurant, a foundation in the mud. We did not turn back but drove over this rough dried river of mud. Thomas Lee knew where to drive since he knew where the road was buried under the ash. Once we crossed the river of mud we were traveling through a very dangerous area. If an eruption occurred while we were in this area, we would be trapped or we were be toast. The van climbed high and soon we were back to green surroundings. We stopped again. We could see steam venting from many places along the side of the mountain. We continued on. Pete commented that we seemed to be driving through a ghost town. No one lived in this dangerous area. In fact, over half of the island was uninhabitable. Some of the roofs had collapsed from the weight of the ash and pebbles. All metal objects were being eaten away by the sulfuric acid in the air. But nearly all the plants were thriving even while covered in ash.

Thomas Lee and Pete look over the ash-covered city of Plymouth, Montserrat after the volcanic eruption.

We stopped at a deserted house high on a hill. We could go no further. Ahead of us was a cliff wall. To our left was the top of the mountain. In front of us below the cliff were the remains of a massive eruption miles long and miles wide. The eruption ran right into the sea. This eruption covered the capital city of Plymouth. Little could be seen of what were once universities, schools, hospitals, shopping centers, businesses, and homes. Plymouth was one of the most attractive towns in the Leeward Islands. The only thing left were swirls of volcanic ash in the air.

Later in the day we looked down on what was the airport and the town nearby. The town was gone. Even the runway right next to the ocean was partially covered by an eruption. Thomas Lee's beautiful home and gardens were buried under this eruption. Nothing could be saved. He and his family were lucky to make it out alive. Thirty-nine others did not survive. The day of the eruption Thomas was at the airport with his taxi van. A warning came over the radio to evacuate immediately. Thomas filled his van with all the people he could carry. As he sped up a hill away from the airport, the eruption quietly flowed down the mountain behind him. An airplane on the runway barely outran the pyroclastic flow of mud and boulders.

One of our last stops was at the Volcanic Meteorological Investigation Center. Seismic sensors located all over the island were monitored there. Computers were everywhere. Often commercial aircraft were diverted around the volcanic clouds. The home used as the Investigation Center was at the top of a hill. The volcano buried the original center. The cloud over the volcano was once again very dark. Could this be another eruption? We would soon find out. As we entered, a scientist was studying the graph paper being drawn by the seismic sensors.

"We just had another eruption," he said.

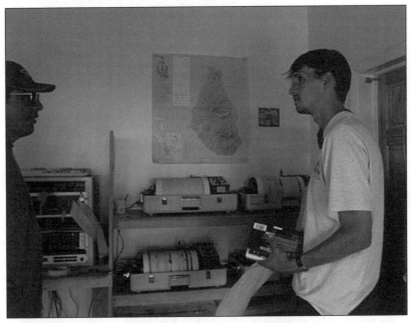

Pete discusses volcanic activity with a scientist in Montserrat during one of the many small erruptions. A map of Montserrat is displayed on the wall. The active volcano consumes the lower half of the island. The seismic sensors between Pete and the scientist were busy registering the eruption.

But this one was very small. We learned that this volcano is much like the Mount Saint Helen volcano in the way that it erupts. We learned that a pyroclastic eruption is much like an avalanche, except that the mud and lava are over 3000 degrees. This volcano was very active and had been erupting nearly every day.

61

Neither of us slept well during our last night at Montserrat. Was the building wind and ocean swell keeping us awake or were we fitfully dreaming of ash clouds and lava flows?

# Antigua

On April 16th we motor-sailed into the wind away from Montserrat and to the vacation island of Antigua.

I thought of Antigua as a holiday island because the only places on the island I had visited before our cruise were along the coast. I found that the interior of Antigua is nothing like Jolly Harbour, Falmouth Harbour, or English Harbour. There are mostly white people at the harbors but black people in the interior. High volcanic hills and rugged cliffs surround the harbors while the interior was surprisingly flat. Surrounding the harbors were quaint shops and vacation villas. The interior had dilapidated buildings and often shacks for homes. The harbors contained beautiful yachts while the interior had cows, goats and donkeys. The harbors had small air conditioned groceries with freezers and American food including skim milk while the interior had an open air produce market and an open air meat market where livestock was butchered and sold off in chunks.

# Guadeloupe

On April 26th we sailed from Jolly Harbour Antigua to Pigeon Island Guadeloupe. The sailing conditions were great with a 15 to 20 knot wind on our beam. We saw a family of pilot whales. These whales were only about 25 feet long and were black and swam slowly.

We trailed a fish lure behind us. A large fish struck the lure. As Pete reeled it in, the fish jumped out of the water. It was a large mahi-mahi (dolphin fish). Pete yelled for me to get the gaff and his heavy glove. The fish was at least four feet long by one foot wide. It finally tired and was riding flat on top of the water. Pete handed me the pole and I reeled in for a while. When the fish got 30 feet from the boat it found extra energy and dove hard. I thought it might break our 90-pound test line. I was getting tired but then the fish surfaced again. I reeled in some more line. The fish was now only ten feet from the boat. Since we were under sail the boat was heeling about twelve degrees. Pete held the gaff out over the water. I tried to get closer to Pete while still holding the heavy pole. The fish was finally tired and

Pete was nearly ready with the gaff. The gaff brushed against the taut fish line and cut it. Our prized fish was gone.

Later we caught two barracudas but let them go because we thought they might be poisonous.

We arrived at Pigeon Island Guadeloupe at 5:30 p.m. We ate dinner and soon fell asleep.

On April 27th we sailed from Pigeon Island, Guadeloupe to Les Saintes Guadeloupe. In the 26 miles we traveled we had plenty of variety in the wind. We caught a wahoo big enough for two meals for each of us. Les Saintes are small islands south of the main island of Guadeloupe. They are a colorful French vacation spot. There were bright yellow kayaks and Hobie Cats with rainbow colored sails on the clear turquoise water. There were also ferryboats, cruising sailboats, open fishing boats and even wind surfers. Under *La Boatique* were plenty of fish. Above us on the green hills were orange-roofed white cottages with big porches.

We decided to go ashore. While we looked down on the anchorage from a hill we saw local fishermen snorkeling with spear guns near *La Boatique*. While we were walking through town they were stringing a net around *La Boatique*. Jay Wright from *Nokandolah* watched and wondered if maybe there were two nets. No, a fish net that was being drawn tighter and tighter surrounded *La Boatique*. Then the fishermen noticed our anchor ball and our Cleveland anchor also within the circle of the net. They could not pull up the net with that anchor in it, so they brought our anchor to the surface, carried it over their net, and dropped our anchor and chain in a heap. Jay protested their actions but they paid no attention to him. They then drew the net in tighter and dragged it under the keel of *La Boatique*. They had trapped all the fish that had gone to *La Boatique* for safety. *La Boatique* drifted over against a French boat and the owner had to fend off the two boats until we showed up. By the time we got on site, the fish were being hauled aboard the open fishing boat. Pete was fuming mad. But there was nothing we could do except re-anchor. That was enough of Les Saintes for us. We left the next morning.

# Dominica

On April 29th we had a very fast sail of about 22 miles to Portsmouth, Dominica. We had constant wind of 20 to 30 knots from the east. Pete had the sails trimmed just right. *La Boatique* heeled about 23 degrees and cruised along at 6 to 7 ½ knots. We had a great ride. We anchored at the north end of the large Prince Rupert Bay. The boat next to us had gasoline stolen out of their dinghy while they were ashore. We found that music from shore was too loud so the day after we arrived we moved to the quiet south end of the bay. We hooked onto a sturdy and free mooring ball at the Coconut Beach Hotel. At the hotel we enjoyed the ice cream and cheap beer before arranging an all-day island tour.

Dominica is known as "The Nature Island of the Caribbean." The lush wet island is 29 miles long and 16 miles across. It has four mountains over 4000 feet with the highest being 4747 feet. Dominica is an island of tropical fruit — especially bananas, mangos, and coconut. It is also a tropical rain forest island of abundant and spectacular waterfalls with fresh water pools at their base great for swimming. Volcanic activity is present and there are numerous hot springs. Native flora includes 74 species of orchids and 200 species of ferns. The songs of birds and frogs are nonstop.

# The Valley of Desolation and the Boiling Lake

On May 4th I reached the limit of my endurance when I climbed and hiked the strenuous trip to the Valley of Desolation and then on to the Boiling Lake.

This journey is for experienced hikers and requires a guide. My group included Larry and Angie from the boat *Tao 8* and Jim and Mona from a nearby hotel. All of us were in our forties. None of us were overweight. I am not an experienced hiker but I try to stay fit and walk when I can. We were charged $160 U.S. dollars for our group. We had two guides, Tom and David. We also spent about four hours in a van getting to and from the trailhead.

The narrow trail starts in a dense rain forest. Soon the trail became rugged and we were either climbing up or down steep rough

**Sailing** MAGAZINE

P.O. Box 249
125 East Main Street
Port Washington, WI 53074
262-284-3494
800-236-7444

date _10-12-02_

name _Robert Schmidt_

address _665 Culpepper Dr_

city, state _Reynoldsburg Ohio_

zip _43068_     phone ( _614_ ) _864-3077_

1 year subscription _____

2 year subscription _____

3 year subscription _✓_

SAILING Designs IV _____

SAILING Designs V _____

SAILING Designs IV & V _____

Total Amount $ _53.00_

Cash _____
Check _____     Credit Card _____

☐ New subscriber     ☒ Renewing subscriber _(EXTEND)_

Rec'd. by

wooden steps. As we got close to a streambed the steps were rocks. When we stopped for a break, mosquitoes attacked us. We climbed to the top of a high ridge at the level of the clouds only to plunge down deep to a roaring rocky stream that we forded. There were no bridges on this tough trail. Then we climbed back up ever higher and steeper. About a dozen times the trail was so steep that we were rock climbing using our arms along with our legs.

Wafts of smelly volcanic sulfur filled our hard-working lungs. We tried to keep out of the mud and keep our feet dry but at the Valley of Desolation, the rain started. Gone was the dense rain forest. The ground near our feet was bubbling hot but the pouring rain cooled us. The earth here was very unstable and delicate. A landslide that occurred only a few months prior to our visit had changed the whole look of the valley. It seemed the ground was percolating hot water and steam all around us. The colors of the earth were amazing. They changed from mustard yellow to black to orange to silver to bright green from the moss.

Then up another rock climb and back we were into another rain forest. On we climbed in the rain to the boiling lake.

When we finally arrived at the boiling lake all I saw at first was a waterfall pouring into steam. The rain stopped. The steam cleared away. Down in the 50-yard wide volcanic crater 200 feet below us was the gray turbulent boiling water. We rested and ate.

On the way back we stopped at a natural hot spring pool fed by a gentle warm waterfall surrounded by lovely tropical greenery. I was in awe. But I could not linger long in the pool because we were running out of daylight. Soon I was hiking and climbing again. Lucky for us the return trip was mostly downhill. Angie and I relaxed again in another pool. Still our legs felt like Jell-O. We were soaking wet. Every one of us slipped on the slippery rocks and muddy trail. We no longer looked for dry ground as we tramped through the muddy rain forest. We arrived at the van minutes before dark.

Was the adventure worth the exertion? Yes. Absolutely. Few places on earth could you immerse yourself in such an awesome non-commercialized habitat.

The next day we relaxed with a guided two-hour boat trip on the Indian River. This $10 trip was an easy way to see the gentle side of nature.

On May 6<sup>th</sup> we motored 16 miles to the capital city of Roseau at the south end of Dominica. We had no wind until we tried to anchor. Pete's back was sore and his legs itched from insect bites. I had a slight ear infection from too much swimming and my muscles were sore from the Boiling Lake trail. What a crew! Even *La Boatique* did not get off easy since we towed Larry and Angie on *Tao 8* out of the anchorage. We anchored in 35 feet of water right near shore in a 25-knot wind. Oscar Services helped us run a 250-foot line to a palm tree. Joe and Marge from *Dream Weaver* were anchored near by. They were able to get a mooring ball near the Anchorage Motel. Jay and Sandy from the boat *Nokandolah* left us at this point and headed north to Connecticut. We felt sad that we would not cruise with them again.

Roseau is the capital city of Dominica and had all the services we desired including a great cyber café called Corner House. However, there was no good anchorage for our boat. The anchorage was deep and *La Boatique* rolled back and forth over the Caribbean ocean swell.

# Martinique

On May 8<sup>th</sup> at 6:30 a.m. we motor-sailed away from the lush green island of Dominica to the French island of Martinique. As we neared the end of our 42-mile cruise Pete felt a vibration. I did not. I smelled diesel fuel. Pete did not. We began to pay close attention to the engine. Then Pete smelled diesel fuel too. Injector pipe number three had leaked back in St. Thomas. Now it was leaking again. Pete tried to stop the leak only to find the leak got worse. We limped to Fort-de-France, the capital city of Martinique. Sometimes it seems that *La Boatique* is nearly overloaded with spare parts and tools. But we sure were glad we had spare injector pipes.

Even though we do not speak French, checking in and out of this French country was easy and even free of the usual fees charged by other countries. Martinique is known for its French cuisine. However, Pete does not like French food so we had great tasting burgers and fries at McDonalds. We strolled the busy city streets. I purchased a tight fitting very French looking two-piece dress with slits on each side and shorts under the skirt. The tag said, "Made in America" and the store was called San Diego.

On May 10<sup>th</sup> the wind was twenty to thirty knots on our nose so we decided to motor only seven miles to the fishing village of Anse

D'Arlet, Martinique. During the short morning trip another huge fish ran off with another one of our lures. The anchorage at Anse D'Arlet was picture perfect with clear turquoise water, a white sand beach, small fishing boats, and restaurants with bright umbrellas.

# St. Lucia

On May 11<sup>th</sup> at 6 a.m. we were off to an early start to St. Lucia. Again the wind was nearly on the nose. We had plenty of daylight so we could afford to sail instead of motor. We tacked back and forth and enjoyed an easy comfortable ride. We caught a barracuda and released it. We were having a good time.

We arrived at Rodney Bay, St. Lucia before 1 p.m. Joe and Marge from *Dream Weaver* were already at the marina. Our slip was only a few slips away from theirs. We spent our free time with the folks from *Dream Weaver, Winona II*, and *Argonauta*. John Hayes from *Stardust II* was moored right next to us. *Stardust II* was also a Port Clinton, Ohio boat. The dock fee was only about $18 per day. The marina showers were free. The marina complex included a laundry, a great bakery, restaurants and an e-mail place.

My computer aboard *La Boatique* was babied compared to our other electronics. However, the hard disk drive had been having repeated read and write failures. Since Elaine from *Winona II* was flying to Miami for a week, I sent the computer home with her for repairs. She sent it on to Ocean PC. They replaced the hard drive and installed some additional RAM.

Pete really liked St. Lucia. The 238 square mile island is 1,300 miles southeast of Florida. The people were friendly. The cost of living was fairly low. Rodney Bay was very protected. Hurricanes rarely come this far south. I liked the produce because it was locally grown and quite varied. Gregory, the boat boy, delivered fresh homegrown produce to our boat every day.

While Elaine was in Miami with my computer we visited with her husband, Ingmar. On May 23<sup>rd</sup> Joe drove Ingmar, Pete, and me to the resort where Joe and Marge were staying for a week. The resort, called Windjammer, was a very large complex. Their Spanish style villa included their own small swimming pool. The light airy rooms were open and birds flew in for handouts. This was the first time Joe and Marge had spent a night off their boat in a year.

Marigot Bay, St. Lucia

On May 28th we filled both our water and fuel tanks. We then sailed nine miles to Marigot Bay, St. Lucia. Marigot Bay is completely sheltered in a deep narrow valley. It was a spectacularly beautiful anchorage that was nearly being loved to death. Soon after we anchored a parade of head boats circled through the bay until sunset. Most of the head boats were 60-foot catamaran sailboats loaded with people from cruise ships and hotels. John Hayes on *Stardust II* rafted off *La Boatique*. All three of us used the kayak at different times to explore the bay. John made spaghetti supper and I made garlic bread.

I think I ate too much garlic and onions because soon after dinner I could taste the garlic and I didn't feel good. I slept well but early in the morning I felt worse. At 5:15 a.m. on May 29th even though I was feeling poorly, we set sail for Bequia. We had over ten hours of sailing that day and I was sick for most of the journey. Pete enjoyed the sail as best he could while I often had my head in the bucket. It might seem hard to believe that I also enjoyed the sail, well, some of it at least.

# Bequia

I had heard a great deal about Bequia being the ultimate Caribbean island. Pete loved the island so much that he planned to spend the millennium there. At 4 p.m. on May 29<sup>th</sup> we had arrived at Bequia. We dropped our anchor next to *Stardust II* off a shoreline of palm trees and white sand in the huge Admiralty Bay. The bay may be huge but the island itself was small. It was

Hawksbill turtle in Bequia

about six miles long and a mile wide.

On June 1<sup>st</sup> Pete, Julius (from *Argonauta*), and John (from *Stardust II)* rode a ferryboat to Kingstown, St. Vincent. A crowd of men waited at the ferry dock. As the ferry neared the dock three or four from the crowd jumped onto the ferry. The ferryboat crew tried to stop the crowd from boarding but was unsuccessful. There was much confusion and yelling. Pete could not figure out what the crowd was up to. He soon found out since he was their target. He looked like a tourist to the crowd of desperate taxi drivers boarding the ferryboat. The unwanted taxis drivers grabbed luggage right out of people's hands. Two drivers were nearly playing tug of war between themselves and the luggage. Few tourists visit this island because it is known for its poverty and high crime rate.

Once Pete, John, and Julius ran the gauntlet of taxi drivers, the street vendors and the panhandlers accosted them. The three of them finally found their destination, Napa Auto Parts. Julius needed oil filters and was forced to pay five times the price he would have paid in the U.S. Then they walked the town. After a few beers they were in great spirits. They arrived back at *La Boatique* full of smiles and laughter after completing yet another adventure.

On June 2<sup>nd</sup>, Pete and I along with Julius and Sally walked six miles to Bequia Head at the northern tip of the island. During our walk we rested in a hammock on a palm-fringed beach. We stopped at the turtle sanctuary where we saw hawksbill turtles. On our walk back from the sanctuary, a coconut fell from a tree onto the road a few feet in front of us. Julius cut open the coconut and drank the sweet milk. Mango trees shaded our path. We refreshed ourselves by peeling and eating a few of the mangos lying on the ground. That was the way I liked to get my exercise for the day.

## Hurricane Season Begins

Hurricane season along with the rainy season began June 1st. Even though we should have been far enough south now to avoid a hurricane, we paid close attention to single side band weather reports. We were at 13 degrees north latitude and 61 degrees west longitude. We listened to Eric at 6:35 a.m. at lower side band frequency 3815.0. We also listened to David Jones at 8:30 a.m. at single side band frequency 8104. Eric was south of us while David was north of us. Our first experience with a tropical wave came on May 5th. We had lots of rain squalls during the day. We put on our bathing suits and let the rain soak our skin. We wiped down the wet deck with a washcloth. We had not seen rain in a long time and it felt good. Thunderstorms came during the night. This was the first lightning we had seen in nearly six months.

## Controlling Our Sails

Bringing our sails down in strong wind and big waves has been a challenge. We were always looking for ways to get the sails down safer, faster, and easier. In St. Thomas we installed Dutchman bat cars that rode in the mast track so that the sails would slide down faster. They did not work well. While in Bequia we had sail packs made by Anvell Davis at Grenadine Sails. Our sail packs were used to catch the sails and then protect the sails from the sun when we were not sailing. We needed to try out our new sail packs. So on June 9th we departed Admiralty Bay, Bequia at 9:15. Pete raised the mainsail. We had plenty of wind pushing us out of the big bay. Then Pete unrolled the jib. *La Boatique* heeled as we rounded the western tip of Bequia and headed for the tiny island of Petit Nevis.

Surprisingly, Petit Nevis had an active whale rendering facility that was used during the winter months. Two whales were taken earlier in the year. We walked around the whalebones and then around the island. The island was so beautiful with its desolate palm-fringed pebbled beach. How ironic that the scene of such beauty was also the place where the whales were butchered.

Sue discovers whalebones at an active whaling station on Petit Nevis. Two whales were butchered a few months before our arrival.

During our return sail to Bequia we raised the mizzen and the jib. A squall with wind gusts over 30 knots and heavy rain arrived soon after we left Petit Nevis. We were glad that we did not have the mainsail up. The mizzen alone was enough sail. The torrents of rain ran down the mizzen sail. Once the water got to the boom, the sail pack trapped the water. The water then ran forward toward the mast. I was at the helm in front of the mast. The funneled rainwater cascaded down on my head and then into the cockpit. Pete laughed. I laughed. Nice shower, but a change was needed.

When we arrived in Bequia we tried to zip up our sail packs with the sails inside. The sail pack for the main sail was too tight. On June 10th we removed the pack including the mainsail and returned it to Grenadine Sails for some rework. On June 11th Anvell Davis returned with the corrected mainsail sail pack and added holes to the mizzen sail pack so that the rain would not fall on my head. We really liked the sail packs from then on.

Later in the day we hoisted the mizzen, the mainsail, and the jib. We had pictures taken of us under sail by the professional photographer, Ken Moore. The pictures taken with his camera were beautiful. He also took a few nice shots with our digital camera.

# Dinghy Disaster

On June 14th we were still in Bequia. The weather had been very windy and stormy but not hot. The tropical waves came one right after the other. Sometime during the night on Saturday June 12th a huge gust blew so hard that it flipped over our dinghy. In the morning we saw the dinghy upside down with the propeller sticking up in the air. The motor was under the waves of salt water. The anchor had sunk. The paddles floated away. The bailing pump floated away. Pete jumped in the water and righted the dinghy. We removed the motor. Pete spent a few hours trying to get the salt water out of the motor. The motor started. We put the motor back on the dinghy. Pete motored around *La Boatique* a few times but the motor stalled often. The dinghy (a Force 4 from New Zealand) was not made for tropical sun. During the last month the inflatable tubes had been disintegrating. The tubes were now sticky and loosing air. Pete started shopping for a new dinghy and maybe even a new motor.

La Boatique

Later in the day we watched the Bequia Carnival Parade. The parade consisted of two trucks containing a few musicians and people surrounding the trucks wearing all sorts of costumes. It was the smallest parade I ever saw. But everyone was having a great time.

We had planned to take short, easy island hops south for the next few weeks. We could have used the southern Windward Islands as stepping-stones south to Trinidad. We could have had easy island protected sails through the Grenadines. We could have stayed with the majority of the cruisers. But we were not ones to stay with the crowd. We must have been looking for more adventure, more of a challenge.

When Gill on the boat *Moon Dancer* asked over the VHF radio if anyone had an interest in sailing to Tobago, we replied that we did and so did two other boats, *Mike 'N Mic* and *Stinger*. Few cruisers venture to Tobago. Ironically, we would be heading from Bequia, one of the most favorite islands of yachtsmen, to one of the least visited islands. We eventually found Tobago to be one of our favorite destinations.

On Wednesday, June 16th at 7 a.m. with a great weather forecast we set sail for Tobago. So much for weather forecasts, we were not even out of sight of Bequia before a squall hit us. The squall was over in a few minutes.

Pete tossed out our fish lure. About an hour later I saw all the signs of great fishing. Boobies were diving for fish. Fishermen in small open boats were trolling nearby. Sure enough, a kingfish struck our lure. Pete fought the fish and got it on board *La Boatique*. Filleting the fish on the heeling boat was not easy. While skinning the fish I put a small cut in a finger. I tossed the guts and bones of the fish overboard and stored the large fillets in the refrigerator. There was enough fish for at least three meals apiece.

The trip soon became grueling. During the day we used the motor off and on to try to point higher into the 20 to 25 knot easterly wind. Up and down we rode over the 10 to 15 foot seas. Often breaking waves slapped the hull throwing salt-water spray everywhere. Large breaking waves slammed onto the deck covering even the top of our bimini cover over our heads with salt water. We were soaking wet from salt-water drenchings. Salt water found ways to leak into our cabin. During the night we sailed on but the waves continued their assault.

We thought we had rough conditions but poor Steve and Susan on *Stinger* had their engine overheat. Steve worked through the night over the hot engine in the pounding seas while Susan was left to sail the boat alone. Then their dinghy davits worked loose and Steve had to tie down the dinghy.

# Tobago

Morning arrived with the sight of Tobago ahead and better conditions. Relief was in sight. Little did we know that the worst torture was still to come.

Tobago's shape and orientation is about the same as Lake Erie's shape and orientation. The 116 square mile island is long east to west. When we rounded the southwestern tip of the island 25 to 30 knot winds hit us right in the face. We had to sail right into 20-foot seas. The 4-knot current was also against us. Pete throttled the diesel engine to full power. The taut sails strained against the wind. We tacked back and forth. The waves were confused and way too close together. The ride was awful. For five hours we battled our way nine miles east to Scarborough, the only port of entry for the entire island.

This trip was challenging, but not the adventure we desired.

Pete found out when he arrived at customs that we were not required to have the boat in Scarborough. We could have avoided the five-hour pounding, anchored on the north side of the

Beach Barbeque at Store Bay, Tobago

island, and taken a taxi to the customs office.

On June 20th we easily sailed from Scarborough to Store Bay. Store Bay is on the southwestern tip of the island. It is protected from the easterly trade winds. It is probably the calmest of the bays for anchoring. The beach that runs from Store Bay to Pigeon Point is beautiful with golden sand and plenty of palm trees. I kayaked often and hoped to do some snorkeling soon. We were anchored in front of a fancy hotel called Coco Reef Resort. The nearest dinghy dock was nearly a mile north at Pigeon Point. When we went to shore we carried our small dinghy high onto the beach above the breaking waves. People with large dinghies really had a difficult time landing on this beach. Yachts with large dinghies anchored off Pigeon Point so that they could use the dinghy dock.

I took two island tours. One was with a world-renowned tour guide while the other was with a local young guy who probably had never given a tour before.

On June 23ʳᵈ Shirley and Gene from the boat *Mike 'N Mic* and I went on a bird watching tour led by the world-renowned guide, David Rooks. David Rooks worked with David Attenborough to film *Trials of Life*. David Rooks was also a magazine photographer and journalist. We had a rough start on our tour because David had to change a tire on the way to Little Tobago Island. We drove from the south end of Tobago to the north end. We then boarded a glass bottom boat for a short ride to Little Tobago Island. Little Tobago Island was a wildlife sanctuary. Many birds nested on this rugged wind swept island. David brought along binoculars and a small telescope for us to use to watch the birds. There were over 200 species of birds on Tobago and Little Tobago. While we watched the birds from the top of a cliff wall, David explained how award winning wildlife scenes were filmed from that very spot. I knew that "birders" would really have enjoyed this trip.

While I was on the tour Pete repaired part of our teak flooring by the galley sink. Then, while the varnish was drying, Pete helped the local fishermen and a hundred other people pull in a large net loaded with fish onto the beach. The fish were passed out to all that helped.

On June 25ᵗʰ Steve and Susan from *Stinger*, along with Pete and me went on an island tour. Pete rented a car for $250 TT. (Six TT equal one U.S. dollar. TT stands for Trinidad and Tobago currency.) Wayne, the local water bike renter, was our guide. At first Pete really enjoyed driving the winding roads, but as the day wore on driving got tiring. We drove along the coasts and stopped at some of the sandy bays and small villages. We visited three waterfalls, Argyle, Angel, and Kings Bay. The Kings Bay waterfall was dry because the water was still being diverted to fill a reservoir. The small Angel waterfall was deep in the rain forest. The rock wall behind this waterfall was golden yellow.

The most spectacular of the falls we saw was Argyle. Pete thought that he liked it even better than the ones in Dominica. Argyle had three levels of falls with three pools for swimming. We took many pictures because we wanted to try to capture the striking beauty of the tumbling water through the lush jungle.

On June 28th both Pete and I helped pull the fish net onto the beach at Store Bay, Tobago. Only about a dozen large fish were kept. A bin full of small yellow jacks were kept for making soup. This was a very small catch compared to the one a few days ago. For our effort, we received the best fish. The fishermen even cleaned the fish for us. I sautéed it and we had it for lunch. It was fantastic. We looked forward every day to helping pull in the net.

Pete, second from the left, helps pull in the net.

Our confidence as capable cruisers had increased, but we still often referred to ourselves as "baby cruisers" since we had been cruising for less than one year. We were proud that we not only made our way to Tobago, but we were self sufficient enough to enjoy Tobago. After all, since few yachts came here, there were no services for yachts at all. There were no marine stores. There were no docks, not even one fuel dock. The local water was not safe to drink. We had to anchor in relatively unprotected bays. To go ashore we had to land our dinghy on the beach between the ocean swells. The swells were huge by Lake Erie standards. For example, on June 30th one swell turned the dinghy sideways and flipped it upside down with Pete still aboard. Pete and our outboard motor were thrown hard into the sandy bottom. Surprisingly, both survived intact after a complete wash down.

There were no big grocery stores like in the U.S. The products sold there were not what we were used to. There were no sugar free or non-fat products. There were no health clubs. However, the population was slender and physically fit. Chicken foot soup is a delicacy that we did not try. Street venders not only sold homemade ice cream, they also sold pickled beef skin in a cup. The pickled beef skin tasted to me like pickled fat. It was awful.

My favorite beverage was one unattainable in the U.S. It was coconut water. In the U.S. only ripe coconuts are sold. In the tropics the coconut was picked while still immature and green. A machete was used to hack open a hole in the coconut. Fancy places provided a straw and served the coconut chilled. When the water was gone, the machete was used again to cut open the coconut and to create a spoon out of part of the husk. Inside the coconut was a jelly that had a mild coconut flavor.

On June 29th Jerry Skinner from the boat *Persephone* from Oswego, New York arrived. Jerry was a single-hander (sailed alone) and quite young for being a cruiser. Jerry was still in his thirties. We had previously visited with Jerry while we were in the U.S. Virgin Islands. Jerry had been cruising about the same amount of time that we had. On July 3rd Jerry's younger brother Dan arrived to spend some vacation time.

Since Independence Day is the biggest holiday of the summer back home, Susan from *Stinger* suggested we do something special. I had a special day already arranged. We waded through the surf to catch a ride on the glass bottom boat called Millennium 1.2000. We stopped at three places. At one of the stops the water was about waist deep over what looked like dead coral. However, when the coral rocks were turned over, the undersides revealed bright colors of beautiful corals. Hundreds of fish descended on the overturned rocks. The bright blue parrotfish made loud crunching sounds as they bit off what looked like pieces of colorful rock. The other hungry fish gobbled starfish and other creatures hiding under the rocks.

When we arrived back on the beach an island barbecue awaited us. Simon, the local fisherman, prepared the meal as his way of thanking us for our assistance with pulling in the fishnets. Joining us were Sue and Steve from *Stinger*, Jerry and Dan from *Persephone*, and five local fishermen. We ate grilled fish with a light sauce, rice pilaf, and a cucumber tomato salad. We worked off our food attempting chin-ups on an exercise bar hanging from the cliff wall above the beach. The local fishermen made us look like weaklings. They not only did chin-ups, they also did somersaults over the bar.

That night Simon and the rest of the fishermen drove us in an old car to the village of Buccoo. The fishermen were well-dressed in dress slacks and vests. I wore my tight fitting very French dress that I bought in Martinique. The event we attended was called "Sunday School." It began with about a 12-man steel drum orchestra. The early music was for listening. Of the music they played, my favorite was the Hallelujah Chorus. Then they moved onto music for dancing. Simon asked me to dance. The dance floor was empty and I love to dance. We did a mixture of ballroom and jitterbug dancing, very Latin American.

When the steel drum band finished, we moved onto what Simon called ballroom dancing at what we would call a partially enclosed nightclub. All of us danced until way past 1 a.m. Pete and I were really getting into the Latin rhythm. For refreshment we picked and ate little round green ganip fruit off an overhanging tree.

The people of Tobago were wonderful. They were honest and fun loving. Few yachties came here and even fewer people from the U.S. fly here. The locals were as interested in learning about us as we were about learning about them. After Pete provided his explanation of "Uncle Sam", Pete became known as "Uncle Sam" and I as "Auntie Sam."

# Trinidad

On July 15th at 5:30 a.m. we motored from Store Bay, Tobago toward Trinidad. We looked forward to what should have been a great sail. After all, prevailing winds would be at our back. There was no wind as we left the anchorage, but at dawn the wind is normally calm. The horizon behind us was filled with storm clouds. As we

Pete prepares to spear a fish.

78

motored on in the calm wind a squall paralleled our course for hours. Later squalls were all around us but we stayed under a ray of sunshine. Ribbons of rain came and then disappeared close to us. A few of the squalls brought wind that we could see racing over the water. But the wind, like the squalls, missed us. Pete spotted a huge sperm whale that looked as if it had swum under *La Boatique*. The color of the ocean changed from the bright blue of the Caribbean to the dark greenish brown color of the mighty Orinoco River from Venezuela. One short downpour finally drenched us as we approached our anchorage at La Vache Bay, Trinidad.

At 1 p.m. after 45 miles at sea the anchor was down. But *La Boatique* did not behave as expected. She tended to creep toward the steep jungle hills instead of the ocean. Pete used the stern anchor to try to keep us away from the shore. The three-foot tide controlled how we swung at anchor.

Only one other cruiser was anchored in the large bay and they were nearly a half-mile away. Our neighbor cruiser, a French family, had just finished spear-fishing their dinner. Pete quickly prepared his spear gun. We wore wet suits because the water was only 67 degrees. Here we were nearly 10 degrees from the equator and the water was colder than Lake Erie's water. Not only that, while the Caribbean water was salty, this water seemed fresh in comparison.

Pete speared what looked like a large red snapper. But when he got it to the surface, we found it was not large, but small. We let it go hoping that it would either recover from its wound or provide a good meal for some other fish. Later in the day as we watched green parrots and brown pelicans parade overhead, Pete saw a large bird of prey swoop nearby. The bird was a corbeaus (vulture). We both watched the large black bird with broad wings swoop down and grab the bright red snapper with its talons. The bird carried the fish to the beach and set it on a log. The vulture held the fish with its talons and tore the fish into bite size pieces with its beak.

I was hungry for fresh red snapper. We received a pleasant surprise when our neighbor brought us two large red snappers that he speared. Great, we had grilled red snapper for dinner.

On July 16th we again had no wind so we motored 20 miles to Chaguaramas Bay, Trinidad. There we met up with Julius and his daughter, Amanda, on *Argonauta*. There were thousands of boats in Chaguaramas. We have never seen so many boats in one place. There were boats at anchor, boats tied to docks, boats up on the shore, and boats in huge buildings. There also was every kind of service imaginable available for cruising boats.

The reason there were so many boats was that this location was considered south of the path of hurricanes. Also, Chagauramas had a great natural harbor. The U.S. navy used Chagauramas Bay for years. The yard abandoned by the navy had turned into a great area for cruisers and the businesses that serviced them. The U.S. dollar went a long way. Many items for the boat were cheaper than in the U.S. We decided to take advantage of the inexpensive services and get new cushions custom made for the salon. The only problems with Chagauramas were the extremely high humidity, the hot weather, bugs and the rain. Mold and mildew were starting to become an annoying problem.

On July 19th we moved from the anchorage to a slip at Coral Cove Marina. At Coral Cove we transitioned to civilization. At the boat we had electricity, cable television, all the fresh water we wanted and even an air conditioner. Coral Cove provided us with a swimming pool and a nice shower facility.

We hauled the boat out of the water on July 30th at Peake Yacht Services because boat storage on shore was safer and less expensive than in the water.

We flew home to Ohio on August 3rd. August and September were spent in Ohio away from *La Boatique*.

We had a pleasant visit in Ohio. But after eight weeks of being away from *La Boatique*, we were ready to return to the cruising lifestyle. Pete was filled with excited anticipation as we flew from Cleveland to Miami and then Miami to Trinidad on September 28th.

We were concerned about getting our luggage through customs. While in Ohio we had made many purchases. Most items we had shipped to Trinidad through Marine Warehouse in Miami. But we still had plenty of brand new stuff to carry on the airplane. We had prepared typewritten lists of boat parts and other items we were bringing back with us. But the customs officer in Chaugaramas sent us on our way without us even showing him a single list or any of the items in our luggage. Getting through customs and immigration was much easier than we had anticipated.

We found *La Boatique* resting on sinking jack stands in a field of mud. Soon the rain started and standing water covered the mud. As we contemplated how to get to *La Boatique's* ladder without sinking up to our knees in muck, ants covered our shoes and socks. We were standing on the only high spot around — an anthill.

The high humidity made the heat hard to take. But the common downpours of rain broke the heat temporarily. We were thankful to have the rented air conditioner. Otherwise, *La Boatique's* cabin would have been very hot and damp. Even with the boat all closed up when night came we were fighting off mosquitoes in the cabin.

On October 1st we ordered a new GPS since two of our old ones did not survive the GPS changes that took effect in August. While we were out shopping for the GPS, Peake's boatyard moved the boat *St. Pauli* next to us. However, by the time Barb and Manfred returned to *St. Pauli*, we would be back in the water and back at our comfortable dock at Coral Cove Marina.

## Storm hits the Anchorage

On the afternoon of October 5th a bitter storm brewed off shore. The normally eastern trade wind shifted to the south and then to the southwest. The anchorage was unprotected from a southwesterly storm. The dust blew through the boatyard. The waves began to build in the anchorage. The rain came down in torrents. The southwesterly wind picked up. Lightning and thunder entered the dark sky. The VHF radio became active with reports of boats dragging through the anchorage. The waves in the anchorage grew to six feet. Masts swung through the air as the yachts rode up and over the large waves. Debris, including large trees, washed into the water from the shore. A snake, possibly poisonous, climbed from a floating log onto a sailboat. For once we were glad we were still in the boatyard secure on the ground. We walked over to Coral Cove Marina for a planned potluck appetizer supper. The boats in the marina fared no better than the ones in the anchorage. The large waves bouncing off the dock wall were especially nasty. Some yachts looked as if they were riding a bucking bronco. Their dock lines strained as they were slammed by the waves. But the wind had stopped. The nasty waves subsided. By morning the anchorage was totally calm.

On October 8th we launched *La Boatique* and had a quick five-minute boat ride to Coral Cove where our dock was waiting for us.

On the morning of October 13th Lady Charlie, the leader of the cruising community, announced over the VHF radio that 25 whales lay stranded on a beach. Help was needed to save the whales. So fifteen of us from Coral Cove squished into a van and headed toward the beach. Little did we know that the local radio stations were calling for all to assist if they could. The beach was a long hot cramped two-hour ride away. Before we could even see the Atlantic Ocean, we got tied up in a traffic jam. It seemed to me that half of the island decided to save the whales. So much for us being of much help. At least twenty soldiers from the Trinidad army stood around with M16 rifles to make sure the crowd did not get out of hand. We found out that the whales were feeding in the shallow water and then about 6:30 a.m. became stranded at low tide. Help was needed early in the morning. By the time we arrived after noon, nine pilot whales lay dead in the sand. There was not enough help early in the day to save all the whales. All we could do to help was to splash the dead whales with seawater so that they would be fresh for the autopsy, which was to happen later in the day.

On October 26th we were told the results of the autopsy of the dead pilot whales. The whales' stomachs and intestines were empty. The whales were very weak from hunger. I believe that the whales died because they could not find enough fish to eat.

We sold our old Force 4 Dinghy and purchased a new eight-foot Caribe inflatable with a fiberglass floor. The Caribe is twice as heavy as our old dinghy and is much sturdier. Barb and Manfred also bought an eight-foot Caribe. Barb and Manfred have been busy trying to get *St. Pauli* ready to go in the water. We fell into a routine of half work (on the boat) and half play (sight seeing).

# Salybai Waterfall

At 6:30 a.m. on October 16th Jesse James and his tour van arrived to take us along with eight other cruisers on an adventure. For two hours Jesse drove us from the west side of Trinidad to the east side of the island. We drove from divided highway to two-lane road, then over one-lane bridges to a rugged rutted path. When the van could go no further, we got out and walked. We had two guides, Alexander and Christopher. We had barely begun our hike when a fellow hiker sank knee deep in quicksand. The clicking buzz sounds of locusts mixed with various tropical birdcalls. One of our guides killed a poisonous snake only after it had slithered across the path between two of the hikers. Soon we were hiking deep in the rain forest. A channel-billed toucan yelped from the treetops but we could not see it. With snakes, quick sand, rocks and slippery tree roots under foot we rarely felt comfortable looking up into the thick canopy of foliage for monkeys and birds.

While Pete was fording a stream he injured his shin on a sharp rock. I saw him wince in pain. Then I saw the bloody bruise and his leg already starting to swell. When he described his injury to the other hikers, that was all I needed to make me feel faint. The others wondered what was wrong with me. Pete said that he gets the injury and I get the pain. I splashed water from the stream on my face as I sat on a rock with my head down between my knees. I wished I had some smelling salts. One of the guides gave me a lime peel to smell. The smell revived me enough so that I could continue hiking.

Eventually we arrived at Salybai Waterfall. After what we went through to get to the waterfall, we were disappointed. The clear fresh water pool at the waterfall base was great for swimming but the temperature up in the rain forest was cool. The pool water was cold. None of us swam for long. The waterfall was beautiful, but not spectacular.

Salybai Waterfall

Near the end of the walk back I caught up to some teenagers carrying birdcages. They had illegally trapped wild birds called semps for the pet trade industry. Semps are in the tanager family and are bright yellow and deep blue. They are known for their musical calls. Baby orange-winged parrots are also often caught for pets. The parrots are so numerous here that they are often pests.

On our way home we stopped at Donut Boys to load up on Pete's favorite, jelly and custard filled donuts.

I had a great birthday on November 3$^{rd}$. The day was beautiful, warm and breezy. There was not even any rain. Pete and I washed the top of the boat together and then went for a swim in the pool. We had a light lunch which included bacon wrapped plantains. We loafed in the afternoon. Julius and Sally from *Argonauta* joined us for dinner at Crews Inn. Crews Inn is the fanciest restaurant in the area. The sunset at dinnertime was a picture perfect sky of reds and golds reflecting from the sky to the bay. I had my first steak dinner since September. All the meals were delicious including the chocolate cake and ice cream for dessert.

Barbara chooses a pineapple while Manfred and Pete carry the produce bags.

Barb, Manfred and Pete shopping at the Trinidad Central Market

**Trinidad Central Market**

On November 6$^{th}$ we squished into a maxi taxi for a trip to the Central Market. Joining us were Julius, Sally, Barb and Manfred. The Central Market was similar to our flea markets in Ohio. This exotic market covered acres. Tropical produce was most plentiful and inexpensive. Fresh fish and shellfish were also in abundance. Eggs, baby chicks, live chickens, ducks and even a live turkey were for sale. The chickens were killed, plucked, and dressed before our eyes. The chickens could not be much fresher than that, but I was not a buyer.

Chicken was not on our menu — fish was. We chose blue marlin from one of the many fish stalls. The butcher used a machete and a heavy thumper to cut through the fish's backbone so that we could have one-inch thick steaks. We also purchased pineapples, a watermelon, a tropical fruit similar to a mango called golden apples, oranges, tomatoes, broccoli and green beans. On a previous run to the market I had purchased fresh herbs, limes, lettuce, onions, and eggs.

When I got back to *La Boatique* I made salsa, a golden apple chow, and a tropical fruit salad with a fresh ginger honey dressing. We had grilled blue marlin, mashed potatoes and broccoli with lime butter for dinner.

(Pete wrote this next paragraph.)

The next morning I had to go up the mast. Sue began the strenuous effort of cranking me up, but one-third the way up she felt weak. She left me hanging part way up the mast in the hot sun while she cooled off down below in the cabin. After a while she returned and was able to get me up and down safely. I mentioned to her about being another year older and that her birthday had some effect. But with all due respect, it was a very hot and muggy day with temperatures in the upper 90's.

# LASIK Eye Surgery in Caracas

On November 8th we flew from Trinidad to Caracas, Venezuela, so that Pete could have LASIK eye surgery. If the procedure was successful Pete would no longer need glasses except maybe for reading.

We hired Aleksandar Uldfrian to drive us around when needed and be our interpreter since neither of us spoke Spanish. We believed that Aleksandar's services were well worth his fee. He stayed with us all the time we were at the clinic and made sure we felt comfortable.

We stayed at the Royal Hotel in the Sabana Grande district of Caracas. Caracas is a huge city with a population of 5 million. It is nestled in a long narrow valley at an elevation of three thousand four hundred feet. The mountains to the north are impressively steep. The

Savana Grande district is packed with hotels, restaurants and shops. It is an outdoor mall. Sabana Grande is only safe during daylight hours. At night we stayed off the streets and in the hotel.

The hotel food was inexpensive and good. However, since we did not speak Spanish, our meals were always somewhat of a surprise. On November 9th, our first day at the clinic, Pete had his eyes checked and measured. The machine took a picture of his eyes in three dimensions. Five different machines were used the first day. Pete looked at pictures, lights and parallel lines while the machines gathered statistics about his eyes. He had no pain at all. The procedure took half an hour at most. Dr. Rodregues then explained that Pete was a good candidate for LASIK.

The second day Pete took pills all day to keep him sedated. At the clinic early in the morning he put on a hospital gown, cap and blue slippers. He sat in a comfortable recliner. Eye drops were added to his eyes. An overhead TV showed the procedure live of a preceding patient. Then it was Pete's turn. A clamp held Pete's eye open. A thin layer of the cornea was lifted up as an instrument called a microkeratome glided across the cornea. Then in less than 60 seconds, ultraviolet light and high energy pulses from the eximer laser reshaped the internal cornea. The cornea was then closed without the need for stitches. Next the other eye was done. After the surgery plastic shields were taped to his eyes. I called Pete "fly man" because of his bug-like eyes.

Pete's vision was clear sometimes and blurry at other times. That was to be expected during recovery. He could read without glasses. His distance vision came and went. He would need about a month or so for recovery. Pete said that it was nice getting up in the morning and not having to grab glasses. The cost for the surgery including the examination, doctor and clinic fees was $974 for both eyes.

Pete and I had good friends heading off the East Coast of the U.S. to the Caribbean Islands. I listened to Herb on the SSB (Single Side Band Radio). He was nearly impossible for us to hear during daylight hours. We had not heard him talk to our friends on the boat *Elysia* as yet. Pete did hear Herb call *Mutual Fun* sailing to Bermuda, but he could not hear *Mutual Fun*. The SSB used too much power for us to leave it on for hours at a time. Sometimes Herb was clear but most of the time there was too much static. Coral Cove Marina was like a black hole for radio communications. We heard Herb talking to boats from the East Coast all the way to the Canary Islands. He sure did have a lot of boats to talk to!

We were trying hard to get the boat and ourselves ready for departure in a few days. We had extremely unusual wind. Normally the trade winds blow out of the east every day. However, we had mainly westerly winds for nearly two weeks. The cause of the west wind was the storm that became Hurricane Lenny. Trinidad was about the only safe place to be in the Eastern Caribbean during this hurricane. We had a swell come through that rocked the boats for a few hours, but other than that we were fine.

Pete's eyes were doing much better. His vision was very clear most of the time. His only problem was with bright lights at night. He still needed to rest his eyes to continue the recovery from the LASIK surgery.

We had a Thanksgiving turkey meal at Comos' house. Comos rented us our air conditioner. Cosmos was 68 years old and was always looking for new services to provide to the cruisers. After all, cruising sailors had much more money to spend than most people who lived in Trinidad. Cosmos often invited his customers over for dinners. He seemed to enjoy standing in the background listening to them talk about the cruising life style. Cosmos lived in a wealthy community and had a large home even by U.S. standards. We had dinner with Cosmos three times.

Life ran at a much slower pace in Trinidad than in the U.S. You could not be in a hurry. Our departure was delayed. I don't think we saw anyone leave on the day they expected to leave. We took a maxi taxi to the Hi Lo Grocery at the Mall with the intent of getting lots of groceries for the next few months. The clerk said that the store would take us and our groceries back to Coral Cove. However, when we arrived at the checkout with our full cart, the delivery guy was gone. We left the groceries at the store and they were delivered the next day. Our dodger was gone off the boat getting alterations. Our motor lift that we ordered months ago still had not shown up. Our new Kiss wind generator had not been delivered or installed. Pete was off helping Manfred try to figure out what was wrong with some other boat's engine. And Pete told yet another boat that he would try to help the guy get his engine started.

I wondered if we would be ready to leave by Sunday or Monday.

We planned to visit a few anchorages in Trinidad and then head north to Grenada and the Grenadine Islands.

Over four months had passed since we last sailed *La Boatique*. Two of the four months *La Boatique* spent high and dry while we flew home to Ohio. Nearly one month was spent with the details of Pete's eye surgery. The remainder of the time was spent working on *La Boatique* improvements and visiting Trinidad.

| **List of New Items (or Improvements)** |
|---|
| 1. Gypsy (that does not work well) for the windless |
| 2. Autoprop Propeller (that works great) |
| 3. Shaft lock |
| 4. Shaft coupling |
| 5. VHF radio |
| 6. VHF antenna |
| 7. TV antenna |
| 8. GPS |
| 9. Traveler |
| 10. Halyards |
| 11. Main boom and mizzen boom repairs |
| 12. Wind Generator |
| 13. Modifications to the dodger |
| 14. Caribe 8 foot long dinghy |
| 15. Dinghy cover, gray and burgundy |
| 16. Dinghy anchor |
| 17. Interior cushions with foam |
| 18. Tupperware containers |
| 19. Stove with oven and broiler |
| 20. Clothes wringer for washing clothes |
| 21. Bathing suits |

| | |
|---|---|
| 22. | Sandals |
| 23. | Shorts |
| 24. | Sun glasses |
| 25. | Cruising guide books |
| 26. | Charts for the Western Caribbean, South Pacific, Australia, and New Zealand |
| 27. | Sewed chart covers for storing charts |

# Grenada

Our planned departure was for an eight-mile trip on November 29th, but we just could not get ready in time because it takes time to turn *La Boatique* from a "house" back into a "boat." By November 30th we were ready. The forecast was for great sailing conditions (15-knot southeast wind) with a chance of a severe thunderstorm for excitement. The winds were to die off during the night, which would allow us a comfortable night sail. The forecast started out correct and deteriorated from there.

At 9 a.m. Pete raised the full mainsail while we were still in the protection of the Chagaraumas anchorage. Then we motor-sailed out of the Gulf of Paria and into the Atlantic Ocean. Pete unfurled the jib and we soon were under sail power only.

We were happy to be underway out on the ocean swell. But my sea legs were gone. I did not throw up but I felt seasick nearly the entire trip. The sailing was great with the 15 to 20 knot wind on our beam. We were sailing much faster than anticipated. As Trinidad disappeared behind us, the horizon changed from dark green hills to building thunderstorms. We both took naps so that we would be prepared for night sailing. Storm clouds grew closer. The wind began to build, staying above 20 knots. Pete put a double reef in the mainsail. But the lazy jack snapped off the boom and got caught on a batten near the top of the sail. The dark clouds descended upon us bringing nearly 30 knots of wind. The misty rain that fell for a few minutes felt cool and refreshing. With the rain came lower winds but not for long. We reeled in a small dolphin fish (mahi-mahi) but lost it at the boat.

With darkness came foreboding flashes of lightning. Another storm came and went.

While I was at the helm Pete watched the radar screen as it displayed more nasty storms heading toward us. The wind built to 25 knots with higher gusts and the next storm was still miles away. We were flying along at over 8 knots, a speed above our hull speed, too fast for our boat. We needed to get the mainsail down. The night sky was inky black. The lazy jack was still caught on a batten. The seas were too rough for me to head into them to totally release pressure off the mainsail. Still, we had to get the mainsail down before conditions got worse. Pete tried to get the sail down while it still was under pressure from the wind but it would not budge. We tried again with me quartering the waves, the traveler line let out, and the main sheet all the way out. Luckily, just then the wind let up to 18 knots and the sail came down billowing out over our sail pack, but down it was. Minutes later the wind was over 30 knots abaft our beam. We were running with the wind and the storm on a reefed jib alone.

At the rate we were traveling instead of arriving at Mount Hartman Bay, Grenada at dawn, we would arrive at midnight. This is not an anchorage to be entered during an inky black night sky. So we altered our course to head up the west side of Grenada. The storm clouds cleared away. The lights of Grenada showed in front of us. At 1 a.m. on December 1st we anchored in Grand Anse Bay off the beach at St. Georges, Grenada for a short sleep. (Pete had anchored here before while on a charter boat.) Some of the hotels along the shore had been washed away by Hurricane Lenny. We had covered 97 miles in 16 hours averaging 6 knots per hour.

At 7 a.m. on December 1st we raised the anchor and the double reefed mainsail and were under way again. The ocean was calm because the east wind was blocked by the island mountains. But around 10 a.m. when we got to the north end of Grenada we got blasted with 25 to 30 knot northeast winds. It was no fun motor-sailing into this wind. At 1:30 p.m. we anchored in Tyrrel Bay, Carriacou. As I backed down on the anchor we heard a squealing sound. We had forgotten to reel in the fish line and now 90-pound monofilament fish line was wrapped tightly around the propeller shaft. Pete was not supposed to go in the water because of his eye surgery. Therefore, I would have to dive down to cut away the line. When I dove down I saw an inch thick wrap of line around the shaft. The 90-pound line was so strong that I could only cut away a few

Sue enjoys the view of Sandy Island.

wraps before I needed air. Cutting away was a long process but I continually whittled away at the line until the shaft was free.

On December 2$^{nd}$ we rode a mini bus to Hillsborough to check into Carriacou (part of Grenada). While there we enjoyed ice cream cones. Hurricane Lenny had destroyed many businesses. On December 3$^{rd}$ we visited the Carriacou Yacht Club. A travel lift was being added. Pete contemplated Carriacou as a place to haul out *La Boatique* during the next hurricane season.

Tyrrel Bay was beautiful but our next destination was awesome. On December 4$^{th}$ we motored 3 ½ miles to Sandy Island. This tiny strip of white sand was less than ¼ of a mile long and wide enough for a single row of palm trees. Heaps of coral and colorful shells broke the ocean swell on the north, east and west side of the island, while the south side where we anchored had the white sandy beach. I had fun kayaking and snorkeling. I was told that Lenny had radically changed the size and shape of the island.

What was renowned as the best cruising grounds in the Caribbean was not for us because of the weather.

We had to leave the picturesque anchorage at Sandy Island because the wind became very strong. The wind, waves, and ocean swell drove us out. We motor-sailed four miles back to Tyrrel Bay, Carriacou on the afternoon of December 5$^{th}$.

## The Grenadines

On December 7$^{th}$ we motor-sailed to Clifton Harbour, Union Island. We were no longer in the country of Grenada. We were now in the country of St. Vincent and the Grenadines. The Clifton Harbour anchorage was protected from the ocean waves and swell by reefs but it offered no protection from the wind. December 8th was a dreary, stormy day. During the night the wind became uncomfortably strong.

After sunset on December 8th the wind piped up to 20 to 30 knots in the anchorage. The bracket holding the wind generator to the mizzenmast was vibrating, we had more than enough power, so we turned the powerful KISS wind generator off for the night. On December 9th we headed north from Union Island. We planned to stop at Mareau but both Chatham Bay and Salt Whistle Bay looked too rolly so we motor-sailed to the island of Canouan. We considered anchoring in Corbay but ocean swells were rolling in there also. So we turned around and entered Charleston Bay, Canouan. We anchored way up in the northern tip of the bay behind the protection of some rocks. However, the ocean swell found us there too. Pete used the dinghy to deploy a stern anchor so that we could point *La Boatique* into the swell. But we still were uncomfortable. We were the only boat in the anchorage until a charter boat arrived. Most of the people on the boat were from Cleveland. One woman named Linda (Miller) Sobel attended classes at Cuyahoga Heights School with my sister Carol. I may have even met her and her husband at my cousin Paul's funeral. Small world, isn't it?

Canouan looked inviting from the deck of *La Boatique* on the morning of December 10th. So we decided to take a dinghy ride to shore. However, when we got close to shore we found that the dinghy dock had been destroyed by hurricane Lenny. Many of the shoreline structures had been damaged. The beach was about gone. There was no easy way to land the dinghy with the large ocean swells rolling in. There would be no visiting Canouan for us. We decided that we might as well head north to Bequia. We mostly motored the 27 miles north into the 20 to 25 knot northeast wind. We arrived at 2:30 p.m. in Admiralty Bay, Bequia. We anchored in the northwest side of the bay for more protection from the ocean swells.

Bequia was planned as our Christmas and Y2K holiday island. Here in Bequia (south of St. Vincent) the weather had been perfect but quite breezy. We were away from the hot humid weather of Trinidad.

On the morning of December 13th we found we had a booby on our bowsprit. The booby thought he had found a good place to watch for fish. But Pete chased him off since boobies don't use the head (toilet). They just shit on the boat. Bobbies are not afraid of humans and so are difficult to chase away.

Bequia is a gathering place for many cruisers. Joe and Marge from the boat *Dream Weaver* were there. So were Ingmar and Elaine from the boat *Winona II*. Barb and Manfred from the boat *St. Pauli* were still in Trinidad. We heard on December 16th on the single side band that Manfred was in the hospital because of an infection in his foot. We later heard that Barb and Manfred flew back to Canada for better medical treatment.

## The Solstice Moonbow

As darkness descended on December 22nd a bright white glow showed above the hills of Bequia. The full moon began its rise peeking through rain filled nimbostratus clouds. As I watched the moon to the east, Pete spotted the moonbow to the west. The moonbow looked like the ghost of a rainbow. At first the moonbow's arc was translucent white. But then as the clouds cleared away from the moon the colors of a rainbow became clear, though still muted in ghostly white. The moonbow began at the southwest end of the anchorage, reflected from the clouds, curved over the night sky, and back down toward the north side of the anchorage.

The winter solstice happened to also be the night of the full moon. This full moon was at least 7 percent brighter than a normal full moon. The moon was much closer to the earth than normal. These conditions along with the addition of the nimbostratus clouds caused this highly unusual, possibly once in a lifetime event.

Christmas day brought unusually light wind and a sunny sky. It was a great day for fishing, walking, and taking pictures. We shared a Christmas turkey dinner with Julius and Sally on *Argonauta*. They cooked the turkey while we made the pumpkin pie and mashed potatoes.

Bequia was very crowded with boats during the holidays.

Admiralty Bay, Bequia

# 2000

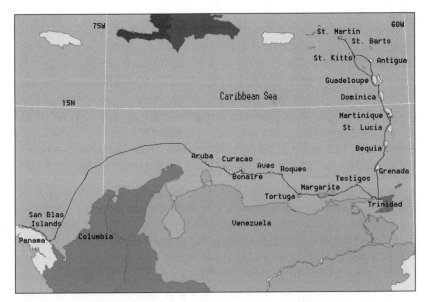

*La Boatique's* travels during 2000 from Bequia north to St. Martin, then south to Trinidad and west to Panama.

## Island Bureaucracy

We rarely sent or received packages because of the hassle. But we needed a new regulator for the engine. The regulator was sent Fed-X on December 30th, 1999 and delivered in Bequia on January 4th. I went to Solana's Boutique where the package was delivered. Solana's is the Fed-X agent. I signed for the package and was given a form to take to Sam's Taxi. Sam's Taxi is the exporter. Pete delivered the form to Sam's Taxi and was told to return in two hours for the completed paperwork. The woman at the desk was clearly not busy. The forms took no more than five minutes to complete on a previous occasion but she would not complete the forms while Pete waited. Pete returned at 2 p.m. She told him the price was $31 EC (Eastern Caribbean Currency, $2.68 EC equals $1.00 U.S.) Pete had a $100 EC bill and a $20 EC bill. She did not have change. So she settled for $20 EC. She gave Pete six pieces of paper.

Pete then went to customs to pick up the package. The customs agent told Pete that Pete needed a $5 EC stamp. He directed Pete to the revenue counter next to the customs counter. A sign at the counter said, "Closed due to inventory." Since Pete could not purchase the $5 EC stamp, the customs agent would not give Pete the package.

The next morning Pete arrived before customs opened only to find a long line. When finally Pete got his turn at the counter he was told that his paperwork performed by Sam's Taxi was incorrect and therefore they would not sell him the $5 EC stamp. Pete walked back to Sam's Taxi. The woman did not see anything wrong so she walked the paperwork back to customs. She returned to Sam's Taxi to inform Pete that Sam's Taxi had forgotten to stamp the paperwork. Since the paperwork had yesterday's date, the papers would need to be redone. Pete was to hand over $30 EC and come back in two or three hours.

Pete was angry. He certainly was not going to pay them $30 EC for their mistake. Pete asked the women to put the stamp on yesterday's paperwork. He then walked back to customs and purchased the stamp. The customs agent had Pete open the box and explain the use of the regulator. The agent told him that ordinarily a customs agent would accompany Pete to the boat to make sure that the item would stay on the boat and not be resold in the Grenadines. Luckily for Pete they were too busy and let him depart with the regulator.

If the Fed-X box had been labeled "hold at Fed-X" we could have picked up the box at Solana's on January 4th and avoided all the trips to customs and Solana's and the expense of the $5 EC stamp and the $20 EC exporter charge. Island bureaucracy can be perplexing.

# Bequia to St. Lucia

After a month in Bequia of strong winds nearly every day we were ready to move on. Instead of using the jib as we usually do, we dug the staysail out of sail locker. Pete raised the staysail along with the triple reefed mainsail. The sails formed two small triangles near the bottom of the main mast. *La Boatique* was set for heavy wind and could gracefully sail through a gale. As Julius (from *Argonauta*) saluted us by blowing his conch shell horn, we waved goodbye. The date was January 12, 2000. The time was 6:40 a.m.

While we were still under the protection of Bequia the wind blew at a strong 20 knots. Between Bequia and St. Vincent the east wind on our beam increased. Even with very little sail area raised *La Boatique* sped along at over 8 knots at times. The beam sea swells were large. One 15-foot swell broke while we were broadside to it and broached us as I was steering. From then on I paid more attention to the waves and pointed *La Boatique* into the large ones. The frequent gusts of wind were just reaching gale force at 35 knots. But, except for a few annoying swells, the two-hour ride to St. Vincent was comfortable. Along the lee shore of St. Vincent the wind and seas were down. We enjoyed the view of the rugged tropical shoreline as we ate hard-boiled eggs for breakfast.

At the north end of St. Vincent we needed to head northeast. Our sail changed to a beat. We used the motor to assist the sails and help us stay on course overcoming the wind, waves, and easterly current. For the next five hours we sailed toward St. Lucia in wind from 20 to 35 knots. Again the ride was comfortable and our speed was great. The coastline of St. Lucia gave us diminished seas and wind along with beautiful scenery. Jutting out from the shoreline the towering twin Pitons were bathed in sunlight while a squall drenched the small town of Soufriere nearly hidden in a valley. A rainbow reflected from the steep slope of Gross Piton.

## St. Lucia

We entered the narrow Marigot Bay, St. Lucia, as the sun set. We had covered 71 nautical miles in 11 hours, a fast run for us. We were glad we arrived during daylight since the anchorage was full of sailboats. We squeezed into a tiny spot and spent the night uncomfortably close to other boats. In the morning almost every boat in the anchorage left so we re-anchored in a better spot away from the dock.

Marigot Bay is spectacularly beautiful as well as sheltered by mangroves and palm trees. What better place for a lazy afternoon kayak ride. Both Pete and I enjoyed the obliging breeze and warm sun as we paddled around the bay.

On January 14th at 9 a.m. we set sail. The entire day's sail would be along the lee shore of St. Lucia. The island of St. Lucia would block the ocean swells. We had nearly perfect sailing conditions under a double reefed mainsail and partial jib. There was plenty of wind. *La Boatique* cut through the tiny waves. This is the Caribbean sailing people dream about; palm trees, bright blue water, smooth ride and a warm breeze.

This was too good to be true.

When Rodney Bay came into sight our sail would soon end, or so we thought.

Our last mile into the bay was also into the wind. Pete decided to take down the sails and motor in. As Perky (our engine) purred along we pondered the wonderful day.

Then suddenly without warning Perky sped up and then stalled. We unfurled the jib and turned back out to sea. Pete went below to try to get the engine running.

Pete makes use of the dinghy pump to clear the fuel line.

Before long the engine was running again. We rolled in the jib and headed back toward the bay. Again the engine quit, and again we were back to sailing. This time we decided to sail all the way into the bay. Luckily for us Rodney Bay is huge with plenty of anchoring room.

Anchoring was easy. Keeping the engine running was not.

Poor Perky was starving to death. The vacuum gauge on top of the Racor filter was registering high. Perky could not suck in fuel. Pete disconnected the fuel line at the two-way valve that leads to the tanks. The lines to the tanks were clear. The line from the valve to the filter system was blocked. We dug out the dinghy pump and used it to blow the blockage out of the line and into a plastic cup. The engine purred once again.

We were ready to enter the narrow channel leading to the quiet lagoon, or so we thought.

When Pete reconnected the fuel line to the filter system he accidentally bumped the valve handle on the Fuel Purification System. This mistake allowed fuel to go to the sump area instead of the engine.

La Boatique races along

Perky was once again starving and stalled outside the channel. We quickly re-anchored, discovered the problem, and got Perky running once again. We finally tied up to a slip at Rodney Bay Marina and had a cold beer.

## La Boatique Races for the First Time

January 21st and 22nd were predicted to be perfect days for sailing, good wind with diminished seas. But we did not cruise to Martinique as a sensible cruiser would. We were game for high adventure. *La Boatique* would race for her first ever race in a Heineken International Regatta in St. Lucia. Pete would take the helm. David Bell from the yacht, *Wind Spirit* would be the tactician and man the starboard jib sheet. I would man the port sheet and the mizzen sail. Brenda Collins from *Wind Spirit* and Susan Abel from *Abel Lady* would handle our mainsail.

Before the race we unloaded our biggest anchor and 300 feet of

Racing crew of La Boatique

chain along with an assortment of other items. Pete attended the skipper's briefing. We checked to make sure everything was carefully stowed.

For our first race we had our mainsail, mizzen, and jib fully raised. *La Boatique* was like an Arabian mare in a horse race with thoroughbreds. She was beautiful and fast but not competitive against sleek racing yachts. After all, we were racing our house. We were in awe as the 63-foot swan, Eva, galloped past us. Then we were embarrassed as a tiny 21-foot local sailboat somehow got ahead of us by sailing close to shore. After 10 hours at sea racing we were dead tired and poor *La Boatique* was a mess. That night we went to the yacht club and watched the video highlights of the day. There was *La Boatique* looking as pretty as could be as the racers sped on by. Our energy was renewed.

Even though we were tired and sore, our second day of racing was much easier. We were all better at our jobs. We used only the jib and reefed mainsail. *La Boatique* still sailed fast, often getting up to 8 knots. We thought we were doing great but we lost every one of the four races we entered. We had last place solidly locked up.

On January 26th we took an island tour of St. Lucia accompanied by eight other cruisers. Rodney Bay where we started the tour is at the northern part of the island. As we traveled south the terrain got more mountainous, the vegetation more lush. We tasted different foods like the flat grainy cassava bread. As we drove along the western shore of St. Lucia we were either climbing or descending winding roads with hairpin turns. We stopped at the scenic overlooks and snapped our pictures. Near the Pitons we visited a volcano with steaming sterile earth and bubbling pools at a smelly place called Sulfur Springs. Later we walked through well-tended gardens to get to the Diamond waterfall.

## Martinique

The following day, January 27th, we sailed out of Rodney Bay headed toward Martinique. We used a partial jib and double reefed mainsail. The wind was stronger than predicted and was blowing at 20 to 25 knots. *La Boatique* galloped along on a beam reach as if she were still racing. She passed the other cruising boats easily. All of a sudden I spotted a huge whale on a collision course with us. Pete fell off course so that we circled around the whale lazily floating on the surface. We sailed 31 miles and averaged a very fast 6.9 knots. We ended the day in the fishing village of Anse D'Arlet, Martinique. Next to us was *Blue Gull* from back home (Toledo, Ohio).

On January 28th we only had to travel eight miles in water protected by the island of Martinique. We anticipated a placid tranquil motorsail. Instead we got surprised by a very windy morning. The wind was blowing at 30 to 35 knots nearly on our nose. Even with only a double-reefed mainsail *La Boatique* heeled over. The wind caught the tops of the short choppy waves. A salty mist of water sprayed all over the boat and us. The capital of Martinique, Fort-de-France, looked so close. But getting there seemed to take way too long. Lunch was at Pete's favorite, McDonalds. We must have arrived back into civilization.

# No Land under Foot for Four Days

Civilization did not last long. The morning of January 31$^{st}$ would be our last step on land until the afternoon of February 4$^{th}$. Before we left terra firma we swallowed our third McDonalds meal in four days. The next five days would bring sailing during the day. The remainder of daylight was used for food preparation, fixing things, and study time. We reviewed the weather predictions received on our single side band radio and printed the weather maps on our computer. We analyzed the predicted wind speed and direction. We studied our large-scale passage charts and small-scale individual island charts. We read the cruising guide to determine how to approach each anchorage and where to drop the hook. We decided what sails we would use the next day and had them semi ready for action. We woke early each day so that we would have the anchor well set before dark. These four days brought a new cruising companion who sailed with us only for these days. His name was Rex and his boat was called *Paspartout*. He was from of Ketchikan, Alaska.

We left Fort-de- France on January 31$^{st}$. We sailed on jib alone. We glided along on an easy 15-knot breeze abaft our beam. *La Boatique* gave us a level ride, no heeling today. This was one of those placid tranquil sails. A group of dolphins swam past and two jumped straight up in the air clear out of the water. After 12 delightful miles we had reached our destination of St. Pierre, Martinique. Rex and I enjoyed a refreshing dip in the cool clear water before dinner.

The morning came early since we set sail at 5:45 a.m. We had nearly 60 miles to cover and then get safely anchored before dark. To sail from Martinique to Dominica involves 30 miles of ocean between the islands. The wind varied from 8 to 38 knots. The 8 to 10 foot waves were annoying and choppy. Squalls came about once an hour all day long. We were constantly adjusting sails for the conditions. The second half of the trip along the coast of Dominica was gentle with no waves. I nearly fell asleep; the sail was so relaxing. But then another squall came so relaxation time was over. We made good time getting our anchor set by 3:15 p.m.

Rex was caught by surprise by a strong gust of wind.

On February 2<sup>nd</sup> we sailed on from Portsmith, Dominica, to Isle Des Saintes, Guadeloupe. Gusty winds off the steep shoreline of Dominica caught Rex by surprise and almost knocked his boat down. Pete snapped a picture just as it was happening. Pete decided to sail on jib alone since he expected a down-wind sail. But, instead, the wind was on the beam. Our speed was slow. We probably would have had a better ride if we had used the triple reefed mainsail and the staysail. But once we were out in the big waves, neither of us wanted to go forward to raise the mainsail and hank on the staysail. Worse yet, Rex alone in a smaller boat was passing us. The 8-foot waves lifted the starboard side of *La Boatique* and then we rose up high only to roll down the backside of the wave. The ride was uncomfortable. Hanging on was a chore. Often breaking waves would slap the side of the boat and spray us with salt water. Thank goodness we only had four hours of this to deal with. We found out that evening in the anchorage that Rex motor-sailed the entire way. No wonder he was so fast.

We woke early on February 3<sup>rd</sup> even though we could have slept in. We decided that we might as well get sailing so we were out on the ocean by 7 a.m. We had a wonderful day of sailing. We had an easy downwind sail to the island of Guadeloupe. The two short squalls with wind gusts to 35 knots did not even bother us. The remainder was an easy pleasant ride with no waves since the island protected us. Just before we reached the anchorage of Deshaies, Guadeloupe, we landed a wahoo for dinner. I pan-fried the delicious fish. The day did not have a perfect ending since Rex ran out of fuel while anchoring. Rex could not get his engine going so Pete spent the evening on *Paspartout* bleeding the engine.

Deshaies was not one of my favorite anchorages and this visit confirmed my feelings. The last time I was here there were two funerals. At least no one died this time. The wind gusts howled out into the anchorage at over 30 knots. *La Boatique* groaned and then swayed back and forth. We were tired, but sleep was difficult. In the morning Pete suggested staying for a day of rest but I convinced him to press on. I wanted out of there.

On February 4<sup>th</sup> we left Deshaies with a bad-tempered wind propelling us out of the anchorage. Deshaies seemed to be saying good riddance. We raised the small staysail and triple reefed mainsail. *La Boatique* sped away on 30-knot winds. As the island of Guadeloupe disappeared so did the bad-tempered gusty wind. *La Boatique* slowed way down resulting in us rocking in the beam swell. We unfurled our big jib to resume our speed. We cut through the swell much better. As we approached the southwest side of Antigua the swell disappeared. The watercolor changed from deep ocean blue to bright turquoise. Pete looked down and could see the sandy bottom, an unnerving scene miles out in the ocean. The dappled water caused by the shadows of small clouds made reading the water depth by sight difficult. We were alert. At least the sea was calm. Cautiously we approached Jolly Harbour, Antigua. We had covered 53 miles in 8 hours.

We smiled and hugged once the dock lines were set. We were tired and hungry. We could finally relax and sleep easily.

# Antigua

We spent a week at the dock in Jolly Harbour. We took a bus ride to English Harbour, read, watched TV, worked on the boat, and ate well. The Epicurean Grocery store at the marina had many of our favorite foods imported from the U.S. We had skim milk and edible ground beef for the first time since our summer visit in Ohio. The fresh milk that we did find, if we were lucky, down in the southern islands often had curds in it. People don't seem to drink milk or eat beef in the Caribbean. At Jolly Harbour we got fat and lazy and slept well.

We needed an early morning start to get to St. Kitts, but there was no way to leave the marina much before 9 a.m. The lines from the boat next to us hemmed in our boat. We needed the marina's assistance to cast off lines and then retie them after we had left. So, on the afternoon of February 12$^{th}$ we departed Jolly Harbour for a short four-mile trip around the corner north to anchor in Five Islands Harbour. We traveled less than four miles but went from the touristy Jolly Harbour to the uninhabited Maiden Island in Five Islands Harbour. Condos and restaurants lined the shoreline at Jolly Harbour while egrets, pelicans and boobies roosted on Maiden Island. The yachts in Jolly Harbour rested quietly at the dock while at Five Islands there was action. Sleek racing yachts with bright spinnakers chased each other around three marks in Five Islands Harbour. Jolly Harbour's grounds were perfectly manicured gardens of red and yellow flowers evenly spaced between towering palm trees. Nature had reclaimed the grounds at Five Islands where sugar was once grown and milled. Way off in the distance Pete spotted the garbage dump. With the dump for a neighbor, Five Islands Harbour had a good chance of being left to nature.

At 6:15 a.m. on February 13$^{th}$ in the quiet of dawn we left Antigua. A dark squall covered the northern portion of the island. We could not be sure this squall with high winds would not catch up with us out in the ocean. We figured on a windy downwind run to St. Kitts. But the wind was insubstantial early in the morning. We used a different sail combination. We raised the jib and mizzen sails. That way we had a large triangle raised at our bow and a somewhat smaller triangle raised at our stern and no sail in the middle. These sails ended up being a great combination for the 25-knot winds we received later in the day.

At 8:15 a.m. Pete turned on the single side band so that we could listen to the Safety and Security Net followed by the Caribbean Weather Net. Just as Pete called in our weather statistics the wretched squall caught up to us. While Pete held on down below with the microphone to his mouth, I was holding the ship's wheel with rain pelting my back. The wind increased from a mere 12 knots to 36 knots in seconds. *La Boatique* had too much sail up for this much wind so she wanted to fishtail from side to side. It seemed to me that whenever we called in to the Weather Net we were in a storm. I began to wonder if other cruisers thought we continually traveled under a storm cloud. By the time the Weather Net was over, so was the storm. Pete reefed the mizzen to make our ride more comfortable. The wind stayed above 20 knots abaft our beam for the remainder of the day.

## St. Kitts

We anchored in Majors Bay, St. Kitts, at 2 p.m. St. Kitts had the reputation of being a drug island and also being not friendly to cruisers. We never went ashore although we did go swimming. The bay was empty of cruisers except for *La Boatique* and our traveling companion boat for this voyage, *Qwest*. The barges that were there during our last visit in April were still there. We watched cruising yachts approach from the horizon but all cruisers sailed on by. Aboard *Qwest* we played many games of dominos until dark.

A golden dawn greeted us as we headed toward the rising sun peaking through small puffy clouds. I glanced from the golden dawn seascape to my watch, which read 6:10 a.m. We motored through a shallow passage between the islands of St. Kitts and Nevis. The tall islands soon framed the sunrise. We sailed along the windward side of St. Kitts and then on toward St. Barts over 50 miles away.

As soon as we turned north away from Nevis, Pete pulled the halyard to raise the staysail. On this trip we used a partial jib, staysail and triple reefed mainsail. We expected nearly a close-hauled sail since a strong wind was supposed to be out of the northeast. Instead, the wind stayed out of the east and therefore stayed on our beam.

*La Boatique* became an uneven lopsided elevator as we sailed along broadside to the waves. When we were in the trough between two waves we were in the basement with 8-foot ocean swell on either side of us. Then the waves would give us the feeling of being lifted to the first floor. Then back we would go to the basement. Often the ride was even and slow but sometimes the elevator went crazy. There was the high-speed ride. Up, up, up we would go to the top of a wave and then the bottom would drop out. The floor of our crazy elevator averaged an incline of 20 degrees. But our floor never stayed level. It's enough to make a person seasick, but I survived without throwing up. One freak 15-foot wave caught us wrong. Instead of riding up and down we rolled from side to side. Our floor went from an incline of 20 degrees to 60 degrees. The dishes flew out of the cupboard. The dinghy motor was down to the bottom of the trough. The motor was attached to the port stern rail. Its propeller was in the water. The port gunnel was deep under water. Our elevator had gone topsy-turvy for a few seconds. But the end of the ride was finally in sight. St. Barts soon blocked the waves. We anchored in the bay of Anse de Columbier.

I would like to say that I enjoyed my crisp swim to the beach the next day. However, the wind was cool and the water was chilly. It seems to me that this winter in the Eastern Caribbean had been much colder than last winter. But then again maybe I was getting used to the usual heat of the tropics.

## St. Maarten/St. Martin

On February 17th we sailed from St. Barts to the Dutch side of St. Martin, which is called St. Maarten. We anticipated wind either on the beam or somewhat abaft the beam. Our choice of sails for the day would be the mizzen at the stern and the jib at the bow since that combination worked so well for us a few days ago.

On the contrary, this was a bad day for the mizzen. The wind ended up being right from our stern. The 12 miles between the two islands were littered with tiny islets with names like Table Rock, the Groupers, and Ile Fourche. Waves ricocheted off these islets causing choppy and irregular seas. *La Boatique* rocked back and forth from side to side. Pete yelled at me to change course to improve the ride but with waves coming from all over the place I was having an arduous time. The mizzen boom slammed from one side of the boat to the other. That slamming is called a jibe. I did not want to jibe because that slamming is hard on the boat. Next thing we knew a clevis pin used to sheet in the mizzen broke and the boom went flying far to the port side. We should have used a preventer to hold the boom in position. Instead, Pete dropped the mizzen sail back into its sail pack. The remainder of the trip would be a slow one on the jib alone. Since we were sailing slowly we could make use of our deep diving lure to try for a fish. Soon we heard the zing of the line as a fish bit the bait. I went back to the stern to reel him in but he was not hooked well enough and got free.

At 10:20 a.m. we dropped our anchor in Simpson Bay, St. Maarten. We could see and hear every plane land on the runway at the busy international airport. When a huge 747 roared in, Pete could wait no longer. He wanted to get to Jet Blast Beach. He wanted to be at the edge of the runway. He wanted to spy a few topless sunbathers. He wanted to watch the sunbathers get tossed about by the hot blast from the jet engines. He wanted to mingle with the people at the Sunset Beach Bar. I would not mind a refreshing swim off the white sand beach myself. I have to admit that I also have a hard time resisting the excitement as the planes take off and land right over our heads.

Jet Blast Beach totally lived up to every expectation. The only disappointment was that the three hotels across from the beach were closed. Hurricane Lenny had destroyed them all (including the Maho Beach Resort where we stayed in February 1999). Hurricane Lenny slammed into the island of St. Martin with a direct hit. Every tree was denuded. The place looked rather ugly. But the residents were trying hard to rebuild and make the best of what was left.

Racing Yachts at anchor

# The Prestigious St. Martin Heineken Regatta

March 5th was the final day of the St. Maarten/St. Martin Heineken Regatta. This three-day race is one of the premier races for world-class yacht racing. Over 250 sailing yachts in 17 different classes from 24 countries competed. Sailboats ranged in size from less than 20 feet to over 200 feet long. Many of the sailboats were plastered with the signs of well-known corporate sponsors. This is a big money event. On one 12-Meter boat people paid $2000 per person to be in the race. Well over 100 boats were in the bareboat category. The bareboats are basic charter (rental) sailboats. The smallest boats racing were the beach catamarans while the largest boats were the huge tall ships. There were so many boats that two different starting lines were used. Every ten minutes a new group of twenty boats would start. Pete and I volunteered to be on the race committee.

Pete's job was at the helm of the Pin Boat, a small Boston Whaler. He positioned the starting mark. Then he sat at the end of the starting line to see if any boats crossed early. If they did he would announce their number on the marine radio and then watch to make sure that they restarted. Pete's boat also contained two photographers. During the ten minutes between each start Pete gave the photographers five minutes to take exciting action shots as he chased after the racing boats. Then they positioned themselves for the next race. Pete was the captain and race official of his small 16 foot boat. He thoroughly enjoyed his command even though he was often splashed by waves.

I was positioned high and dry on a stable 45-foot catamaran at the primary end of the starting line. I worked three flags on fifteen-foot poles. My primary job was to see if any boats crossed early and if they did then I would immediately stand and raise the individual recall flag. One woman on my boat counted down the minutes and then seconds to each start. As she counted down, the tension rose. Twenty boats would draw near the line each trying to get the best starting position nearest the catamaran. The barked commands of the racing skippers were barely heard over the groaning of the taut sails. As the starting horn blew the boats were often only inches apart in a nearly perfect line from my huge catamaran to Pete's small Boston Whaler. With boats this close collisions were inevitable. Of course, there were always the late starting stragglers. Only a few races had sailboats that jumped the starting horn, consequently I seldom had to stand and raise a flag. The racing yachts then tacked back and forth upwind a mile to the first mark. They rounded the bright orange floating mark to sail toward us downwind to another mark nearby. Brightly colored billowing spinnakers speckled the ocean like bubble gum balls rolling across a blue tablecloth. So began the race around the island. In less than three hours all 250 boats were racing and our official duties were complete.

I flew home to Ohio on March 15$^{th}$ while Pete stayed in St. Maarten to take care of *La Boatique*. I was busy with stacks of mail and income taxes. I sent boat items in for repairs and bought new things that were hard to get in the Caribbean. I got health checkups and visited friends and family.

Pete was busy with boat maintenance, painting and varnishing, and pricing new roller-furlings for our jib and staysail. He visited our cruising friends. He also repaired the fuel system at the Marina. Hurricane Lenny had destroyed all the marine fuel pumps on the island. Pete received many words of praise once he got the fuel flowing.

We planned to start heading south again toward Trinidad. From Trinidad we talked about heading around the world. We knew of about five to ten other boats that had similar plans. A trip around the world would be a huge commitment even for us.

But our plans looked as if they would have to be postponed. Pete had developed a small hernia. He saw a doctor in St. Maarten. He made an appointment with a surgeon on May 8$^{th}$ in St. Lucia. Surgery was scheduled for May 10$^{th}$. With Pete's hernia we needed to take it easy and stay near medical care. The condition of the hernia worsened as days passed by.

Pete's brother visits us.

109

For the first time in a year and a half we were to have an overnight guest. The last guests were with us in Baltimore before we had set sail for the Caribbean. Back then we were preparing for the unknown, for an open ocean adventure. Now we were seasoned blue water cruisers. Now we knew what we were doing. Now for the first time right before our guest arrived I found cockroaches on *La Boatique*. We thought we were being very careful. We thought we could avoid those terrible bugs. During the entire visit we were at war with the roaches.

Our guest, Pete's brother Bill, was to arrive early in the afternoon on March 17th at the Saint Maarten Airport. Pete and I waited at the uncomfortable airport as close as we were allowed to the arriving passengers. We stood in the hot sun nearly surrounded by concrete walls. Little air moved in this enclosed space. There were no chairs for resting. We could not see the planes landing or taking off. We could only hear them. Groups of passengers arrived but Bill was not among them. His scheduled flight arrived without Bill. I finally walked back to the American ticket counter and found out that Bill was now confirmed on the last American flight arriving that night.

We rode the dollar bus back to the boat. I checked our Sailmail e-mail when I got back to the boat. (We retrieved our e-mail at the boat through single side band radio.) Sure enough, there was an e-mail from my mom explaining that Bill would be arriving later. Pete finally met his brother Bill at the airport around 10:15 p.m.

Bill's visit gave us a reason to act like tourists. We took a bus to Philipsburg to see the cruise ships and the expensive boutiques that they attract. The next day we dinghied the length of Simpson Bay to visit the French town of Marigot. We walked by stands selling exotic tropical produce and then on to stands selling T-shirts, jewelry, and artwork. We had an elegant French lunch on a balcony overlooking the yachts at anchor.

On April 20th we decided to go for a day sail. *La Boatique* inched away from her slip of two months like a bed-ridden patient trying to walk. The steering squeaked. The propeller shaft squealed. Black smoke came out of the exhaust. *La Boatique* shuddered. She had very little power. Because the wind was on our bow, we motored. We dropped anchor off a tiny uninhabited desert island called Ill Fourche. The salty turquoise water looked so inviting. Soon we were all snorkeling around the boat. Pete found out why *La Boatique* was so sluggish. Around the propeller and shaft were parts of a rope, a black

110

plastic bag and an orange bag. Pete dove down and with hard work cut the propeller free. Bill and I scrubbed black scum from the hull. Pete scraped away the few barnacles. Swimming in the clear water felt great.

After a quick lunch on deck we set sail back to Saint Maarten. While Pete and I were on the bow untangling the jib sheet lines a wahoo struck our lure. We never heard the fish line roll out. Later I saw the fish dragging behind the boat on the ocean surface. Bill reeled it in and Pete gaffed it. While we had been dragging our fish another fish had bitten off our fish's tail. There was still plenty of fish for us to eat. Just as I finished cleaning our fish Bill said, "Fish on." I thought he was kidding. But sure enough his pole was bent over and he had another fish. We landed a lively three-foot long barracuda, which we released. Later we caught a small wahoo, which we also released.

Julius and Sally from *Argonauta* met us at the dock. Instead of eating the fresh-caught fish that night we enjoyed a delicious Italian meal aboard *Argonauta* as we watched the full moon rise. We enjoyed the fresh fish for the next few days.

# South to St. Lucia

A week after Bill left so did the cockroaches. Our successful war included filling the cabin with Bop insecticidal spray multiple times. We spread a paste of Boric Acid and sweetened condensed milk in various corners. We also used roach traps.

While in St. Maarten we decided to purchase Profurl Roller-furlings for both the headsail and the staysail. The price charged by Ocean Profurl was much less than anywhere else. Our old roller-furling still worked fine but we felt that it had long outlived its suggested life. If it broke it could have taken down both masts and ruined the boat. The only problem we had with the new roller-furlings was that they took much longer to arrive and install than we expected. Because of the roller-furling delay, we got a late start leaving St. Maarten.

Pete's hernia was beginning to bother him. It popped out often. It gurgled. Sometimes it ached. He could no longer walk for miles. When we did walk Pete needed to rest after twenty minutes. He needed surgery to correct the hernia, but we were told by many people to have it done somewhere other than St. Maarten. Pete did not want to fly home and leave the boat. Dr. Richardson from St. Lucia was recommended so our plan was to have the surgery done there.

On the evening of May 2nd a cruising doctor named David Rollins from the boat *Coal Tracker* gave Pete one final examination before our departure. Pete was in no danger unless he could not push his intestines back where they belonged. If this happened the hernia would be strangulated

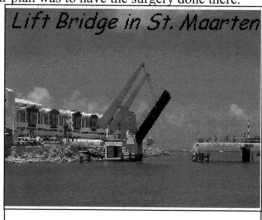
Lift Bridge in St. Maarten

We departed under this bridge.

and Pete would need urgent medical attention. The motion caused by large seas would be painful. If ever we needed gentle seas it was now for this voyage.

At 11 a.m. on May 3rd, *La Boatique* idled in Simpson Bay waiting for the Lift Bridge to open. We were excited about finally getting underway. We were like a caged animal set free as we left the placid confines of Simpson Bay. Minutes after we left the bay our steering broke. A minute or so later Pete had it working again. A bolt in front of the steering chain had worked loose and fallen off. There would be no sailing today because the wind was on our bow. Julius and Sally on *Argonauta* followed close behind on our three-hour 15-mile trip to Columbier Bay, St. Barts. Heading into the waves for three hours was no fun for Pete. His hernia ached. At Columbier Bay we swam and cleaned the bottom of the boat. Pete's hernia ached that night and we were only just beginning our trip.

At 6:40 a.m. on May 4th *Argonauta* and *La Boatique* headed 47 miles south to Majors Bay, St. Kitts. Pete needed calmer conditions for his hernia. We needed to cover many more miles than the previous day. The east wind on our beam dropped from 15 knots down to 11 knots. The gentle four-foot seas dropped down to nearly calm two-foot seas, perfect sailing conditions. From any distance *La Boatique* must have looked majestic with four full sails flying. We probably looked like a mini tall ship with our jib, staysail, mainsail and mizzen. A grand dame of the sea is how Julius described us.

112

At 3 p.m. we dropped anchor, but we stayed less than three hours. The bay was rolly and the nearby barge was running a noisy motor. So at 5:30 p.m. we headed five miles further south. At dusk we anchored for the night along the coastline of Nevis. We were off Pinneys Beach. There was no bay to anchor in by Nevis. The lee shore of Nevis was a rolly anchorage. Sleep was difficult for me so I had no trouble being awake for our 5:30 a. m. departure.

Our day's passage would be over 80 miles, a lot of miles to fit in during daylight hours. Looming in front of us was the volcano at Montserrat. A warning had just been issued for a predicted major eruption within the next two months. The eruption could occur at any moment but would most likely be triggered by rain. The sky did not look like rain but there were some dark clouds near the mountaintop. If the volcano erupted as we sailed by, we would be toast. We decided to make haste and motor-sailed as fast as we could on past Montserrat. I stared up at the volcano. Sally stared down at the water and saw pumice stones floating on the surface.

Once we passed Montserrat a fresh 15-knot breeze gently carried us another 40 miles to Guadeloupe. Under our jib, mainsail and mizzen we had a calm ride going 6 to 7 ½ knots. The seas were still way down from normal.

We anchored for the night off Pigeon Island, Guadeloupe. St. Maarten, St. Barts, St. Kitts and Nevis looked like deserts compared to the lush green and flowering trees of Guadeloupe. I could even smell the foliage. At dusk small tree frogs chirped their nighttime serenade. Sally and Julius joined us for a hearty dinner aboard *La Boatique*. We had tossed salad, roast beef, mashed potatoes and carrots.

May 6th meant another leg to the trip to St. Lucia. On this day we motor-sailed 48 miles from Guadeloupe to Dominica. Pete caught a 40-inch long barracuda that we threw back. We had to beat into the wind that built to over 20 knots. But still the seas were uncharacteristically low. We shared a huge anchorage off the Coconut Beach Hotel with only *Argonauta* and *Cahoots*.

Martin Carrierre, a local from Dominica, with the boat called *Providence* came out to our boat. He provided services to passing yachts. He got us some juicy fresh-picked grapefruits. He used his stable boat to help Pete change anchors. We decided to use the Max anchor as our primary anchor instead of the Cleveland anchor. Pete thought that the shovel shaped Max might grab quicker than the plow shaped Cleveland. The Cleveland anchor is heavier than the Max but the Max might make up for its weight by digging in deeper.

The forecast for May 7th was for continued light wind out of the northeast but that is not what we got. Along the lee coast of Dominica there was almost no wind and the hot sun beat down on us. At the south end of the island the wind immediately went to 20 knots. The sky filled with dark gray clouds. The wind gusted to 30 knots. The rain followed. The seas became choppy. The squall ended in 15 minutes, but another squall followed. About halfway to Martinique the sky cleared. The wind settled in at 15 to 20 knots from the east and the 6-foot seas became more regular. The trade winds had returned.

We stopped for the night at Saint Pierre, Martinique. The Max anchor did not give a best first salt-water performance. We had to drop it three times before it set.

Our trip to Marin, Martinique, on May 8th was even more difficult than we expected. We had to head south along the coast and then east to Marin. Heading east against the trade wind is tough. But our problems began even before we turned east. Pete noticed that our vacuum gauge read high. The engine was having trouble getting enough fuel. So we shut the engine down. The wind along the coast was erratic but I had no trouble sailing along while Pete purged the FPS (Fuel Purification System). He then changed the Racor filter. We did not realize it at that time but we were running low on fuel on tank number 2, the tank we were using to power the boat. While still low on fuel we ran the engine again and made our turn east. We were at the southwest corner of the island with a steep mountain beside us. Ahead of us lay the barren Diamond Rock, a very tiny island with sheer cliffs on all sides. Diamond Rock is so menacing that the British Navy commissioned it as a warship. It was called HMS Diamond Rock and included cannons to fire at passing ships. We planned to motor through the pass between Diamond Rock and the island. The mountain ashore and Diamond rock funneled the trade wind and seas against us. Our speed dropped from 6 knots to 3 knots. We inched along. The wind gusted to 30 knots. Suddenly there were huge waves in front of us. The bowsprit seemed to rise almost straight up before crashing down. Our forward progress was stopped. The cliff walls seemed to nearly close in on us as if the ghosts of the British Navy would not let us pass. So we turned around to the open ocean. We motor-sailed an extra 12 miles into wind and seas to avoid the ghosts of Diamond Rock. We made our way to Marin before we realized what was wrong with the fuel system and changed to tank number 1 there.

With all the trouble we had getting to Marin we assumed that there would be no other boats there. But to our surprise we found more boats than even at the huge Simpson Bay in St. Maarten. There could easily have been 1000 boats in this beautiful and huge protected bay. We had a few days to spare before we needed to be in St. Lucia so we decided to spend the days there. We visited the many boat stores. The chandlery prices were expensive but the French wine and cheese on this French Island were cheap.

On the morning of May 11$^{th}$ at the anchorage in Marin I was at the helm while Pete stood on the bow. The electric windless lifted up our anchor chain and deposited it neatly in the chain locker. The chain that had been lying on the bottom of the bay was totally coated in gooey mud. Soon the mud was flicked up on the deck. Pete sprayed the chain and the deck with the salt-water wash down hose but mud still clung to the chain. The max anchor had buried itself deep in the mud. But soon the anchor was up and we were off toward St. Lucia.

For once in a long while we were not trying to claw our way east. On this 27-mile trip we headed south-southwest. The sailing was easy in the 15-knot easterly wind. We used the jib and mizzen sails.

We sailed all the way into Rodney Bay until we were nearly to shore. Then we dropped the anchor to further clean the chain. A thin line of mud coming off the chain was visible in the crystal clear bright blue water. We raised the anchor once again and headed to our slip at Rodney Bay Marina.

# Health Care

Since our health insurance (through Blue Water Insurance) had a large deductible, it paid for us to shop around for the best health care at the most affordable price.

On May 12$^{th}$ Pete had his entire body checked for skin problems by Dr. Didier, a dermatologist. No problems were found. The cost was $28. On May 15$^{th}$ Pete had his hernia examined by Dr. Richardson and the surgery date was set for May 19$^{th}$ at Tapion Hospital in Castries, St. Lucia. Long ago the Tapion Hospital building started out as a hospital on an outcropping overlooking the ocean. Then the building was turned into a hotel, but the hotel went bankrupt. Later on a group of doctors bought the building and turned it back into a privately run hospital. The surgical theater had an extraordinary view of the ocean. If I were to have an operation I would have concentrated on the magnificent view, not Pete. Pete saw much more to hold his interest.

Pete's hernia operation was done with only a local anesthetic. Pete propped himself up so he could observe the operation. As Dr. Richardson cut and stitched Pete's groin, the operating table dropped lower and lower at 15-second intervals. Pete said, "It feels like the hydraulic cylinder that holds up the table is leaking."

Dr. Richardson said, "It is leaking. Nurse, pump that cylinder back up to raise the table."

Now Pete, always trying to fix things, changed his focus from the operation to the hydraulics holding up the table.

Dr. Richardson said, "A hydraulic specialist came in and told me that it would be cheaper to buy a new operating table than to fix this one."

Pete saw that the valve was leaking. During the operation Pete showed the doctor and the nurse what was wrong and then said that they did not need a new operating table, they only needed a new valve. Pete joked that if he had brought his tools and a valve, he could have fixed the sick table. All in all, Pete was very satisfied with the entire operation and particularly Dr. Richardson's skills as a surgeon. Pete wanted to especially thank Sally's friend Elaine Richard for driving him to and from the hospital.

We found hospital costs to be much more expensive in the U.S. than at other places around the world. The cost for the doctor and the surgical theater at the hospital was only $750. The pain pills were an additional $8. Pete was back on the boat resting comfortably until the local anesthetic wore off. Then he spent an uncomfortable night after the operation. *"La Boatique"* became *"La Boatique* Clinique" and infirmary. Julius and Sally stayed close by and provided needed medical advice during the first week of recovery as Pete moaned with pain.

# St. Lucia to Bequia

After three weeks of recuperation time, Pete was ready to sail on. So on June 12th we cast off our lines from Rodney Bay Marina, St. Lucia. A few minutes later we dropped the anchor in Rodney Bay in order to clean our propeller. Pete went for his first swim in a long time and it felt great. The water was warm and clear. Many fish swam close by. He cleaned at least an inch of thick growth of barnacles from the propeller. The hull was surprisingly free of growth. *Argonauta* filled up with fuel and soon motored out into the bay to join us. The wind was slightly abaft our beam. We gently glided along under our jib and mizzen sails. There were only 2-foot waves since we were sailing along the lee shore of St. Lucia. We stayed close to shore and enjoyed the view. Burnt orange colored cliff walls plunged to the sea. Valleys with beaches separated the cliffs. Along white sand beaches were hotels. Beach catamarans with bright sails raised stood in a row along the shore. Palms waved in the breeze. The cliff walls isolated each hotel complex. At the top of the cliffs were often beautiful homes. We sailed on past the capital city of St. Lucia, Castires. Pete spied the Tapion Hospital where his hernia surgery had been performed. We then sailed past a huge oil storage facility run by Hess Oil. The next bay was Marigot, our destination for the day. We had covered nine splendid miles. Too bad cruising couldn't always be like this. The following day would not be so pleasant and easy.

At 5:30 a.m. the next morning we raised the anchor and set the double-reefed mainsail along with the jib. Once again we were sailing along with *Argonauta*. The early morning was another gentle ride along the lee of St. Lucia. The 30-mile sail from St. Lucia to St. Vincent was an uncomfortable ride. The 20 to 25-knot east winds were great for sailing but the sea conditions were annoying. The 8-foot waves abaft our beam seemed to come at us with jolts. It felt like we were bouncing over boulders instead of waves. That bad old seasick feeling was beginning to affect me while Pete's incision ached. Clyde, our autopilot, did not like the ride either and chose a course that wove back and forth. I counted down the hours and miles to go until we would be in the lee of St. Vincent.

Along St. Vincent we saw a pod of over 100 dolphins swim past away off to our starboard side. The ride along St. Vincent was gentle and gave us a nice break. During our 16 mile leg from St. Vincent to Bequia four dolphins rode our bow wave for a minute. We had covered nearly 64 miles in 10½ hours including the 45 minutes we spent anchoring.

The Tobago Cays

# The Tobago Cays

Our destination for June 17<sup>th</sup> was the Tobago Cays, which are nowhere near Tobago. Getting there, we had a wonderful 28-mile sail south on jib and mizzen. The Tobago Cays are a protected park and are about halfway between St. Vincent and Grenada. They are a group of four tiny islets too small in themselves to offer protection from the rough Atlantic Ocean. In fact, we anchored on the windward Atlantic Ocean side of these islets. The islands had been cleaned up of trash left by squatters. The squatters for the most part were no longer present there. We had no protection from the strong 20-knot Atlantic trade wind. But in front of us the 8-foot Atlantic swells smashed themselves into white frothy bits because just a few feet under the ocean surface was a horseshoe shaped reef that ran for miles.

The coral reef presented the best snorkeling water I had ever seen. The clear aquamarine water was full of neon colored fish. In a few places I saw cloudy water but on close inspection the clouds were schools of transparent baby fish. Some of the adult fish swam in schools while others swam alone. Some fish swam over to see me. The corals were of every size and color. Some corals formed natural archways. The neon colored fish loitered in and around these arches. Many corals rose so close to the surface that I could not swim over them. I had to search for paths around the high coral sections. The current was very strong and even with my flippers I had to swim hard to make any progress. Drifting back onto a sharp coral was always of concern. I had to swim alone since Pete was not up to climbing in and out of the dinghy. But Pete kept a watchful eye on me from the dinghy tied to a mooring close by.

## Mayreau

The following day was humid, hazy, and overcast. But the northeast wind still blew at 20 knots. After I baked a coconut custard pie we decided to move on. We only had three miles to our next anchorage. Our destination was a small bay that looked like a tropical paradise. Its name was Salt Whistle Bay on the island of Mareau. The bay was beautiful all right, but huge swells found their way into the bay. We went for a stroll on the beach hand in hand. We looked out to the bay and saw *La Boatique* rocking up and down and from side to side. We would only be staying one night. We could handle it.

The late afternoon and evening were full of entertainment. A neighboring sailboat brought out an old wind surfer. The guys trying to sail it were nearly out of control. They were falling about as much as they were sailing. Pelicans and boobies dove for fish while laughing gulls circled and screeched overhead. A Hobie Cat sailed in and out of the bay. At the end of the day two cabin cruisers from Trinidad joined the five sailboats to fill the anchorage for the night. The uncomfortable rollers continued making sleeping difficult.

At 5:30 a.m. Pete got up and said, "I have had enough of this. Let's get out of here." So off we went south in search of a more comfortable anchorage.

## Grenada

The wind was from the northeast at 20 to 25 knots as it had been for days. This was unusual since in the summer the wind is usually much lighter and from the southeast. Our weather was much more typical of winter than summer. The northeast wind made our sail for the day downwind and fast. Since all the miles covered that day were spent threading our way between reefs and islands we kept the motor running for safety and used only the small staysail. After a few hours we were at Tyrrel Bay on the island of Carriacou in the country of Grenada. We took a bumpy bus ride to Hillsborough to check in. Later in the afternoon we swam over to *Maritime Express* and then to *Argonauta*.

Because of the continued strong northeast wind even Tyrrel Bay was rolly. The forecast was for continued northeast wind for the foreseeable future. We were tired of rolling so we decided to sail south to the island of Grenada. On June 20th we had a downwind trip that was fast and easy. It was so easy that I even made a loaf of bread and calzones with pizza style fillings while under sail. We sailed the leeward side of Grenada and anchored in Mount Hartman Bay at the southern end of the island. The anchorage was calm — no rollers. Mount Hartman Bay had cliff walls covered in lush vegetation. The bay cut deep into the island and had reefs protecting it from the ocean.

Grenada was a pleasant surprise. The water even in the anchorage was clear and blue. The reddish brown cliff walls dropping down to the water had a smooth sculptured appearance. There were frangipani trees with white flowers and tall slender cacti. At the water's edge were creamy colored sand beaches enclosed by clumps of mangrove trees. The mangroves were loaded with oysters. Doves and herons roosted in the branches. The climate was perfectly warm and sunny except for one day. That day, June 28th, we had rain all day and at dusk a nasty thunderstorm arrived with wind often over 30 knots. The storm was originally forecast to become a hurricane but then it fizzled out. Just as the storm descended upon us its strength increased. The wind pushed *La Boatique* back and forth against the anchor chain. A can of soup I had just opened slid across the counter and I caught it just before it dropped to the floor. One large gust over 50 knots whistled through our rigging before the storm began to let up.

I took two kayak trips from Mouth Hartman Bay. On the first trip I toured the edges of the bay. On the second trip I got a strenuous workout. I found a kayak partner from another boat. We paddled out of Mount Hartman Bay and then circumnavigated Hog Island. The upwind legs were tough paddling but the tropical scenery was exquisite. The following day Pete and I enjoyed a beach barbecue on Hog Island with many other cruisers. We took an all-day island tour and learned about nutmeg cultivation and processing. During the tour we noticed that the poorest villages seemed to be the fishing villages. The fishermen don't seem to use ice or refrigeration. I would not want any of the fish I saw sitting out in the hot sun. Near the end of the tour we stopped at the Concord Waterfall where I enjoyed a refreshing swim.

On June 29th we prepared for departure. We motored a few miles to Prickly Bay. Prickly Bay is open to the ocean while reefs nearly encircle Mount Hartman Bay. A nighttime departure would be much

120

easier from Prickly Bay than from Mount Hartman Bay. We took one last swim. Pete cleaned the propeller and knot meter of a tiny bit of growth. Since the trip to Trinidad is too long to be covered during daylight hours, our departure time was set between 1 and 2 a.m. on June 30th. We seldom sailed at night in the Caribbean because the islands were close enough together for day sailing between them.

We departed at 1:30 a.m. with *Graffiti* and *Mike-and-Mic*. The ocean along the south coast of Grenada was very shallow. I kept a nervous eye on the depth meter and called out the depths to Pete. We had a GPS way point set clear of any reefs. But Pete believed that maybe we should head a little west of the waypoint. Yet we did not want to get too far west because of Glover Island. Motor sailing through the shallow water with Glover Island on one side and a reef called the Porpoises on our other side made us nervous. What looked so easy during daylight seemed puzzling at night. About a half-hour after we reached deep water I noticed a dark cloud ahead. It was Pete's turn to take the helm so I pointed the cloud out to him. In the dark of night I could not foretell what potential this cloud could hold. Minutes later the wind speed doubled. The wind pushed hard against the only two sails we had out, the jib and the mizzen. Pete turned downwind to take some of the pressure off the sails. We were getting wet more from salt-water spray than from the rainsquall. I could not anticipate the waves spraying us nor the rain nor the wind gusts. Even though I had my light raincoat on I was cold and shaking. I hate to say it but some of the shaking was from fear. We had too much sail up. *La Boatique* was crashing through the waves at over her hull speed. The GPS was set to warn us when we sped along at anything over 8 knots and it was crying out as if to shriek "slow down." I let the jib line loose so that I could furl in most of the sail. The jib flogged in the wind adding more clamor until we had it properly set at a smaller size. The storm lasted less than an hour. I was not feeling too good. The wind let up some but the seas were still annoyingly rough. If only dawn would come so that I could see the waves maybe I would not be so seasick. But dawn was over 2 hours away. Pete did not need my help so I slept fitfully until around 9 a.m. By then Pete needed a break from steering and I felt better. Clyde, our autopilot, did not steer a good course at all so we hand steered the entire 14 hour trip. Clyde may have done a better job had we used the mainsail instead of the mizzen. The wind was not abaft our beam as we had expected it to be so we had chosen the wrong sail combination.

About 20 miles from Trinidad Pete noticed turbulent water ahead and thought that maybe it meant increased wind. But we found the turbulent water was caused by upwelling of deep ocean water. Our speed became very erratic. One strong current pushed us along at 8.9 knots. I enjoyed the hour-long ride through the turbulent swirling water. Soon the green northern mountains of Trinidad rose above the horizon. The end of our overnight trip was in sight.

# Trinidad

We tied to our favorite dock at Coral Cove Marina and set our haul-out date. We planned to keep *La Boatique* out of the water until mid September. In Trinidad the cost to be out of the water is much less than the cost to be in the water at a dock. Also being out of the water is much safer.

*La Boatique* was hauled out on July 4th at Coral Cove Marina and was set on jack stands near the water's edge. Living on the hard in a boat was like living in a tree house. We climbed a ladder with uneven steps to get to our home. Birds flew by at eye level. Pelicans roosted on the marina dock posts below. When they got hungry they dove from their roost for a fish dinner. Lush green rain forest hills nearly surrounded us providing us with only a narrow view of the ocean.

To celebrate Independence Day a group of cruisers got together and formed a band. About four local Trinidadians joined in. Of course you cannot have music here without at least one steel pan. (Steel drum or pan music was invented here in Trinidad.) A nine-year-old local boy who was as good as any professional musician played the steel pan. The music went on for five hours and included jazz, patriotic tunes, Trinidad ballads, instrumental arrangements and sing-a-longs. Some musicians played the entire program while others played or sang only a few numbers. I really enjoyed the variety.

After the evening of music the following week was spent with boat chores.

Julius and I decided to participate in an organized hike on July 16th to an enchanting waterfall in the rain forest. The hike was much more arduous than we expected. We should have brought along more water. The hot air was heavy with humidity. Maybe we should have taken notice when we found out the organizer was known as "Snake," and he wanted his money even before we started hiking. There were about 40 hikers and 5 guides. The 9 of us cruisers were the oldest of the bunch. The local Trinidadians all looked like athletes to me. One of the guides carried a large roll of bright yellow polypropylene rope. I had not been on a hike where rope was required. I pondered if we would be expected to use that rope for climbing. The rest of the guides carried machetes. "Snake" told us to be on the lookout for the poisonous mapepe snake, which is often seen in this area. However, this snake has no bright markings making it difficult to spot. The hike started out as a gentle climb. But then we kept on climbing step after step higher and steeper. I was breathing hard. My heart was pounding. On we climbed. The air was thick with water. To catch my breath I took tiny steps. We were supposed to stay together but I was having trouble keeping up with the athletic Trinidadians. I was falling behind but I had to set my own pace.

Julius was 59 with two artificial hips. He began to fall even further behind and I thought he might turn back. Soon he was out of my sight but still climbing with a slower group. I climbed on with a local Trinidadian woman who matched my pace. While hiking Julius fell on a rock so sharp that it cut his leg and his pants. Blood soaked trough his pants but he kept on climbing. None of the guides brought along any first aid gear.

The jungle closed in on us. Unseen birds hidden in thick growth sang haunting calls and warbles while frogs chirped. I kept my eyes focused on where I would place my next step without getting tangled in a vine or slip on a rock. I don't know if my clothes were more wet from sweat or from the high humidity. Finally, high on the mountain the air became cool and then rain cooled us further. The view of the ocean and surrounding jungle hills from the lofty cliff wall was stunning. Then we climbed way down to get to the Habio Falls. The trek down was so steep that in one area the rope was tied to a tree and then we repelled down a cliff wall for 20 feet. Hikers in front of me found a small poisonous mapepe snake. The guides caught it and put

Baby turtle in Pete's hand

it in a bottle to be released later at a snake farm. The trail was overgrown. The machetes were often required to hack our way through. Progress became very slow but I did not mind because I enjoyed the slower pace. I was certainly ready for a rest when I arrived at the falls. Not long after I arrived, Julius came trudging through the forest with the remaining hikers.

After an hour's rest and swim at the falls we started the return trip back to civilization. Somehow the trip back was not nearly as bad as the trip to the falls. But my legs were sore for the next few days.

# Leatherback Turtles

Leatherback Turtle

On July 18<sup>th</sup> Pete surprised me with a present. He reserved an evening trip for both of us to Matura Beach to watch the largest turtles in the world lay their eggs under a full moon. Matura Beach is about a two-hour ride from the marinas in Chaguaramas. From March until August the 500 plus pound leatherback turtles lumber onto the sandy beach to lay their eggs. There are only a few places in the world where these prehistoric creatures come ashore. Soon after we arrived our guides located some baby turtles nearly ready to make their run to the sea. Then a huge dark five-foot long turtle began to climb her way up onto the sandy beach. She searched for a good spot and then began the laborious task of digging a deep pit using her huge rear flippers. She could not see the perfect shaped nest she dug. She could only feel the proportions of her nest with her flippers. She then deposited about 80 soft white round eggs. She would make about eight trips to shore to lay more eggs during the six-month season and then she would not return for at least two years. She covered the eggs with sand and then camouflaged the area to make it hard for predators to dig up the eggs. The leatherback turtle has long flippers and is very streamlined compared to other turtles. As we watched her get ready to head back to sea, other turtles began to make their way to shore. We

124

watched a second turtle deposit eggs while baby turtles from other nests swam out to sea.

Rear view of leatherback turtle laying eggs, hand holding the rear flipper up so that the eggs can be viewed

## Sneak Attack in Trinidad

(Pete writes)

Susan left me stranded in Trinidad and flew home on July 20th. She had no idea what distress I would soon be in. While she was in Ohio I had lots of jobs to get done but back pain was slowing me down. Still I removed the cap rails and resealed the hull deck joint. I paid a local Trinidadian to sand the bottom and get ready for new bottom paint. I removed the two existing fuel tanks and contracted to have new poly tanks made. I ordered new anchor chain and new batteries. I flew to Venezuela to have my eyes checked and had another LASIK procedure performed. As the weeks went by I developed the most agonizing pain in the lower back just below the ribs spreading around to the front of the abdomen and often extending into the groin area. The pain came in waves. I noticed some blood in my urine. I talked to Julius from *Argonauta* and he said, "Congratulations, you are giving birth to a kidney stone." Julius recommended that I see a doctor as soon as possible.

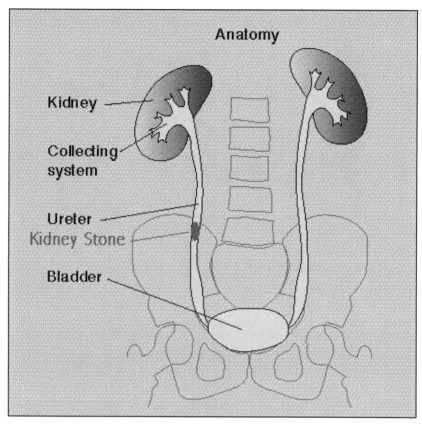

**Anatomy**

Kidney

Collecting system

Ureter

Kidney Stone

Bladder

I went to a doctor and described my pain. I had an x-ray and found out that I indeed had a kidney stone on the warpath. The doctor gave me a prescription for pain pills that would help pass the stone. Ten days went by and no stone passed. The pain was down. I went back to the doctor who then did a die test to show where the stone was. Well it was stuck in the ureter between the kidney and the bladder. The right kidney was blocked. The doctor made an appointment with a specialist two days before I was scheduled to fly home. I wanted to see if it would be OK to travel. The day I was to see the specialist I developed a fever over a hundred degrees and the specialist sent me straight to the hospital that night. I had surgery at 7:00 a.m. the next morning. They tried lithrotripsy. It did not work. So they went in the hard way to remove it. They used ureteroscopy: sending instruments up through the urethra, the bladder, and into the ureter to grab the stone and pull it out. That afternoon I was back at *La Boatique*, getting ready for my flight home the next morning.

August 17th I flew home on schedule. Talk about a fast three days! I was feeling a lot better, but when I would get back to Trinidad the doctors would have to go back in and remove the stent (a small tube that was inserted between the kidney and bladder).

While at home we purchased some boat supplies to take back to Trinidad with us. We tried to visit as many friends as we could in the short time we were in Ohio.

# Kidney Stones in the Tropics

(Susan writes)

Kidney stones are common in hot climates because we sweat so much more than in a cold climate and therefore not enough water makes its way to the kidneys. Pete needs to drink at least 3/4 of a gallon of water a day. While in Ohio Pete was uncomfortable because of the plastic stent inserted in him between his kidney and bladder. He did not need to see a doctor while in Ohio. On September 7th we flew back to Trinidad. We hoped to get going on boat jobs, but Pete took a turn for the worse and ended up back in the hospital.

St. Augustine Private Hospital provided excellent care when my kidney stones were removed

Pete is in the hospital in Trinidad. Sue is glad to see him doing better.

(Pete writes)

Yep, I am resting again. I had a pain attack on Saturday the 9th of September. I called Dr. Khan. He said to meet him at the hospital. So off we went after finding a car to rent. The pain was bad. Dr. Khan said that probably there was a little infection from the stent. He considered operating that night. The x-ray looked OK so he gave me a shot in the butt. The pain was soon gone so he put off surgery until Monday morning. The hospital staff got me ready, and off I went into dreamville. Dr. Khan went in and removed the pile of rocks that remained in the bladder. Apparently many stone fragments remained as a result of the procedure that was done in August to break the huge stone that clogged the ureter. The doctor left the stent in and added two more tubes. When I woke up I had saline solution being forced in my arm and drained out my penis to bags next to the bed. Talk about a back flush! So I spent the night with what felt like a faucet running through my system all night. In the morning after breakfast the fun began. Three nurses (cute ones) came in and removed the tubes and the stent. It was a peculiar feeling having them removed from my penis. Being fondled by six hands was different.

Now after a week, I feel so much better. It is hard to believe a little thing like that stone can put a person down. The strange thing is that my backaches are gone. I went to do Dr. Khan today, September 19th, and he gave me a clean bill of health.

During our time here in Trinidad we have been getting ready for a Pacific Ocean crossing. I had the cap rails removed and I resealed the hull and deck joint. Tony Tinto, a local carpenter, helped me with the cap rails and made a wooden box to fit over the rear lazarette. We installed the new fuel tanks. We replaced all the batteries. I sanded and painted the bottom with Sea Hawk 44. We installed a Garmin 100 fish finder and a Garmin 130 GPS, which includes a map of the world. We plan to use the fish finder mainly for finding an acceptable place to anchor. We installed new 5/16 high-test chain 287 feet long. I started to install the new Nexus autopilot, which we named Harvey & Joyce. Susan's parents would have liked to have come along but they can't, so they bought the autopilot. This way they can take their turns at the helm. We thanked them again and again.

We have been putting things away and making space for new stores. And of course I have been messing with the engine. Also we got rid of the microwave, which gave the cook (Susan) more room in the galley.

(Susan writes)

During the morning of September 22nd *La Boatique* was launched back into Chagauramas Bay. We motored over to a dock at Coral Cove Marina. Our good friends Julius and Sally on *Argonauta* launched later the same day. It sure felt nice to be back in the water

128

where we belonged. Little did we know that in only a week we would go through the major expense of pulling *La Boatique* back out of the water.

# Hurricanes, an Earthquake and Other Close Calls

On September 27th Joe from the catamaran *Ladybug* offered to help us carry jerry cans of diesel fuel to *La Boatique* from the nearby Power Boats Fuel Dock. Dave, Stacy, Joe and Mat aboard *Ladybug* (from Wisconsin) would soon be our cruising partners. Poor Joe ended up performing all the heavy lifting. Joe and I motored his dinghy full of yellow 6-gallon plastic cans back and forth between Coral Cove and Power Boats. Pete dumped the fuel into *La Boatique* and then marked a dowel rod showing how full the tank was after each 6-gallon can. In hot 90-degree sun with no air we loaded 47 gallons into tank one and 56 gallons into tank two for 103 gallons overall.

Hurricanes were brewing out in the Caribbean and Atlantic on September 28th. Hurricane Isaac was far north of us but it may have been the cause of a ground swell that sent *La Boatique* wildly rocking for 5 hours at the dock. We were lucky to escape without damage as *La Boatique* was nearly thrown against a cement pier. Many boats were not so lucky. Much more threatening than hurricane Isaac was hurricane Joyce. Joyce was taking a very unusual southern path and was heading directly for us. On September 29th we reluctantly hauled *La Boatique* back out of the water to be better prepared for the hurricane. That same day there was a huge crude oil spill that fouled everything in the water. *La Boatique* was lifted out of the water just as the oil arrived. For the most part we were spared from the mess the crude oil made on other boats.

Pete thought that the steering seemed mushy when he drove over to the boatlift. He decided that we should try to bleed any remaining air out of our hydraulic system. When he opened up the system expecting air and hydraulic fluid, he got drips of water. Water in the hydraulic system would ruin our steering system including our new Nexus autopilot, Harvey & Joyce. While everyone else prepared their boats for a hurricane, we flushed our hydraulic system repeatedly with air and new hydraulic fluid. How could water get in there? We found that the Vetus hydraulic fluid that we added when we had installed the new Nexus Autopilot contained water. We were lucky to have found the problem before any major damage was done to our steering.

Ironically, a hurricane with the same name as my mother, Joyce, caused us to use our new steering system that led us to bleed the system that ended up saving our autopilot named Harvey & Joyce. So, Hurricane Joyce helped to save Harvey & Joyce. That was a close call.

Another close call was hurricane Joyce now heading directly for us. However, contrary to all the forecasts Hurricane Joyce suddenly dissipated. By the time Joyce arrived on October 1st she brought no more than two cool dreary rainy days.

We had plenty of excitement in one week with the ground swell, water in the hydraulic system, the crude oil spill and an approaching hurricane. But the excitement was not over yet. On October 3rd while our boats were still held up by jack stands, Pete and Julius were busy under the boats cleaning the oil slick off the hulls. I was in the cabin sitting at the navigation table working on the computer. The boats began to shake and then to jump. I held on to the armrests of the chair I was sitting in.

Earthquake!

The rigging from all the boats made a terrible clatter. Pete and Julius quickly backed away from the boats. They saw the earth move in waves. I thought about what would happen to me if *La Boatique* fell off the stands. I hoped falling boats would not crush Pete and Julius. Just as I was thinking that I was safer in the boat, Pete yelled up to me to get off the boat. He thought that he was safer on the ground. The boat was still shaking as I climbed onto the cabin top. Seconds later the shaking stopped and I climbed down the ladder to ground level. All the boats at Coral Cove Marina were still standing. However one boat at another boat yard did fall off its stands. The quake registered 5.9 and was centered about 50 miles from us out in the ocean.

*La Boatique* went back in the water again on October 4th. We spent the next week preparing *La Boatique* for being away from boat stores, grocery stores and other trappings of civilization.

# West to the Pacific

We took a break from preparing *La Boatique* on Saturday, October 7th. Julius and Sally invited us to ride with them aboard *Argonauta* for a day trip to the island of Chacachacare. There in a pleasant breeze Pete and Julius installed solar panels. They then made sure the water maker was working properly and the wind generator was charging the batteries. Then we all went for a refreshing swim. We decided that we should visit this place again on *La Boatique*. As we headed back to Chagauramas dolphins were all around and often leaping and splashing. A squall with 30 knots of wind made for a rainy end to the trip. One nice thing about the squall was that we were able to see the new Kiss wind generator put out a large 30 amps of power.

We finally left Chagauramas on October 11th. We motored west along the lee shore of three Trinidad out islands. We anchored in the huge bay at the island of Chacachacare. Until about 30 years ago Chacachacare was a leper colony. When a cure for leprosy was found, the colony was abandoned. The jungle has been reclaiming the land. We did not go ashore to investigate. We needed to relax and take it easy. Late in the day the catamaran, *Ladybug* joined us. The night was quiet, calm, and peaceful.

## Venezuela

At 8:45 a.m. on October 12th Pete raised our mainsail for the first time in months. We were finally sailing again. We were sailing across a narrow passage between Trinidad and Venezuela. Commercial vessels heavily use the passage. We saw a car carrier, a container ship, an oil tanker, small freighters and even a cruise ship. We kept our motor running to help us maneuver through the traffic. Along the coastline of Venezuela the wind swirled around making sailing difficult so we motored the rest of the way. We had gone 23 miles. Our anchorage was Cabo San Francisco, Venezuela. We were joined by *Ladybug* and then later on by *Argonauta*. *Argonauta* was on a fast run to Puerto La Cruz, Venezuela so they were off sailing with the sunrise.

Fishing boat at anchor in Cabo San Francisco, Venezuela

Only one family lived in Cabo San Francisco. Their home by a babbling stream had no walls. Palm fronds covered the roof that was supported by wooden posts. The furniture consisted of hammocks strung between the posts. Dinner was cooked over a fire. The inhabitants were friendly and waved as I paddled by in my kayak. Behind their home tall mountains of rain forest rose abruptly from the sea. Unseen howler monkeys called from somewhere deep in the jungle. Ashore there were no cars, no roads, no electricity, no refrigerators and no television. We cruisers shared the bay with fishermen. The next morning a pirogue pulled along side our boat. The young Venezuelans aboard wanted batteries for their boom box. Pete found two batteries that we could spare. Later in the day from the shoreline at the edge of the dense rain forest came the melodies of Latin rhythms. Stacy from *Ladybug* joined me on a kayak trip. We investigated the edge of the bay where the rain forest mountains met the Caribbean ocean. We kayaked along shaded by dense vegetation and overhanging cliff walls. We discovered caves and tiny bays concealed by huge forest trees above. We kayaked under a fresh cool waterfall and remained long enough to drench our heads.

Spectacular!

I would like to have stayed longer. Maybe we should have stayed but our plans were to move on. So on October 13<sup>th</sup> at 5 p.m. we set sail for an overnight passage to Los Testigos Islands 80 miles to the west-northwest. *Ladybug* followed us.

As the mountains of Venezuela towered behind us the sun set to our left followed by a full moon rise to our right. Now all we needed was some wind. The annoying ocean swell was even subdued. Later in the night lightning flashed. We traced the storm's path on radar. The wind picked up and remained at 10 to 15 knots for the remainder of the night. We decided to motor sail to try to outrun the storm. We were successful. The storm tracked along beside us. Our Harvey & Joyce (Nexus) autopilot performed amazingly well. We were in the most difficult of conditions for an autopilot. We were on a beam reach but later on we were sailing downwind with following seas trying to throw *La Boatique* off course. The 2-knot current pushed us along much faster than we expected. Since we did not want to arrive at these islands during the night we rolled in the jib and the staysail. We were still traveling along at nearly 7 knots. Pete took down our reefed mainsail. We were still going along at nearly 5 knots over the ground. The current was still 2 knots and as we coasted along under bare poles at 3 knots. Unbelievably Harvey & Joyce kept right on course. We arrived at the islands at sunrise, perfect timing.

We anchored off Testigo Grande at Playa Real (Royal Beach) named for the royal palms set on white sand next to blue water. Los Testigos are beautiful if you are looking for tiny islands with sun, sand and stunted palms. They certainly were a contrast from the huge lush vegetation of Cabo San Fransisco. About 100 fishermen and their families lived on these islands. Their homes had one or two walls. They used simple hammocks as their main furniture. However, I did spy a TV antenna along with a wind generator. I also saw electric poles. Yet, there were no vehicles of any kind and no roads. A fisherman and his wife asked us for cigarettes. We don't smoke and don't like to assist in a bad habit, but we were told while still in Trinidad to purchase cigarettes for trading. We traded one pack of cigarettes for two small fish for dinner.

# Margarita

On October 16<sup>th</sup> we woke with the sun and set sail for a 50-mile trip to Margarita. The ocean and the wind were gentle. We sailed on a broad reach using the genoa, the mainsail, and the mizzen sail. Dolphins rode our bow wave. Boobies dove for fish. *La Boatique* glided along at an easy five and a half knots. How much better could it get?

Zing! Fish on!

The crew of Ladybug aboard La Boatique, (from left) Dave, Stacy, Joe and Mat helped us finish off the dorado caught earlier in the day.

The *Ladybug* crew has a fish dinner aboard *La Boatique*

Pete ran to the stern and grabbed the pole. A huge mahi-mahi leaped out of the water. Pete tried to stop him from taking all our line. I turned off the autopilot and turned the boat nearly back toward the fish. Pete was able to begin to bring in some line. The fish jumped again. Then the line went slack. Maybe we lost him. Pete kept reeling and then the fish started fighting again. We still had him. Pete let him drag behind the boat to try to wear him down. We did not want him fighting hard when he was next to the boat. As the fish began to tire Pete reeled him in closer. I took the fishing rod. Pete gaffed him through the gills and lifted him over the stern rail. Pete squirted alcohol into his gills to finish off the fight. I cleaned the fish with a lot

134

of assistance from Pete. I used two nice pieces to make a fish chowder for lunch. We froze some of the fish and had the remainder on the grill for dinner after we had anchored in Margarita. We invited the crew from *Ladybug* to join us for the dinner.

The island of Margarita was warm and dry with lots of tall buildings. We checked out a huge grocery store called Ratan. We planned to stock up on some items later.

We liked Margarita. The water in the anchorage was clean and clear. Food was inexpensive and good. Stores were well stocked. We even found 1% milk for Pete. He still loved milk even after the kidney stones. Offshore Marine was an especially good boat store. The American dollar had a great exchange rate. Internet cafes were very cheap. At one comfortable air-conditioned place with high-speed lines Internet time was $1.25 an hour and Polar beer was 40 cents a bottle. The climate was warm with a pleasant breeze. There were no bugs. But there was not much vegetation either.

We had not used our Pur 80 water maker in months. When we finally went to use it on October 20th Pete found that it worked but it leaked salt water. When he took it apart he found that the stainless steel cylinder had corroded. Pete tore the pump apart and put it back together four times trying to stop the leak. No luck. We could make some fresh water, but a lot of salt water leaked out of the water maker and into our bilge. We would have to buy water from a water delivery boat the next morning instead of sailing off as planned. Purchasing water delayed our start time by two hours.

October 21st was a day of sight seeing and sail changes. We spent the day sailing the southern shore of Margarita. We saw fishing huts with no walls. We saw oil storage facilities. We looked out over a desert climate. For over three hours we sailed along under our big billowing orange spinnaker and our small mizzen sail. This was the first time we had used the spinnaker since Lake Erie. We did not pole out the spinnaker. Instead Pete wrapped a bridle around the rolled up jib. The spinnaker was attached at this point. It pulled us along on an amiable ride.

The wind stopped so we used a very long white plastic bag called a sock to capture and pull over the sail. Then we dropped the thick white sock containing the sail on the deck. Minutes later a beam wind came up. Then when we turned the corner at the west end of the island a 24-knot north wind surprised us with wind on our nose. We ended up using every sail except our mainsail. We anchored for the night off the western coast of Margarita.

# Rescue at Sea

We decided to get an early start on October 22$^{nd}$, so we were on our way at 6 a.m. heading west from Margarita. There was no wind. The ocean was calm. We motored along under the small staysail and mizzen sail. Once in a while a breath of air would give us a little push. Two and a half hours out to sea we spotted a fishing boat off our bow. As we got closer Pete saw someone on the roof of the boat waving his arms. Then the person started waving a shirt.

Pete said, "They look like they are in trouble. Turn the autopilot off and head to them."

Yes, they were in trouble. "Bateria" was all we could make out since we did not speak Spanish. They lowered a tiny tipsy wooden dinghy. Two of them paddled it over to *La Boatique* while Pete dug out jumper cables and our starting battery. Off they paddled back to their boat to try to get it running.

In the meantime we used our single side band radio to call David Jones at the Caribbean Weather Net. The sailboat *Wind Spirit* was anchored in Polamar, Margarita where Brenda listened to the weather on her single side band. David asked for a response from any boat in Polamar. Brenda responded and began connections to authorities in Margarita.

The fishermen could not get their boat started so they returned our battery and cables. Pete decided to see if he could get their engine started so he motioned for them to paddle the dinghy back. Pete brought along our battery and a bag of helpful items including the book <u>Spanish for Cruisers</u> by Kathy Parsons.

Once Pete got aboard their boat he saw that their wiring was bad and their engine was half under water. Their load of fish had spoiled and was beginning to stink. Water was over two feet deep in the boat. *Spanish for Cruisers* with its emphasis on boat repairs helped Pete explain to the Venezuelan crew what he intended to do to help them. Pete used his voltmeter to find wires he could use to get the bilge pump and radio working. The bilge pump drained the water out of the boat. The captain of the stricken vessel was able to contact help using the radio. Pete was nearly able to get the engine started, but the starter motor was too wet and the wires smoked.

136

While Pete was working on the fishing boat I motored *La Boatique* close by. The sailboats *Lulu* and *Feisty* heard the single side band reports. They were not far away so they altered their courses to lend additional assistance if needed. I was busy motoring *La Boatique*, talking on the VHF radio to the boats close by, and talking on the single side band to Brenda and to David Jones. A half-hour later Brenda verified that authorities in Margarita had the location of the vessel and that a towboat was now on the way.

Pete got back aboard and reinstalled our battery. Off we continued on calm seas to the west. Later that day a towboat dragged the fishing boat safely back to Margarita.

Fishing hut on the island of Tortuga

## Tortuga

For the remainder of the day as we motored on to Tortuga fishing for us was great. But the wind and seas were zero. We caught a barracuda that we threw back. We could not gaff a very lively dorado that put up a great fight and deservedly got away. Then a small fish let go of our lure when it saw the boat. Late in the day dolphins often swam along beside us so close that they touched the boat.

We arrived at the island of Tortuga, Venezuela at 4 p.m. where we saw the clearest light blue water ever. The water was so clear that *La Boatique* seemed to be suspended above the ocean floor. We met up with *Maritime Express* and our old cruising buddies on *Argonauta*. The next day all six of us enjoyed walking the white sand beach and swimming. Only low scrub grew on this desert island. We saw a few fishing huts on the 12-mile-long island, but there were no roads and no motorized vehicles. We topped off the day with fresh caught live lobster that we purchased from local fishermen.

On October 24th we sailed downwind beside *Maritime Express* and *Argonauta* to the northeast end of Tortuga. We would sail with *Maritime Express* and *Argonauta* all the way to Panama. The next day all six of us again walked the shoreline, watched fishermen repairing their nets, and went for another refreshing swim. We discussed departure times for the 85-mile sail to reef-studded Los Roques. A compromised midnight departure was set so as to arrive at the reefs during daylight.

# Los Roques

The wind was at our back the entire 85 miles. We started out with a reefed mainsail and the genoa. We motor-sailed during the night to keep our speed up and to try to make the ride a little more comfortable. At dawn we raised the mizzen sail and the mainsail.

The Roques are a group of tiny islands covering 14 by 25 miles protected from the pounding surf by a coral reef on the eastern and southern side of the island group. The islands are a Venezuelan national park seldom seen by tourists since they are far from shore. At the southeast corner of the Roques is an entrance of deeper water through the reef. However, from the ocean looking toward the reef all we could see was white water ahead. The surf roared as it crashed against the reef. The entrance was supposed to be near a lighthouse. But the GPS coordinates from our guidebook showed it further north than we expected. We motored slowly north searching the surf for calm blue water. We circled back and looked some more. A mistake here could cost us our lives. *Maritime Express* and *Argonauta* held back. No one wanted to be first. We headed to the GPS coordinates and there was an opening through the coral reef at 11.46.6 North and 66.34.85 West just as our guidebook said. Once inside the reef the water was calm and clear. We could easily see the depth by the color of the water. We headed for the darkest deep blue water as we traveled north now surrounded by reefs and small narrow islands. We anchored off the mangrove-covered island of Buchiyaco. I snorkeled for some exercise to the island and even swam between the mangrove roots. In the dim light under the trees I saw lots of fish. I watched four live conch in only about three feet of water.

On October 27th we stayed inside the reefs and headed north and then west. We caught a 12-pound big-eyed jack that made a great

Sue holds up a big-eyed jack that we caught in the Roques Islands.

meal for the six of us. Then we anchored off the uninhabited island of Sarqui. Sarqui contained three small ponds favored by wading birds like stilts, sandpipers and herons. As we appreciated a pink sunset, pink and black birds flew from the direction of the setting sun toward us.

Pink flamingoes!

They spent the night at Sarqui. When the pink sky of dawn arrived off they flew to the west. The flock contained nearly 100 birds.

Near the waters edge we saw wooden crosses. We believed these marked graves. Often in these locations we also found parts of broken boats. At one location on Sarqui part of a broken boat was propped up near a cross.

On October 29th we accidentally hit coral with the bottom of *La Boatique*. We barely bumped coral while leaving the mooring ball at Sarqui and then bumped coral again while trying to get into the anchorage at Cayo De Agua Island.

# Las Aves

We left the Roques on October 30th and headed for the islands of the Aves, the bird islands. We sailed nearly all 32 miles using the spinnaker. As we approached the Aves we could see swarms of birds from way off in the distance. The tree-covered islands were loaded with boobies and their nests. There were also plenty of frigates, pelicans and great blue herons. Frigates are designed for flying and rarely land. However, here they were roosting in the trees in great numbers. The smell was like a dirty birdcage and dead fish. Bird poop landed on the boat. I would have liked to have stayed and kayaked the little bays but everyone else wanted to get out of there. So we left the next morning for the 15-mile sail to the western group of the Las Aves Islands.

Booby chick

We anchored off Isle Palmeras, a tiny coral island with two palm trees and nothing else. The snorkeling here was excellent. The water was extremely clear and the coral reefs were lively.

# Bonaire

On November 1st we sailed using our spinnaker for most of the 43 miles west to Bonaire. Bonaire reminded me of Bermuda. Everything from the homes, to the streets, to the ocean water was spotlessly clean and bright. Also, like Bermuda, the island had the reputation of being very expensive. While here we decided to purchase and install a new Spectra Watermaker. The watermaker dealer was very knowledgeable. He was very helpful with our installation and his prices were reasonable. His name was Jan Solberg and he was located at Harbour Village Marina.

Bonaire was known as the "Divers Paradise." We saw people with diving gear everywhere at all times of the day and night. The diving was great right from the shore. We watched divers swim right by our boat.

We were not divers. Since everyone on Bonaire seemed to be going diving, I wondered what was so interesting. So we used our dinghy to motor to two different divers moorings. At one popular sight we waited until the dive boats were done for the day. The snorkeling was good but not as spectacular as the Tobago Keys (north of Grenada) or the Aves (in Venezuela). The advantage Bonaire had was convenient flights and nice hotels. The only way to get to the Tobago Keys or the Aves was by boat and there were no hotels. Bonaire seemed to be trying hard to preserve its coral reefs but not hard enough to properly treat its sewage. Even so, Bonaire had the cleanest water compared to any other populated Caribbean island.

Before 7 a.m. on November 11th we let loose our mooring in Bonaire and headed 36 miles west to Curacao. We had hopes of another spinnaker sailing day. Once we got away from the lee of the island, six-foot northerly swells rocked us back and forth. The five to eight knot wind was very light even for the spinnaker. With the swells the sail would be difficult to handle, so we motored.

Yachts attached to moorings in Bonaire

# Curacao

As the sun rose high a line of squalls paralleled our course. With the squalls came a stronger southeast wind. We went back and forth between the staysail and the big genoa trying to find the right sail for the conditions. About the time that the wind was strong enough for sailing, we were at Curacao. The sight of a flock of bright pink flamingoes greeted us. They circled around and then landed in a salt lagoon barely protected from the sea by a narrow reef.

Curacao is a cactus and scrub covered island of angular cliffs. I did not expect to find much bird life so I was surprised to find many small bright green and yellow parrots, doves, and bright yellow and black birds. Our anchorage at Spanish Waters was very protected with only a tiny entrance to the ocean. Spanish Waters has many salt water finger bays separated by cliff walls, mangrove islands, and low land flat terrain.

*Cherokee* anchored in Spanish Waters, Curacao

# My wallet is gone

On Monday, November 13th, the local cruising sailors hangout called Sarafundi's decided to show the movie *The Perfect Storm* on their TV for free. Our cruising friends were there and we were having a great time. Pete opened his wallet to purchase a few beers. We slouched back in our chairs and gazed at the TV screen mounted up near the ceiling.

The movie started great and ended bad. Our evening started great and ended bad.

After the movie ended we dinghied back to *La Boatique* in the dark. As Pete stepped down into the cabin he slapped his pants pockets and shot me a look of alarm.

"My wallet" was all he needed to say.

I began to picture the American Express commercial. "You are in a foreign land. You have lost your wallet with your money and all your credit cards. What will you do? What will you do?"

Pete retraced his steps back to where we saw the movie, but the wallet was nowhere to be found.

I tried to sleep. But I kept seeing the commercial in my dreams. "What will you do?"

Tuesday morning bright and early we were retracing our steps again. The wallet was gone. Generously Sarafundi's let us use their phone so that we could call the U.S. to cancel and reissue our Discover, MasterCard and Visa cards. Our American Express card was a local call but we rarely find anyplace where it is accepted. The Discover card was of little concern since it likewise can rarely be used outside the U.S. We lived on the MasterCard cards and the Visa cards. Life would be tough without them.

Many cruisers, even some we did not know, offered to give us cash to help us out.

Luckily for us we found cruisers who were flying to Curacao from the U.S. within a week. We had the cards sent to them. Nearly all the cards showed up before the cruisers departed the U.S.

While we nervously waited for our cards, Fred and Renee from *Aldebaran* asked us to go for a walk with them. They wanted to show us a great snorkeling spot. We walked along the ocean edge up high on a cliff. We stopped at many scenic overviews. From above we spotted a tiny secluded beach. We would use that beach as our entrance to the sea.

The snorkeling was extremely good. The elkhorn and fan corals were some of the largest we had ever seen. There were plenty of fish. Not far from shore a steep wall completely decorated with coral dropped out of sight hundreds of feet down.

Back at the boat after the snorkel trip we were again waiting for our cards thinking of all the lessons learned.

---

**What We Learned after the Wallet was Lost**

1. Do not carry your wallet when it is not needed.

2. Do not carry your driver's license unless you will be driving.

3. Split up the credit cards so each spouse carries a different card.

4. Do not carry your passport unless necessary.

5. Have an ATM card that does not have a credit card logo on it. You won't have to cancel this card account if one of the two cards is lost. (ATM's are nearly everywhere.)

6. Have phone numbers handy for canceling the cards.

7. Since 800 numbers do not work in the Caribbean, have long distance numbers.

8. Have e-mail and web sites of the credit card companies handy.

9. Practice accessing your accounts and your account history on the Internet.

10. Open accounts including ATM access with at least 2 different financial institutions.

11. Try to know schedules of other cruisers in case you need something important from the U.S.

---

Enough of our cards showed up with the cruisers from (*Argonauta* and *Lady Bug*) when they arrived from the U.S. to give us access to our accounts. We had my mom call and activate the cards. We tried them out and they worked.

On November 25th we had a fast downwind sail along the coast of Curacao. We were out for only five hours. We hand-steered instead of using the Nexus autopilot. During our stay in Spanish Waters we replaced the head and the rudder indicator of our new autopilot. The head was randomly displaying "error 25" and the rudder indicator glass had not been glued properly. The head needed to be initialized but we could not seem to get the APC initialization routine to perform correctly without "error 34." Once we got anchored we fiddled with the autopilot and finally completed the APC initialization routine. The Nexus autopilot, which we call Harvey & Joyce, is amazingly intelligent but is also very complicated. Once it was programmed the way we liked it, the unit was easy to use. The Harvey & Joyce autopilot is like an extra crew member to steer the boat. With only the two of us on board we often need someone to steer so that we can do sail changes and other tasks. Usually we let Harvey & Joyce do most of the steering.

We anchored for the night at Boca Santa Krus, Curacao. The small bay did not offer much protection from the ocean swell. It was fine when we anchored but during the night rolling seas arrived and woke me up. Sleep was difficult from then on and I got up with a nasty headache. I sure did not feel like sailing, but it was time to move on.

# Aruba

This is how bad days start. Thank goodness we only had to sail out in the big waves for six hours.

As we left the protection of the island the ocean swells and waves were bigger than we had seen in a while. Soon I was seasick. We motor-sailed most of the way with the jib and mizzen. The coastline of Aruba provided great sailing conditions but Aruba provided a terrible welcome. The first terrible greeting was the oil refinery at the southern tip of the island. We have all seen oil refineries but this one was by far pumping out the most polluted air we had ever seen. We had to sail right through the chemical haze. Not far from the oil refinery smell was a huge garbage dump. The garbage was burning and we had to sail through those fumes as well. With this island being only 6 miles wide and 14 miles long when a south wind comes the entire island gets covered in the haze. This is certainly not what I expected of Aruba.

Our first view of Aruba, an oil refinery spewing out pollution

When we arrived at Oranjestad, the capital, the coast guard stopped us. The coast guard directed us to tie up to the cruise ship dock for check-in procedures. The huge cruise ship dock was not designed for sailing yachts with its construction equipment tires next to our boat. While we were tied to the dock, Santa Claus arrived on the island on a tugboat. Nearly all the local jet skis and pleasure boats surrounded the tug and blew their horns. We finally got anchored at 5 p.m. in calm protected water next to the airport runway.

During the night we not only had many huge planes roaring nearby, we also had Julius from *Argonauta* calling. He got a late start leaving Curacao and ended up arriving in Aruba during the middle of the night. Pete drove out in our dinghy to guide him in. Finally at 4 a.m. we got to bed and the planes stopped for a few hours.

On November 27th we went to town. We saw what most people expect of Aruba — glitzy casinos, fancy resort hotels, and lots of places to shop. We found the hardware store, the boat store, and the grocery stores. All were expensive. Lunch was at Little Caesar's Pizza.

# Aruba to Panama

We did not give Aruba its fair share of exploration time. Our thoughts were totally devoted to preparing for our longest passage in over two years. We would have to spend at least four nights at sea. Much of the time we would be far off the coastline of Columbia. We would be too far offshore to see land. We would travel over 500 miles from Aruba to Panama. I was anxious and full of nervous energy. So was Sally. Our cruising companion boats would be *Argonauta*, *Maritime Express*, *Cherokee* and a South African boat named *Bow Bells*. Little did we know that from this time until New Zealand the people on these boats would be our closest companions and dearest friends. All we knew at this point was that we wanted *La Boatique* and ourselves to be in tiptop shape for the long trip ahead of us.

Aruba had the best grocery stores we had seen since Upstate New York. We found nourishing easy-to-prepare food and also some treats. Grocery shopping was easy and fun.

Finding items to get *La Boatique* ready for the passage was another matter. The bilge pump was old and decided to wear out and quit. We did not like having to begin the trip without a working automatic bilge pump. The boat store had bilge pumps but none were strong enough to lift the water from deep down in our bilge. We gave up on the boat store. Pete took extra effort to get our 20 year old bilge pump working. Luckily for us we did not need it during the trip.

The trip from Aruba to Panama should be made during November. Before November tropical waves, storms and hurricanes can cause trouble. After November very strong winds from the northeast switching to southwest build up huge seas making an uncomfortable ride and often a dangerous trip.

We departed Aruba at 6 a.m. November 29th. We were beginning the trip at the tail end of the weather window. The weather forecasts we received over our single side band were for near perfect conditions. But we would be at sea for five days. Rarely does the weather stay pleasant that long.

As soon as we pulled away from the lee shore of the island of Aruba already we had big following seas. We would have liked to have raised a reefed mainsail but we did not want to turn into the big waves. The mainsail ended up being the only sail we did not use. For the next 30 hours we had big wind and big following seas. We headed west-northwest using the mizzen and jib. During the night the wind held at over 25 knots with gusts well over 35 knots. The boats were tossed from side to side by the waves. The ride was uncomfortable. Little food was eaten during the first day of this trip. Sleep was difficult but we took turns in three-hour shifts and managed to get maybe five hours of sleep. At dawn our second day out we gently jibed the partial jib and mizzen sails. We were now heading west-southwest slowly curling to the southwest.

As we got further south the wind and seas dropped gradually. The sail became fun.

At 9 a.m. on December 1st, we raised our new spinnaker. (We sold our old smaller spinnaker to *Lady Bug* and purchased a larger used spinnaker from Atlantic Sail Traders. Our new spinnaker was delivered by a guest on *Lady Bug*.) Less than an hour later we took the big sail down because the immense rolling waves rocked the sail back and forth across the bow. We did not want the sail collapsing. The wind was too light to steady the boat in these conditions. We motored for a few hours and then raised the spinnaker again.

When we tried to drop the sail the second time, the sock got stuck and would not cover the sail so the sail continued to billow out over the boat. With Harvey & Joyce, our autopilot, steering a steady course we both went forward in the rocking seas and tried to pull the sail down and onto the deck. Just when we got part of it on deck a gust of wind caught the sail and pulled it out from us. After the sail billowed out the bottom portion fell into the water. Now we had a heavy wet sail to pull down. Eventually we got the sail on the deck. We were exhausted. Harvey & Joyce continued to steer the steady course while we caught our breath. We did not want to put the sail away wet so we would have to raise it again to dry it out. We had little trouble raising the sail but Pete could see that the sock was caught again. Pete could either go to the top of the mast and fix the problem in the rolling seas, or we could try to pull the sail in again with the good chance that it would get wet again. While we contemplated our dilemma, the spinnaker pulled us along on a nice ride and the seas eased somewhat. I told Pete that I did not mind cranking him up the mast using the winch. Pete said that he would climb as much as he could to help me out. Pete also thought that the photo opportunity would be good so he included the camera with his pouch of tools.

We found out that going to the top of the mast while underway in rolling seas was not as easy as we thought it would be. First, Pete could not climb because he was being pitched out over the side of the boat. I could not crank with my normal strength because I had to wedge my feet carefully to keep my balance so that I was not thrown off the deck. The process took longer than we would have liked, but Pete made it to the top. There he fixed the tangled lines that kept the sock from coming down over the sail. He even had time to take some great pictures of the sail billowing out from under him. When it was time to take the sail down again, it was easily captured in the sock and came down without any trouble.

On December 2nd we caught a sailfish. Pete watched it leap and dance on the water trying to throw the hook while I slowed down the boat. We landed it and cut it into steaks. Later, after we were anchored and rested we provided fish dinner for all our traveling companions.

A few hours after we caught the sailfish the wind switched to the southwest, right on our nose. We still had 80 miles to go. This was not good news. We motored and motor-sailed using the mizzen and staysail. The night brought with it thunderstorms and building seas. *La Boatique* began to pound into the seas. Our bowsprit crashed through the waves. While Pete slept, I went below to plot our course on the chart. While I was below Harvey & Joyce sounded an alarm.

Pete holds up the sailfish we caught.

They could not steer. They could not hold the course. Pete woke up and quickly took control. He could not steer either! The engine was running and sounded good, but we were not going forward. Was there something around our prop or was there something wrong with the engine?

Pete and I quickly changed places. He went below to study the engine while I let out the staysail and fell off course to pick up speed so that Harvey & Joyce could steer again. Our vacuum gauge read high which meant that Perky, our engine was being starved for fuel. Pete removed the fuel filter and found that it was covered in black rubbery stuff. We had thought that our fuel purification system should have removed any particles from the fuel before the fuel reached the filter. This should not be happening. The only way it could happen is if the particles were too small to be detected by the fuel purification system and big enough to be caught by the filter. Pete rolled some of the rubbery stuff into a ball to save it. The stuff looked just like our black fuel tanks. The tanks were installed in September in Trinidad. Once Perky got a new filter she ran along fine but it did not take long for the filter to become black again. We hoped we could get anchored before we ran out of filters. Not only did we have trouble but *Argonauta's* filter also got clogged with black goo. We found out through chemical analysis that the fuel in our tanks had not been properly refined. We fought with the bad fuel problem all the way to Colon, Panama.

# Kuna Indians of Panama

Dawn arrived with Panama in sight. The seas and wind calmed. We made water with the new Spectra water maker. We took nice hot showers while Harvey & Joyce continued to steer to our waypoint miles away near shore. We smelled a pleasant aroma of a cooking fire. Then there was the fragrance of a bouquet of flowers as we got closer to the lush dense tropical foliage. A group of dolphins greeted every boat as we approached our island anchorage. We anchored between the mainland of Panama and the island of Isla De Pinos in calm protected water. Indians paddled and motored by in long dugout canoes.

All we wanted to do was eat and rest. We made a big breakfast of juice, bacon, eggs and toast. Then we slept for a few hours.

# Isla De Pinos

Thump. "Molas, molas" repeated by women and children awoke us. Molas are colorful stitcheries sewn by the women of the nearby Kuna Indian village. The women wear molas on the front of their blouses. The Kuna Indians are the second shortest people in the world. The only people shorter are the pigmies in Africa. The Kuna Indians expected us to buy a mola. They believed that everyone needs molas. We would purchase a mola, but not now.

Later the secretary of the village arrived with a ledger book. He spoke enough English to inform us that we needed to pay $6 to anchor. He printed a receipt for us. The next day we rode our dinghy to the village on the island. The people greeted us warmly and gave us a tour. There were about 30 thatched-roofed homes with dirt floors. There was no electricity. There were a few propane-powered refrigerators used mainly for storing cold drinks like Pepsi, Coke, and Old Milwaukee beer. Running water was available in a few places around the village. Most of the outhouses were placed out over the water. There were no motor vehicles nor were there any carts. People used canoes to carry heavy loads or they carried the loads on their backs. There were two pay phones. The pay phones were connected to a cellular tower at the highest point of the island. The phone system was powered by solar panels. This was the first place where we did not see dogs. There were no dogs at all on this island. We saw one cat and three parrots kept as pets. I did pick out a mola with a sailfish design to purchase for $5. We also bought soft bread sticks for 10 cents each, some cold drinks and a huge squash for $7. Furniture consisted of woven hammocks, wooden benches and plastic chairs. Music came from battery-powered boom boxes. Many of the adults work in the big cities of Panama and come home to the island infrequently.

Later that day a large Colombian trading boat broke down and the guys from the anchorage helped tow it near the town dock. Pete and Julius stayed for hours helping them begin engine repairs on the V12 Detroit Diesel. The engine broke a camshaft.

Two days later we took a 3-hour tour of the island. We walked through coconut gardens and along sandy beaches. While on the walk we saw a crocodile with his mouth open showing his sharp teeth. Colleen (from *Bow Bells*) could not believe that the crocodile was real. She figured that the Indians must have been playing a joke on us. After all, we had not seen a single crocodile and here was one five feet in front of us. Just as I was ready to snap the best wildlife photo of our trip, Colleen decided to toss a stick at what she thought was the fake crocodile. The crocodile was no fake and disappeared at an amazing speed into the water. The only picture I got was of the stick. I decided to put off going for a swim for a while.

Plastic sandals and shoes were strewn all along the path and the shoreline. Many plastic shoes had washed up on the shore from the ocean. After the walk Pete was called aside. It seemed his reputation as a "fixit" got around fast. He was needed to fix an outboard motor. Everyone else went back to the boats for lunch while Pete stayed and repaired the engine. Pete was given a large yucca root for his effort.

Pete tries to explain what is wrong with this outboard engine while clothes dry on the thatched roof behind him.

On December 9th we dinghied three miles to the local airport to meet Renee. Renee flew in from Cleveland, Ohio and was visiting her brother on the boat, *Aldebaran*. She was bringing us some fuel filters and other items we needed. That day the wind was up and the dinghy ride was a rough one. Since there were no cars to be seen and no roads to the airport the parking lot for the airport terminal was a dock partially awash. The airport terminal was a thatched roof hut with no walls. That did not stop the local officials from charging a three-dollar airport terminal use tax. The cement runway was barely wide enough for the airplane as long as it stayed dead center. However, the cement runway was not long enough, and when the plane landed it rolled along into the muddy grass beyond the cement.

After 13 days at Isla De Pinos we were ready to leave. At 7:50 a.m. on December 16th we motor-sailed with the staysail 20 miles northwest. Navigating through the San Blas Islands of Panama requires good daylight and good weather. We would have liked to have left Isla De Pinos days earlier but the weather did not cooperate.

Isla De Pinos is close to the mainland of Panama. In front of us at the end of the island was a reef stretching from the mainland to the island with a narrow break in the middle for boats to pass through. The large ocean swells that had traveled hundreds or thousands of miles smashed themselves into a white spray on this reef. At the time we wanted to leave the seas were high, the wind was strong, and the sky was full of mean dark clouds. The 12-foot waves crashing against the reef and the island made a nonstop roar. With the help of the tides from a full moon the pounding surf crested over its coral wall at the end of the island. The salt water then rushed through the Kuna Indian village. The salt water rose to knee deep throughout the village. Many items used for daily living floated around the thatched roof huts. The people could have gone to higher ground but they did not. Instead they carried on with life as best they could in the knee-deep water. In a hundred years they had not seen a flood like this.

We, on the other hand, carried on with a waiting game. Even most of the local trading boats decided to wait for better weather. I stared out at the white crashing surf and could not even see the pass. Days passed before the weather broke. The wind and waves abated. The pass through the reef became clear. We carefully motored out through the pass followed by *Bow Bells, Cherokee, Maritime Express, Argonauta* and *Aldebaran.*

# Achutupu, Dog Island

We went from the island of no dogs to an island known as Dog Island. Using our GPS to guide us we traveled on from waypoint to waypoint steering clear of many reefs. We arrived at Achutupu at 11:30 a.m. The island seemed to be overly filled with huts. The smell of cooking fires filled the air.

Achutupu means Dog Island and we heard plenty of dogs. A swarm of local village canoes descended upon our six boats. They tried to sell us molas and beaded jewelry. We did buy one bracelet and one mola. For the rest of the day we had a hard time getting anything done because we were pestered nonstop by these sales persons.

When night came the wind varied causing *La Boatique* to swing around. The anchorage off the island of Achutupu had way too many shallow spots of rock hard coral so when we swung to the end of our chain we were usually in too little water. The stern hit bottom so we re-anchored during the night. Then we had to re-anchor again when we swung the opposite way. Then again we swung around and again ended up in shallow water. We got little sleep. Even though we had paid our $5 to stay as long as we liked, we couldn't wait to leave this place.

# Mono Island

On the morning of December 17th we had a lumpy 11-mile ride to Mono Island. We did not raise any sails because we wanted to concentrate on looking out for reefs.

Mono Island was one of our favorite destinations for the following reasons: uninhabited area, lush vegetation, uncrowded secure anchorage, clean water, no bugs, nice breeze but not windy, birds to watch, locals sailing by in canoes, friendly people, clear fresh water stream nearby, and some trails for hiking.

Colleen and John from *Bow Bells* joined us for a dinghy ride to the mainland of Panama. The mainland of Panama is a mountainous rain forest. We glided along in the dinghy up the Mono River. The Kuna Indians live on islands near the mainland. They do not live on the mainland but they do have small gardens there. The Kuna gardens blended into the rain forest so that I had a hard time determining what was a garden and what was the forest. White herons fished along the riverbank while colorful birds called and flew overhead. Fish were easy to spot in the clear water. When the depth got very shallow we got out and pulled the dinghy along. Colleen and I enjoyed a swim and a ride through the rapidly moving current to a small pool. We laughed and all had lots of fun on this trip.

On December 18th Pete and John used a lead line and a GPS to search out a deep-water exit from Mono Island along the Panama mainland shore. Our guidebook, The Panama Guide, did not provide enough information about how to navigate through the reefs close to shore. I then used the information gathered by Pete and John to type up a page of useful waypoints that would hopefully keep us out of danger, in calm water, and cut miles from our journey to Snug Harbor. We printed 10 copies and passed them out to other boats. We then walked around the uninhabited island off our bow and snorkeled off its shore.

Later local officials from the nearby Indian village of San Iganacio De Tupile asked us if we would like to visit their community. They picked us up in the chief's large canoe. Once ashore three small parrots toured the island on Pete's back. One of the parrots enjoyed pecking at Pete's hat more than looking out at the scenery. The Kuna villagers were playing a mean game of volleyball. I noticed the net was set low because there are no tall Kunas. During our tour of the island village we visited with a young woman who was a Peace Corp worker. She was helping the Kuna women with the distribution and marketing of molas. The molas made in this village were sent out to stores near the Panama Canal. Often during our trip through remote areas we met Peace Corp workers. In every case they seemed to be genuinely appreciated by the local communities. They really seemed to be helping people live a better life and were great ambassadors for the United States. On the other hand I cannot say the same for the missionaries.

Colleen and John (from Bow Bells) sat in the front of this large dug out canoe while we rode in the back. We rode about 2 miles from Mono Island to the local Indian village.

John, Colleen, Pete and Sue ride in the chief's dug out canoe.

Before our departure on December 19th Pete decided to check our propeller for barnacles. Soon after he started scraping the propeller he thought maybe the scraper or the knife he was holding had scraped against him. But no, something else was trying to cut into his flesh. Schools of small four-inch man eating fish with oversized teeth were trying for a lunch of Pete's flesh. He began to swing his arms at the biting fish trying to drive them away to no avail. He swam fast for the ladder and climbed it without taking off his swim fins. Our neighbors on the boat *Homeward Bound* called over to us and said that they had never seen anyone climb a ladder so fast wearing big floppy swim fins. The Mono Island anchorage was not so perfect after all.

# Snug Harbor

We followed our waypoints and the guidebook charts for the 12-mile trip to Snug Harbor. The anchorage was empty when we arrived. Snug Harbor was protected by a group of tiny palm covered sandy islands with groups of mangroves and coral reefs. It was beautiful to the extreme. Pelicans spent the day roosting in the palms and diving for fish. White herons fished the shoreline. The Indians fished from their canoes. The Indians often came by with live fish, lobster and crabs for sale. The snorkeling was great. Pete caught a small lobster in the coral cliffs. Each day after we anchored more boats joined us.

Pete writes:

The San Blas Islands of Panama are remote. If things break you must have parts to repair things yourself. Luckily for us we knew of a person coming down to visit with Julie and Barry on *Cherokee* for the holidays. We had him bring a new alternator from Ferris Power Products. The alternator puts out high amps at low RPMs. It puts out an amazing 70 amps at idle. With this alternator we can charge fast using our engine if the solar or wind is not efficient enough. This way we use less fuel. Speaking of fuel, we have had some fuel that was old and plugged up our filters very quickly. You have to check all your fuel you get at the different places. We will use our baja fuel filter to help catch junk in the fuel from now on. If the fuel is bad try not to use it. But the trouble here is that fuel is far and few between stops. Gasoline is available for about 3 dollars a gallon at some villages. Outboard motor parts are hard to find. For some things, if you need them to keep running, it might be cheaper to fly home and get them. Airports are everywhere in the San Blas, but the planes are very small.

Sue Continues:

During our stay at Snug Harbor we enjoyed Christmas cocktail parties and potluck dinners aboard various boats. Some boats had Christmas lights and many decorations. *Cherokee* by far had the most decorations.

# Green Island

On December 26th we headed 29 miles to Green Island. Green Island was similar to Snug Harbor except that the water was clearer at

Green Island. The Green Island anchorage was not as well protected by small islands as the Snug Harbor anchorage was.

Sue holds lively stone crabs. We boil them alive for our dinner.

For the past 3 days starting December 28<sup>th</sup> we had nearly non-stop thunderstorms. I had never seen so much rain. For most of the 3 days we had the dinghy in the water. Eventually when we got tired of emptying rainwater out of the dinghy we put the dinghy up on our davits with the drain plug removed. At first when the dinghy filled up with water, the experience was novel and I took a bath. But then the wind and rain turned way too cold. Being outside in a bathing suit was no fun at all. From what was in the dinghy we must have had between 1 and 2 feet of rain. Our cockpit was soaking wet and the cabin windows were fogged up. Even in the cabin the air was quite damp. We found a few leaks around some windows. We collected plenty of water for washing clothes but I didn't want to start washing if I couldn't get them dry. We had up to 37 knots of wind. The lightening and thunder were very impressive and we had some hard strikes extremely close to us. The wind shifted repeatedly. The boats were turned one way and then a half-hour later they faced a different way and sometimes they turned around in a complete circle.

Everyone's anchor seemed to be holding. However, sometimes the way the boats swung we came uncomfortably close to *Bow Bells*. Getting sleep was not easy. The water around the boat changed from a very clear light blue to very muddy brown from a nearby overflowing river. Much of the rainforest seemed to have been washed out to sea and floated around the boats. In the clear water the reefs were easy to spot when we arrived here days ago. Navigation through the muddy water would be very difficult. It looked to me like we would be staying at Green Island longer than expected. I had no reason to complain since the temperature was in the upper 60's and low 70's. At least we were not having snow and were warm in the cabin.

On December 31st the rain stopped and I washed clothes wringing them out with an antique clothes wringer. The New Year arrived with only a little celebration since we were all tired from the stormy days.

Canoe goes sailing by

# 2001

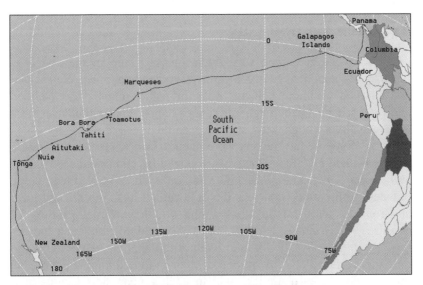

*La Boatique's* travels during 2001 from Panama to New Zealand

## Eastern Holandes Cays

On January 2nd we motor-sailed 15 miles northwest to the Eastern Holandes Cays. The Eastern Holandes Cays are considered the "must" stop for every boat visiting the San Blas Islands of Panama. Most boats enter the San Blas Islands from the north and work their way south. We entered from the south and worked our way north. For the majority of the boats entering the San Blas, the Holandes Cays are one of their first stops. They certainly are magnificent. The Holandes Cays are known as the swimming pool because of an oval shaped area of light blue water near two palm-fringed uninhabited islands. Many cruisers anchor beside the swimming pool for months. However, we were not all that impressed. Yes, the water was clear, the snorkeling great, and the tiny sandy palm islands were lovely. Waves made spectacular crashes as they pounded the protecting barrier reef. The roar from the waves was loud and non-stop. The waves threw salt spray into the air. I did not like the continual roar and I did not like the salt spray. Except for pelicans there was very little wildlife to watch. About 30 to 40 boats were anchored there, too big of a crowd for us. So we moved on the next day. Our companion boats stayed on for a few more days.

# Western Lemon Cays

The Western Lemon Cays were our last stop in the San Blas Islands. We anchored between three tiny islands at 3:30. We relaxed and enjoyed watching pelicans dive for fish. Kuna Indians paddled and motored by in their dugout canoes. Those that paddled came a long way over rough seas since we could not even see any Kuna villages. Some of the Indians were naked. Two Kuna women with a baby who had paddled a long way stopped by and asked for "leche" and "ropa." We knew "leche" was milk so I gave them some powdered milk since that was the only milk I had. We did not have any rope to spare but later we found out they wanted clothes. In Spanish "ropa" means "clothes." By U.S. standards the Kuna Indians live in extreme poverty. I would like to think that we helped them out during our stay. Pete did fix one of their outboard engines, we gave them some needed supplies, paid to anchor near their islands, and purchased items they had for sale. I believe that their lives would be greatly improved if they could practice birth control and had better health care. They have lots and lots of babies knowing that many or most of them will die while still very young.

# Isla Linton

After one month of visiting with the Kuna Indians of the San Blas Islands we headed northwest out to sea away from the islands on January 10th. We motor-sailed 28 miles along the jungle coastline of Panama. Our destination was to tuck up behind Isla Linton. Isla Linton is known as the most protected anchorage from the San Blas Islands to the Panama Canal. Here we thought we could ease our way back into civilization. Little did we know that at the dock we would not be greeted by humans. There were about a dozen boats in the anchorage with about half of them empty.

We decided to motor our dinghy to the dock at Isla Linton. Instead of short Kuna Indians coming out to greet us, three large monkeys with very long strong tails walked upright to the end of the dock to check us out. We had a bunch of small bananas back at the boat. So we turned back for the food. The monkeys really liked the bananas. A few days later we brought them coconuts and bananas.

Wild monkeys at Isla Linton, Panama

There was plenty of wildlife here to view. I noticed that many of the birds were the same kind of birds we see at home in Ohio in the summer. I particularly enjoyed the swallows even though they did perch on our rigging. Arriving with every dawn were the calls of jungle animals, parrots, and songbirds.

Islands and coral reefs protect the coastline near Isla Linton. We could travel for miles through protected waters with our dinghy. To the northeast is Isla Grande, a tourist destination. On Isla Grande there were small hotels, restaurants, beaches for swimming, and beaches for surfing. For people watching, Isla Grande was the place. On the mainland across from Isla Grande was a Chinese grocery with fresh milk and ice cream. Isla Linton contained only monkeys and birds. To the southwest was Isla Palina. Isla Palina was an uninhabited mangrove and palm island. A channel so narrow that it was totally shaded by mangroves separated Isla Palina from the jungle-covered hills of mainland Panama.

On the mainland south of Isla Linton was a dock in a deep bay. We tied our dinghy off on the dock. A bus to the city of Colon, Panama, made a stop there. We enjoyed the view of mainland Panama during the $2 two-hour bus ride. Once the bus dropped us off in Colon we breezed through the check-in procedures with the help of a great taxi driver named Rudy. He charged us $15 to take care of all the details to make us legal in Panama. The bus going back to Linton was extremely crowded. People were squished in as tight as could be. People stood on the steps and hung outside the door as we motored along up over hills and around bends. Pete and I were lucky. We had a seat near the front of the bus.

Isla Linton was so nice that instead of staying for a day, we ended up staying six days. We seriously considered staying for a month or more. However, we wanted to beat the rush of yachts going through the Panama Canal this year so we decided to move on once we were joined by *Argonauta, Maritime Express, Cherokee, Spirit Born, Aldebaran,* and *Bow Bells*.

# Colon, Panama

On January 10th most of the group of boats set sail for Colon and the Panama Canal. Barry, on *Cherokee,* caught an albacore tuna that we all enjoyed late in the day for supper. As we approached the Panama Canal we saw freighters everywhere. Most of them were huge ships at anchor miles out in the ocean. Sometimes we had a hard time determining if the ship was at anchor or was heading our way. Just as we approached the break wall protecting the Panama Canal area, a huge freighter we thought was stopped began heading toward the break wall from the Canal side directly toward us. We spun *La Boatique* around and headed away from the freighter. After the freighter passed by we made our way through the break wall to calm protected water. We then anchored with all the other yachts in an anchorage known as the flats.

We had read and heard from other cruisers that Colon, Panama, was one of the most dangerous cities in the world. The air and water were supposed to be full of pollution. We were prepared to get in and out of Colon as fast as possible. We had planned to stay a month at Pedro Miguel Boat Club in the Panama Canal near Panama City.

Once we stopped listening to others and opened our eyes to Colon, we decided for ourselves that Colon was quite nice. The Panama Canal Yacht Club was pleasant with surrounding grass and shade trees. It had a nice bar and restaurant and inexpensive laundry. Within walking distance in Colon were plenty of stores, a bus terminal, cheap Internet, and plenty of taxis. For us, Colon was more appealing than the run-down Pedro Miguel Boat Club. Yes, we did take extra precautions in Colon and always walked alert and with others. We never saw so many armed police on the streets. Stores were well stocked with reasonable prices. Fresh local fruits and vegetables were real bargains. The water in the anchorage looked clean. We did not go swimming, but we did make fresh water with our Spectra water-maker every day. As many of our friends transited the Panama Canal and moved on, we stayed anchored in the flats. The view off our stern was a nonstop parade of ships bound for another ocean. Tugboats tooted their whistles as they guided the ships through the channels. Off our bow, ships moored to docks to load and unload all sorts of cargo.

Sue is on the bow of *Argonauta* as we begin our trip through the Panama Canal. Barry, Julie, Pete and I volunteered to be line handlers on Julius and Sally's boat. To the left, a tugboat pushes a blue and white car carrier into position. Above the car carrier is a cruise ship going up. To the right, a freighter is in another chamber. The huge ships go up two at a time 24 hours a day.

## The Panama Canal

Many sources recommended to us that before we took our own boat through the canal we go through on someone else's boat. The locks are not designed for the typical cruising yacht. The lock chambers are 110 feet wide and 1000 feet long. The largest ships to transit the canal are 106 feet wide and 965 feet long. Pete transited the entire canal on the 45-foot Island Trader ketch called *Slip Away*. The Panama Canal adviser was named Ruben. Ruben was very professional and did an excellent job. With his expert advice *Slip Away* was able to transit the 50-mile canal in 11 hours. During the open stretches of water a boat must average 7.5 knots to be able to complete the transit in one day. The boat only goes 85 feet above sea level. By comparison, we dropped 570 feet from the level of Lake Erie to sea level. I was amazed that less than 50 miles of hilly terrain separates the Caribbean (Atlantic) and Pacific Oceans. We often took a $2 bus ride from one ocean to the other since we enjoyed shopping in the Panama City stores on the Pacific coast.

Both Pete and I got to transit partway through the Panama Canal on *Argonauta*. Julie and Barry were also aboard. We found the first lock to be by far the most difficult. We were immediately behind a tall car-carrying freighter. We were side-tied to a tugboat that was tied to another tugboat. We did not have the lines tight enough. The lock filled with 52 million gallons of fresh water. We watched it boil up from the bottom of the lock in 15 minutes. *Argonauta's* lines stretched and the bow pulled away from the tug. Julie and Barry used a winch to tighten the spring line and bring the bow back into position.

Once we finished the first lock, we were in fresh water. Since we were not mixing fresh water with salt water, the water in the locks did not seem to boil like in the first lock. We had the routine down and made sure the lines to the tug were tight. We had three up-bound locks before a long scenic ride through Gatun Lake. Our down-bound lock was easy. We had the lock to ourselves and were tied to the wall. The water draining out the center of the bottom of the lock kept us away from the wall. We arrived at Pedro Miguel Boat Club at dusk. Then we had to get a ride to Panama City in order to catch a bus to Colon. As we walked to catch our first ride rain pelted us. We rode in the back of a pickup truck with a cage over the truck bed. We felt like dogs being taken to the pound. We were dropped off at a bus terminal that looked more like a big city airport. We then boarded a new bus to Colon. In air-conditioned comfort in our reclining seats we watched the stupid movie <u>Anaconda</u>.

We assumed our Panama Canal transit would be nerve-racking. But we found preparations in Colon, Panama to be worse than the passage. January 31$^{st}$ and February 1$^{st}$ were two nerve-racking days for us. On January 31$^{st}$ Pete ended up in a seedy Colon police station for six hours. I had no idea where he was and I was certainly worried.

Then on February 1st right off the bow of our anchored boat we witnessed a freighter nearly sink a sailboat. The freighter then passed only 200 feet off our bow.

# Lost Muffler

The story begins as Pete explains his experience:

On January 31st I removed the lift muffler from the boat because it had a small leak. The local cab drivers told me of a welding shop, Donald's Welding. So for a dollar cab ride a taxi took me there. I dropped off the muffler for repair. Donald from the welding shop said to come back around 11 a.m. I went back at 1 p.m. to find out that Donald could not find the leak. He claimed that he tested the muffler with air and soap. There were no bubbles on the muffler. After an hour of working with Donald trying to find the leak I took the muffler without any repairs. I hailed a cab to drive me back to the marina because the neighborhood was unsafe. At the first intersection, which was a double lane street, the cabby missed one car because he did not stop for the stop sign. At the next intersection he did not stop for the stop sign and hit another cab. The words started flying between the two cab drivers and so did the fists. I jumped in to separate them. Then the police were separating all of us. We were each put into separate police cars. I found out my driver had no license. His car was towed away with my muffler in the front seat. We were taken to the police station where we sat for six hours. After some paper work, the police figured I was harmless. I could not understand Spanish and they could not understand English. I was glad I had my passport on me. I ended up signing some papers in Spanish that I did not understand so that I could get out of there.

Sue was looking for me and the rest of the boats had the word out. The police finally took me back to the marina, but without my muffler. I figured I should go while I had the chance. So the next morning, February 1st, I called the police about the muffler. They said they would deliver it. After I waited an hour I asked the local cabbies to go to the police station and look for it. The muffler was finally found by a cab driver who charged me ten bucks for his services.

I learned a lesson. Stay in the cab and let them fight.

And after all that, I installed the muffler and it still leaked. The leak was very small and I was still not sure where it was. I would not take the muffler off the boat again in Panama. As I completed installing the muffler, the freighter *Sierra Leyre* prepared to depart the dock off our bow.

The sailboat's anchor chain is caught on the bulb of the freighter.

# Freighter Hits Anchored Sailboat in the Flats, Colon Panama

Sue continues:

At about 3:30 p.m. on February 1st, 2001 the freighter *Sierra Leyre* pulled away from the dock near the flats anchorage in Colon, Panama. A tug pulled the bow of the freighter around in order to position the freighter to head to the Panama Canal. The line from the tugboat came off. The 20-knot wind pushed the empty freighter sideways toward the pleasure boat anchorage (called the flats) and our boat. The freighter hit an anchored sailboat in front of us. By the time we noticed what was happening, the freighter was already dragging the sailboat by the sailboat's anchor chain. We jumped into our dinghy and rushed closer. No one was aboard the sailboat (*Diana* from France). The anchor chain of the sailboat was caught on the bulb of the bow of the freighter. Andy from the sailboat *Webegone* boarded *Diana*. The anchor chain became tight and the sailboat began to be dragged under the bow of the freighter. Andy released the anchor chain. The chain rushed out of the anchor locker so fast that it stripped the teeth of the gypsy away. The anchor rode tied to the end of the chain and lashed securely to the boat held tight.

Andy yelled, "Get me a knife" as *Diana* was drawn hard against the freighter. While *Diana* was being drawn under the freighter Andy scrambled to the cabin to search for a knife.

Meanwhile, we sped back to get a knife from our boat, but by then Andy had found a knife inside *Diana*. He sliced the anchor rode at the end of the chain to free the sailboat. The freighter departed the flats for the Panama Canal. We then helped tow *Diana* to an anchorage zone buoy where we helped to tie it off. An hour later the owners arrived and re-anchored *Diana*.

The sailing vessel *Diana* sustained major damage. The Panama Canal Commission decided that *Diana* would not be compensated for damage because they claimed that *Diana* was anchored just outside of the designated anchorage. The flats anchorage held nearly 40 closely anchored boats at the time. We found out later that *Diana* was anchored in the flats. We never found out if *Diana* was repaired and who ended up paying the bill.

*La Boatique* transits the Panama Canal

# The Pacific Ocean

## *La Boatique* Transits the Panama Canal

On February 7th we transited the Panama Canal. The United States used to operate and maintain the Panama Canal. The government of Panama has been operating and maintaining the canal now for about one year. They seem to handle large cruise ships and merchant ships in an efficient manner. They should, since each ship pays an average of $45,000 to make the transit. The canal is not set up for cruising yachts. We only paid $500 to transit.

Our day began in the darkness at 4:30 a.m. with Pete picking up our crew off nearby sailboats while I prepared an apple cinnamon crumb cake. Part of our crew consisted of the two muscular guys, Joe and Mat off the catamaran *Ladybug* (Madison, Wisconsin). The remainder of our crew consisted of Joyce, Roger, and their granddaughter Tristin from the sailboat *Austerity* (Cincinnati, Ohio). Soon after we got our dinghy and motor secured, a pilot boat delivered our pilot/advisor, Edwin. As soon as Edwin arrived we headed toward the canal with a strong wind at our back. Before we entered the first lock we turned around facing the wind. We had lots of old black tires and round white fenders tied to the sides of *La Boatique*. We had to be ready for whatever might come against the side of our boat. The first thing along side of us was to be another sailboat. We tied up securely to *Cherokee*. Next, the sailboat *Bow Bells* tied off the other side of *Cherokee*. All three boats tied together then turned and headed into the first lock. In front of us was a 661-foot long container ship called *Cielo Di Livorno*. The lock door closed behind us. Water boiled up from the bottom of the lock. In short order we were through the first three locks. *Bow Bells* released from our group of three boats first. They should have headed as fast as they could through the lake but their advisor had them head toward the shipping channel by mistake. They should have taken the short cut used by pleasure boats. That mistake probably ended up costing them many hours of delays and damage to their boat.

By 8 a.m. we were entering Gatun Lake. Everyone on board *La Boatique* was hungry so instead of enjoying the beautiful scenery, I was down below dishing out orange segments and apple cinnamon crumb cake. Even though we arrived at the lake much before we thought we would, Pete did all he could to keep our speed up as high as possible. The 20 to 30 knot wind behind our jib sail was a big help. We had to keep the motor on all the time because the channel through the lake was narrow and winding. Often islands and the shoreline blocked the wind. After breakfast I got busy using the fresh water from the lake to hose down the topside. The salt, dirt and soot from Colon disappeared. *La Boatique*'s white paint sparkled in the sunshine. Pete continued steering, pushing *La Boatique* faster and faster. We were able to pass ahead of the container ship that was ahead of us in the first three locks. Little did we know at that time that this was a critical maneuver.

We had to time our meals so that all hands would be available any time we were near a lock. We normally have our big meal of the day early but a meatloaf dinner at 10:30 a.m. was even early for us.

The next lock was the first down-bound lock. Pleasure boats always go in front of large ships when going down. Since we got ahead of the container ship we were allowed to proceed to the lock. At this lock a tugboat was tied to the wall. *Cherokee* was tied to the tug and we were tied to *Cherokee*. The huge ship was at our stern.

Joyce and Sue present nervous smiles as the container ship continues its approach.

There was no room for *Bow Bells*. *Bow Bells* was sent back away from the lock. They were delayed for many hours. They had to tie up along various walls and wait. Eventually they were thrown hard up against one wall by the wash of a tugboat and their boat was damaged.

We, on the other hand, were still speeding along. The second down-bound lock was called the Miraflores Lock. Here we were pictured "live" on the Internet. Our friends on *Maritime Express* and *Argonauta* had decided to stay at the Pedro Migel Boat Club. They walked to the observation booth where they waved to us and took pictures. After one more lock we cruised under the Bridge of the Americas and entered the Pacific Ocean. The Pacific lived up to its name and showed us its gentle peaceful side. We anchored next to Isla Flamenco with a panoramic view of the skyscrapers of Panama City, the Bridge of the Americas, and the calm Pacific Ocean.

With uneasiness we stared out at the immense Pacific Ocean from our tranquil anchorage at the end of the Panama Canal. Our view of the Pacific showed gentle calm water with huge ships waiting for their transit time through the canal. Near the horizon to our left was the Bridge of the Americas, the impressive bridge linking North and South America. I was in awe as we crossed under this magnificent bridge at the end of our Panama Canal transit. On the horizon to our right were the bright white skyscrapers of Panama City. Panama City, the capital of Panama claims to be the commercial focus of Central and South America. From our view across the bay the city certainly looked its part. However, since the United States stopped running the Panama Canal the economy has declined.

# The Perlas Islands

Our first venture into the Pacific Ocean was only 30 miles. The sailing conditions were very pleasant. We had 15 to 20 knots of wind from the northeast but the ocean was nearly calm. There was not even an ocean swell. The color was a drab green dark blue combination. Our destination was the Panamanian island of Contadora. We sailed along with *Bow Bells* and *Cherokee*. Along the way to Contadora we spotted dolphins and whales. Once we anchored we watched whales breach and crash back into the ocean. They made huge splashes. Contadora is in the northern portion of the Perlas Islands. Contadora is Panama's island for the rich, famous and very well off. Along the tree-lined paved streets were mansion estates with names instead of house numbers.

The nearest beach for landing our dinghy was the nudist beach. A sign on the shore gave the rules for the beach in about 6 languages. There was no rule stating that we could not land our dinghy, but we did break the main rule of the beach. The rule stressed that no clothing was allowed.

The tides were 16 feet so sometimes the beach was huge and sometimes it was gone. I saw only five nudists. The tropical sun was too intense for sun bathing and the ocean water at 68 degrees was cloudy and very cold for swimming.

Ashore a small convenience store sold the basics along with fresh milk and ice cream. Also available at the store was gasoline and diesel at prices better than at the Balboa Yacht Club near Panama City. A tiny bakery sold fresh bread, cake and donuts.

On February 14th we got to fly our colorful spinnaker during our 16-mile trip south to Isla Del Espiritu Santo. There was no sign of human habitation in this area. The anchorage was scenic and quiet.

Isla Del Rey in the Pacific group of Panamanian Islands

The next day we used our spinnaker again during our 6-mile trip to Isla De Cana. The following day we motored to the southern end of the Perlas Islands. Along the way we saw more pelicans than we had every seen before. There must have been thousands of them diving for fish and resting along the shore. Here there seemed to be upwellings of deep ocean water causing strange currents.

We spent three days at the southeast corner of Isla Del Rey. There were no homes within sight. We walked nearby beaches covered with beautiful shell assortments. We dinghied up a mangrove lined stream where birds fished from the banks and sharks swam around us. We prepared for four to five days at sea. The evening before we were ready to depart the sink drain pipe corroded apart. The pipe was right at our water line so water was leaking into the boat. Pete used epoxy to fix the leak. We hoped nothing would break while we were out at sea.

The weather predictions were for light winds pushing us south with nearly calm seas. So on the morning of February 19th we set off into the Pacific accompanied by *Cherokee, Bow Bells* and *Silver Heels*. *Bow Bells* and *Silver Heels* decided to head straight for the Galapagos Islands while *Cherokee* and *La Boatique* headed south to Manta, Ecuador. The predicted light wind turned out to be much stronger than we expected. The following seas built to an uncomfortable roll our first night. But from then on we could not complain about rough seas. The seas were very gentle providing us a pleasant ride.

Two or three times a day we talked to the other boats using our single side band radio. We used the single side band radio to check our e-mails. I cooked various meals and even made bread while under way. We made water with our great Spectra Watermaker. We took hot showers.

In each 24-hour day we traveled between 140 and 150 miles. We sailed, motor-sailed and motored. Our spinnaker sail was often used during the day but we always took it down before dark. At night we often motor-sailed using the jib and mizzen sails. A 1 to 1½ knot current helped push us south but it also pushed us west. Our GPS provided us with the best course to steer to stay on our rhumb line.

During the trip *Bow Bells* caught a yellow fin tuna, *Cherokee* caught a dorado. We caught no fish at all even though we had the pole out most days.

We crossed the equator at 47 minutes after midnight on February 23rd. We were traveling at 6.5 knots heading south. We had traveled 1948 nautical miles since we put *La Boatique* in the water in Trinidad in September. The moment was exciting but I was tired and soon went back to sleep.

# Manta, Ecuador

As we approached Manta, Ecuador we saw more and more fishing boats. The air smelled fishy. The most common fishing boats were 30-foot long open fiberglass boats. These fishermen set out long lines tied together. Plastic bottles were used to float the lines. The plastic floats were very hard to see until we were nearly on top of them. Then there were so many of them that we could not avoid going over the lines. We caught one line with the fishing pole and another line with the bow of the boat. When we pulled in the fish line to release it from the bow of *La Boatique* we found that squid were used for bait. We saw large fishing boats with nets. We saw large high-tech boats like the one from the movie *The Perfect Storm*. At the low-tech end we saw wooden sailing fishing boats. We ended up steering miles out of our way to avoid boats, nets, and floating lines.

At about the time I saw the mountains on shore I smelled the steam coming off the earth from an early morning rain. I breathed deeply to savor the earthy aroma.

We tied to a mooring ball at the Manta Yacht Club. We were charged $5 per night for the club's services, which included a pool. We were amazed at all the fishing boats around us. There were more fishing boats than we had ever seen anywhere. Fishermen from all over the world were gathered here. Fish processing must be big business in Manta. The fish they unloaded were huge tunas, shark and dorado.

Manta is a big modern city, not the small town we expected. Except for food and drinks at the yacht club, prices were extremely inexpensive. Manta was not a tourist destination. It was a great place for us to see the people at work in their city and at play on their beaches.

We were in Manta during carnival time when everyone seemed to be in a playful mood. A very popular activity in Manta was the use of large volume squirt guns to spray unsuspecting passersby with water. Whole pails full of water were also dumped on people. People on the street squirted people in cars, trucks and busses. People in the back of pickup trucks squirted people on the street and people in other pickup trucks. The cool shower felt great and everyone seemed to laugh it off. When we were walking on a street I cringed when I noticed a large squirt gun aimed my way from a person in the back of a pickup truck. I did not get squirted. We always got squirted when we did not expect it. Often the cool spray surprised us.

The worst thing about Manta was the mosquito bites. We had not had any problems with mosquitoes anywhere in Panama. We were no longer diligent with our screens. Our first evening while we were out on deck tiny mosquitoes flew below into our cabin. From then on whenever it was dark these tiny bloodsuckers were biting us. The bites left welts on our skin that itched for about a half-hour. We could barely see the mosquitoes to swat at them. We tried spraying the boat with insecticide one day. We burned a mosquito coil and filled the boat with smoke another night. We covered our skin up with a sheet or a net but then we got too hot. We ran a fan. Our best defense was to sleep covered in insect repellent. I hoped these mosquitoes were not carrying any diseases like malaria.

I did not know that my last venture ashore to the American continent would be February 27th. The night of February 27th I came down with flu-like symptoms, sore muscles, headache, fever, chills, nausea and most annoying diarrhea. I spent February 28th in bed feeling awful. Manta, Ecuador, is a terrible place to be sick since the air always smells foul with the stench of fish processing. After a few days I felt somewhat better except for the diarrhea.

*La Boatique* at the Manta Yacht Club.

# Passage to the Galapagos

I wanted to get out of Manta to get away from the smell. So did Pete, Julie and Barry. On March 4th *Cherokee* and *La Boatique* wove their way through the fishing boats and headed west into the South Pacific. I tried to stick to a bland diet and eat small portions. Imodium pills really helped me recover.

We had 550 miles between our destination, the Galapagos Islands, and us. The forecast was for calm seas and calm wind. The trip ended up being an easy motor-sail with as expected calm wind and seas. "Perky", our engine, ran nearly nonstop gobbling up almost all the fuel we had on board.

Each day during our four-day passage I felt a little better. Luckily for us, we did not have to work hard. The trip was almost boring it was so easy. The ocean was calm enough for us to wash clothes. We used our antique clothes wringer to remove the soapy water from the clothes. We hung them on the lifelines in the bright sunshine. There was no salt spray in the air that would make the clothes impossible to dry. All day we motored along under our mainsail with clothes of various colors fluttering in the warm air.

Perky, our engine, chugged along while Harvey & Joyce, our autopilot, steered. All we did was supervise. *Cherokee* was by our side the entire four-day passage.

Julie and Barry on *Cherokee* were by our side during the entire passage.

# San Cristobal Island, Galapagos

At dawn on March 8th the Galapagos Island of San Cristobal rose above the western horizon. The ocean became alive with schools of tuna. As we motored along side the island what looked like short fat logs in the water turned out to be sea turtles. Sea turtles love jellyfish and the water seemed filled with jellyfish. The sea turtles here were different from any I had ever seen. The Galapagos' sea turtles rode high in the water. Their shells rose at least five inches out of the water and the shells were often dry from being out of the water a long time.

Our destination was Wreck Bay, San Cristobal Island. The wrecked boat in the middle of the bay seemed to us to have been there for many years. We figured that it was the wreck of Wreck Bay. However, we were told that the boat had run up on the coral reef only two months ago. We found it strange as we motored by the wreck that there were no other visible wrecks in Wreck Bay. The wreck had caused an oil spill that made news around the world. We are happy to report that the bay water was clear and blue and filled with life.

At Wreck Bay we met up with *Cherokee, Argonauta, Maritime Express, Aldebaran*, and other boats. We shared the clear blue water of the bay with sea lions, blue-footed boobies, pelicans, black gulls, magnificent frigate birds, rays, and many fish. None of the creatures were afraid of us. In fact, the main problem was keeping creatures off the boat and the dinghy. Once night came, the birds and the sea lions seemed to prefer to sleep on boats rather than the rocks on shore. Boats with swim platforms usually had a sea lion or two resting on the platforms. The sea lions smell fishy. Many of the local boats had barbed wire strung around their perimeter. Except for a bird that sneaked aboard during one night, we had no problems. The bird, of course, made a mess on our deck.

Checking into the Galapagos was a long process because the rules were in a state of flux. While Pete and Barry listened to the locals argue Julie and I watched sea lions and blue-footed boobies play right outside the Port Captain's office.

A few days later outside the Port Captain's office in a small park two musicians played traditional South American flute music. We sat and listened under stunted shade trees. Sea lions and boobies rested nearby. Local children splashed in the water as they jumped off a pier. Later that day Pete arranged with Juan Carlos (a local yacht services provider) to have diesel fuel delivered to the boat for $1 a gallon. That night Julius, Sally and Ed (their guest) from *Argonauta* joined us for a delicious lobster dinner at the home of Juan Carlos' mother for $10 per person.

On March 11th we took an island tour with a local man named Gustavia. We saw marine iguanas sunning themselves on rocks. I snorkeled with sea lions in a protected bay. They swam right up to me. Further out from the bay were huge breaking waves. A few

Sea lions on San Cristobal Island

surfers rode the waves. The surfers were not locals but instead were "California" surfer guys. We continued the tour. Our next stop was a volcanic crater filled with the island's fresh water supply. Here juvenile frigate birds practiced flying and dipping their beaks in the calm water. Our lunch stop was a vegetable farm where we picked our own produce. Lunch consisted of products from the farm including watermelon and "free range" chicken grown on the farm. Nearly all the trees on San Cristobal were scrubby looking since there was very little rain. However, along our tour we stopped at one huge thorny tree in a protected valley. This tree was well over 250 years old. It had a diameter of at least 12 feet and was very tall. A tree house had been built high up in the tree. This tree house had running water, plumbing, a bathroom, a kitchen, a loft with 2 beds, and a pole to slide down for a quick escape. What was amazing was that the tree house was about 12 foot by 12 foot by 15 foot, but the tree was so massive that the tree house was well hidden in the branches. Under the tree house on a lower branch of the tree lived an owl. We did not expect to see an owl in the Galapagos Islands. But this was the kind of tree that deserved at least one owl.

Before we left San Cristobal we found Pepee, the local giant tortoise. Pepee lived in a garden in a backyard in town. He nearly ran to us when we called his name. He was very old and very large. He liked us to hand feed him. Pete found out that he liked the leaves of the pepper plant.

Barry and Sue and the giant tortoise at the Darwin Research Center

# Santa Cruz Island, Galapagos

On March 13th we motored over flat calm seas 45 miles to Santa Cruz. Santa Cruz is the most populated of the Galapagos Islands. The island is the base for most tourist companies. Supplies are available but they are nearly double the prices we paid in Manta, Ecuador. The restaurants, however, were inexpensive. The grocery store had little competition but there were many restaurants to choose from.

While at Santa Cruz we walked to the Darwin Research Center. The center's main goal is the preservation and repatriation of the giant tortoises. The center had reared over 2000 tortoises and sent most of them on to live in the wild on the various islands that make up the

Galapagos. The center had modern buildings, elevated walkways, nice landscaping, informative exhibits and plenty of tortoises. There was no cost to visit the facility. It seemed to me that the Darwin Research Center was funded by the World Wildlife Fund.

We had to cut our stay somewhat short at Santa Cruz Island because we needed to meet up with *Bow Bells* at Islabela Island.

# Isabela Island, Galapagos

Isabela Island is nearly five times the size of Santa Cruz Island. However, Santa Cruz Island has the largest population and most supplies. Isabela Island seemed at first to us that it should have been much more populated than it was. Isabela Island has a calm bay protected by volcanic rock reefs. There were places on the island of Isbela that got lots of rain. Yet, there were only about 1,400 people living on the island. Later during our horseback riding tour we found out why.

There were nine sailing yachts in the anchorage when we arrived on March 16th. The island has only been open for visiting yachts for a year or so. *Bow Bells* with our boat parts was one of them. Their daughter flew to the Galapagos Islands from Florida with the parts. We made the tenth boat in the anchorage. A few days later *Cherokee* made number eleven. Tiny cruise ships with from 6 to 30 passengers would anchor for a day or so at the entrance to the protected bay.

Colleen and John from *Bow Bells* said that they could hardly wait to show us a magical pool nearly surrounded by lava rocks. The pool had a small opening to the sea at high tide. Barry and Julie joined us. After a three-minute dinghy ride through a lava rock passage we anchored our dinghies in a small bay. Then we swam to an islet of black lava rocks. A path through these rocks led to the magical bay. Our walk had to be fast because horse flies were biting us right through our wet suits. But the walk was worth the view. The turquoise water of the circular pool was partially enclosed by walls of black lava rock. Black marine iguanas sunned themselves on the rocks. The bright green branches of mangrove trees shaded one side of the pool. Beneath the trees under their tangle of above-ground roots were tiny white sandy beaches where sea lions played. We put on our snorkel gear and got in the water quickly to get away from the biting flies. While snorkeling we saw colorful fish. Sea lions swam around us. Then at the bottom of the pool Pete spotted white tipped sharks six to eight feet long. Sometimes they seemed to be resting and other times they were swimming around. They made me apprehensive when I saw them swimming around. The pool really was magical except for the biting flies and large sharks.

The next day, March 19th, we took a horseback riding tour to the volcano of Sierra Negra. There are five active volcanoes on Isabela. The most recent large eruption on the island of Isabela was in 1998. Sierra Negra last erupted in 1979 with hot lava flowing for many miles to the sea for over six months. Included with the all day tour were two hours of riding in the back of a pickup truck, an English-speaking guide, a Spanish-speaking guide that knew the horses, breakfast, and a late lunch. I had not ridden a horse in over 20 years. But I had no reason for concern because my horse was just perfect for me. She was not too spunky and not too slow. She trotted along at a comfortable pace for both of us. Pete's horse was spunky and always wanted to be in the lead because his horse was the lead horse. Pete's horse was just right for him but his saddle was awful. The saddles were made of rebar covered with padding material and rubber. Pete's saddle was loose and during the ride the saddle turned over with Pete still holding on. His shoulder landed on the ground. Pete got red

Barry and Pete study the hot volcanic earth.

marks from sitting on the lightly covered rebar. My saddle was comfortable.

We rode along a scenic trail for about an hour. We went up and down gentle hills through scrub terrain. At the tops of the hills we could see the ocean. We rode along the rim of the world's second largest volcanic caldera. It stretched for miles. A few trees grew here and there. Under the shade of the last big tree we tied up the horses. The rest of the trip would be by foot. Once we climbed over a small hill we were in a lava field. The first plants to grow out of the volcanic lava rocks were cacti. We saw empty lava tubes where hot lava once flowed. We looked into hot fumaroles. Some of the fumaroles sent out hot steam. On one high spot we enjoyed a snack and the far off view of the ocean. From this high spot we could see why few people live on this island. The volcanic earth was still too hot and unstable over vast areas. Then we hiked back to our horses and rode them back on the trail for another hour. We really had a good time. The cost for our group of six including an omelet breakfast and a roast beef and potatoes lunch with soup and dessert was $31 each.

On March 21$^{st}$ *Argonauta* and *Maritime Express* joined us while *Bow Bells* headed out for the Marquesas.

On March 22$^{nd}$ we walked over 10 miles to find the "wall of tears." Henry, from *Maritime Express*, and Julie and Barry, from *Cherokee,* joined us. We walked through town. We stopped at a number of salt-water marshes in search of pink flamingoes and found four of the bright pink birds at one of the marshes. Marine Iguanas and red crabs had a powder white sand beach all to themselves for over two miles. We glimpsed into a lava cave that ran down to the ocean. We walked along a trail through a cactus forest. Many of the cactus plants here look like a combination of a tree and a cactus. In one valley we even had some shade trees. Most of the time we were walking on black lava cinders. The hot equatorial sun beat into our skin. The black cinders beneath our feet soaked up the sun's heat and reflected it back at us.

Pete and Sue by the tree cactus

When we finally got to the "wall of tears", we were hot and more than ready to turn back. The "wall of tears" is an eight-foot thick rock wall that goes nowhere. It was a make-work job done by prisoners of long ago. With little food or water the prisoners were forced to carry jagged heavy lava rocks on their bare backs in the scorching equatorial heat. The rocks often cut into their skin. If they dropped a rock, they were shot. Some of the dead prisoners were then buried inside the wall. The construction of the wall by the prisoners was not stopped until 1959.

April is the recommended month to make the extremely long 2904-mile journey from the Galapagos Islands to the Marquesas. Before we left the Galapagos Pete checked all of our rigging for any signs of problems. He found cracked nuts in two of the turnbuckles. We used replacement turnbuckles since we did not have spare nuts. I pulled out the charts we would need and drew a desired rhumb line course on all the charts in blue pencil. I used our Yeoman electronic chart plotter to help me set up waypoints on the charts and in the GPS. Pete meticulously scrubbed the propeller and the hull below the waterline. The cleaner the bottom, the smoother *La Boatique* would travel through the water and we found it really paid off later in this trip. I went to town for one last chance at groceries. The pickings were slim.

Sea lion resting on a catamaran

A bed and breakfast hotel called the Blue Whale catered to yachties. At the Blue Whale we had our laundry done. We enjoyed great American meals of hamburgers and French fries. I used the hotel's Internet access to update the web page. Pete used connections at the hotel to arrange for fuel. Pete used jerry cans to load *La Boatique* with every drop of fuel she could possibly hold, 179 gallons of diesel fuel and 11 gallons of gasoline. The diesel fuel at $1 a gallon delivered to the dock was a good deal. We still had to haul the cans out to *La Boatique* in the anchorage. A few days after we left Isabela, the island ran out of fuel.

We put the dinghy on the cabin top and deflated it. The evening before we left, the boat, *Some Day is Here,* hosted a farewell cocktail party. Present along with us were the couples from *Argonauta, Maritime* Express and *Cherokee*.

# The Longest Passage

**March 31, Day 1**

We departed Isabela Island, Galapagos, at 9 a.m. *Cherokee, Calypso* and *Hooloplop* followed us out of the anchorage. *Calypso* and *Hoolaplop* are German boats. Even though the other 3 boats were bigger, sleeker and faster than *La Boatique*, we were able to keep up. In fact, we never got more than one hundred miles from *Cherokee* and *Calypso* and we got hundreds of miles ahead of *Hooloplop*. *Cherokee* was slowed down a few days out by a broken rod in their mainsail boom.

We spent this first day sailing along side the island. The wind was fickle or non-existent. The ocean was calm. We motored. We could easily spot huge turtles with their shells rising above the flat ocean surface. Our progress even with the motor running was slow. In our first 24 hours out we only made a disappointing 87 miles. Little did we know that this would be our worst mileage day.

**April 1, Day 2**

Our second day out was hot with almost no wind and nearly calm seas. For much of the day we could not even see a ripple on the flat Pacific Ocean. We tried using the spinnaker and then later the mainsail, mizzen and jib. We ended up running the motor for all but 20 minutes of the 24-hour day. We did not have enough fuel for many more days like that. At least the conditions were easy on the boat and us.

**April 2, Day 3**

We caught a 58-inch long king mackerel. The fish fought long and hard trying to get unhooked. The mate of the large fish stayed right by the hooked fish while we fought to bring the fish aboard. Long after the fish was aboard the mate stayed right by our boat. I felt bad for both fish. Pete enjoyed the fight and considered fishing some more. We had more than enough fish to eat. Even though Pete would have released any fish he caught, I said no more fishing until our fish has been eaten.

*La Boatique*

Wild monkeys at Isla Linton, Panama, met us at the dock

*La Boatique* transits the Panama Canal

Right, Sharks!
Ecuador

Bottom, *Bow Bells* sails
to the Galapagos
Islands.

Left, blue-footed boobies outside the Port Captain's office; right, Marine iguana

The tree, the tree house, and the owl that lived there

Sue enjoys the horseback ride to the volcano of Sierra Negra. There are five active volcanoes on Isabela, Galapagos Islands.

During our walk to "the wall of tears" we found four bright pink flamingoes in a salt-water marsh, Isabela, Galapagos Islands.

Pete holds the king mackerel as its mate watches from the water.

*La Boatique* anchored at Fatu Hiva in the Marquesas

Left, Hardy and Carol on *Calypso;* Right, Kia Ora Hotel on the Pacific Atoll of Rangiroa

The Heiva Parade, Tahiti

Cooks Bay, Moorea

Top, dancers from California perform for the local Polynesians in a backyard on the island of Huahine. Bottom, professional Polynesian dancers perform for American tourists in Tahiti.

Bora Bora

From left, Henry and Gail from *Maritime Express*, Barry from *Cherokee*, Pete and Sue from *La Boatique* contemplate when to depart Bora Bora to begin the long trip to the Cook Island group.

Aitutaki was one of our favorite islands.

Tiki in Aitutaki, Cook Islands

Pete and Sue enjoy seeing Aitutaki by motorcycle.

Top, clear shimmering water leading to a cave in Nuie

Bottom, Sue kayaks in Swallows Cave, a favorite destination from Anchorage Number 7 in Tonga.

Deep-sea fishing while under sail was a strenuous work out. Pete puts his muscles into the fight with this fish.

During one of our bike rides in Tonga, we visited with this man while he prepared a pig roast. First, he cooked the pig on the spit and then he spread out the hot coals. He put the pig in the hot pit. He added root vegetables and then covered the food to let it cook in the ground.

These boys paddled their outrigger canoes to *La Boatique* for a visit at Anchorage Number 7, Tonga.

*La Boatique* in Anchorage Number 8, Tonga

Top, Sue loves walking through the tree fern forests in New Zealand.

Center, summer begins at Christmas time in New Zealand. The pohutukawa tree with these bright red and gold flowers is very common. It is known as New Zealand's Christmas tree.

Flying Fifteen's race to the finish during one of the many races.

We drove along over the flat ocean and gave a large portion of the fish to *Cherokee*. We ate king mackerel for a least one meal per day for the next week and I put some of the fish in the freezer.

We continued to have light wind and calm seas but at least we were able to turn the engine off for about 9 hours. We got a pleasant surprise when we calculated our fuel consumption. We only used half a gallon per hour of engine running.

### April 3, Day 4

At 10 a.m. we had 8 knots of wind from the east so we put up the spinnaker. The spinnaker sail is supposed to billow out over the bow of the boat. Our spinnaker is striped with the bright colors of a beach ball. The spinnaker has to be tended all the time so that it does not collapse and catch on the rigging when the wind shifts. We took turns closely watching our course so that the wind would fill the sail. The day wore on. Spinnaker tending became tedious. But we were making progress and not using the engine. At dusk we took the spinnaker down and raised the jib, mainsail and mizzen sail for the night.

### April 4, Day 5

*La Boatique* took off during the afternoon. Our GPS keeps track of velocity made good nautical miles (VMG). The VMG miles are the miles we make toward our destination. The usual reason on this trip that we were not sailing directly toward our destination was that the wind was coming nearly from our stern. We sail fastest with the wind on the beam. Anyway, on the afternoon of April 4th we were making 7 VMG miles per hour. That is a fast speed for us. But during the night squalls came. We did not get much sleep.

### April 5, Day 6

The wind died down. The wind picked up. The rain came. The wind died down. The wind picked up. The seas were choppy and confused. Our ride was uncomfortable. During the night we had lots of rain. This was not much fun.

### April 6, Day 7

The morning brought another squall followed by no wind. The ocean became calm so Pete added fuel to our tanks from jerry cans stored on deck. In the early afternoon a dark severe looking storm approached from behind us. We got ready for terrible weather.

However, the storm was a fooler. The wind gusted to only 24 knots and then died away to nothing. After this storm the wind switched directions blowing first from the southeast and then from the northwest. Wind is not supposed to blow from the northwest here. Then small squalls formed a circle with a clear eye of sunshine. We tried to ride in the eye. Twice we went through these circular storms.

Neither of us got any rest during the day. We were both very tired when night came. The wind nearly disappeared but the seas were still rolly and uncomfortable for sleeping. During the night we began snapping at each other. We both felt run-down. We even turned the engine off for a while and let the boat drift. By 5 a.m. no one wanted to be on watch. We only made 91 difficult miles on this day.

### April 7, Day 8

A very light wind from the west-southwest blew for a while on April 7th. This wind was right on our nose so we motored nearly all day. We also got plenty of sleep.

That night a full moon brought with it clear skies and a light east-southeast wind. When my shift arrived at 1 a.m. Pete greeted me with a twinkle in his eyes and a smile on his face. He was full of enthusiasm. He wanted to raise the spinnaker. After all, the conditions were perfect, except that it was the middle of the night. At first I thought he has got to be kidding. But as I looked around I realized he was right. So under the bright spotlight of the full moon our spinnaker went up easily and carried us along for a comfortable ride the rest of the night.

### April 8, Day 9

Our spinnaker night was followed by a wonderful day of sailing. This was not so bad after all.

### April 9, Day 10

So far when we used the spinnaker we attached it to our roller-furling headsail. On this day we used our whisker pole. The 14-foot whisker pole is cumbersome to manhandle and set up, however, it takes the pressure off the roller-furling headsail and it also allows us to travel a more downwind course. On April 9th we sailed with the poled out spinnaker for the whole day. Our excitement for the day was a one-foot long flying fish that flew right into our dodger windshield. It was like hitting a bird with the windshield of a car.

186

At 4 p.m. we took the sail down because a storm was approaching. The 10-minute storm took the wind with it so we motored most of the night.

**April 10, Day 11**

We got the wind now, a 25-knot southeast wind! But when the wind picked up, so did the seas. We sailed along bumping over 12 to 15-foot waves. The waves were uncomfortably close together. Pete picked 11 dead flying fish off the boat. One fish flew over the boat between the cabin top and the mainsail. Twice during the day I cranked Pete up the mizzenmast so that he could position the wind generator to better catch the wind. Since our wind generator will not turn completely around on its post, it sometimes ends up facing the wrong way. Pete used some string to stop it from turning the wrong way. Day 11 was *La Boatique*'s fastest ever day. We made 153 VMG miles averaging 6.4 knots per hour. The average wind for the day was 22 knots with gusts to 34 knots.

Sue on the night watch

**April 11, Day 12**

We had a nearly perfect sailing day. The wind was down to 10 to 18 knots on the beam. The seas were down somewhat and were more comfortable. *La Boatique* sped along all day and night. We went so fast that we broke the record set the previous day. We made 154 miles.

**April 12, Day 13**

The great sailing conditions continued. Even though we were traveling very fast, the ride was smooth. I was able to make honey white bread, from scratch of course, and a spaghetti dinner.

We broke the *La Boatique* miles per day record by 6 miles. In 24 hours we traveled 160 VMG miles at 6.6 knots per hour. The great conditions were making us over confident. After all, we were not in a race.

**April 13, Day 14**

In order to get a nice sailing angle we traveled farther south than we wanted to go. To go more downwind and stop going too far south we tried a wing and wing combination with our sails. We had the jib poled out on the port side of the boat while the main and mizzen sails were way off to the starboard side. Yes, we could go more downwind but our progress was slower and the ride was not as comfortable.

Soon after dark we saw lights from either a freighter or a very large fishing boat. The closest the boat got was eight miles from us off our stern. We thought we knew of all the sailboats nearby. During the night I used the VHF radio to report our position, heading, and speed in case there were any vessels in the area. The sailboat, *Lady Katherine* responded to the VHF radio call I made. *Lady Katherine* was a fast 60-foot Australian boat heading toward home. A husband and wife were on board. The husband had just lost his balance and taken a bad fall cracking his head open to the bone. Medical attention would be many days away. The wife, Katherine, did the best she could to clean the wound and tape his head back together. Even though *Lady Katherine* got within a mile or so from us we never saw any running lights. Once in a while we would see a strobe light at the top of their mast so that we could spot them. We used our radar to track them along with the large fishing boat.

Instead of getting our needed sleep we were talking with Katherine on *Lady Katherine*.

We usually reef the mainsail for the night, but the weather had been so good for the past few days that we left the full mainsail up. I spotted little tiny squalls on the radar. We should have reefed then. While Pete was busy talking to Katherine I was at the helm and the first squall hit. I ran with the squall line wind. It got up to 34 knots. After the squall we should have reefed the mainsail. But my shift was over and I was tired. Pete had not been sleeping, as he should have been. Pete took over. I went to sleep. Pete woke me up. He had gone through more squalls. Now he was very tired and I was half-asleep. Worse yet, the hand held unit on the autopilot was not allowing us to steer properly. We needed to reef the mainsail and finally did. Then we disconnected the hand held unit from the Nexus autopilot. Our steering problems went away. By the time dawn arrived we were both very tired.

### April 14, Day 15

We started off the day very tired. We did not even bother to raise the mainsail the entire day. We did not care if we went slowly. All we wanted was sleep. So Pete slept through the morning and I slept through the afternoon. Even taking it easy we still made 137 miles. For the past few days the alternator had been chewing up belts. We were not sure what was wrong. Maybe the belts were of poor quality. We found out much later that they were the wrong belts.

### April 15, Day 16

The going was slow. The wind was from the stern. We considered using the spinnaker but the wind was often too strong. We tried changing tacks a number of times. The plotting line of our course for the day looked like a poor quality zigzag stitch. Our VMG mileage was poor. We only made 109 miles for the day.

During the early part of the night we had the engine running. We thought we were charging the batteries. The autopilot was busy steering. We were making water with the water maker. I was busy typing away e-mails on the computer. We had lights running. We thought we could use lots of power, but the alternator quit working and we were quickly draining away our power. As soon as we noticed the problem we shut everything down including the autopilot. I hand steered while Pete worked over the hot engine.

At first Pete assumed the regulator was bad, so he replaced the regulator. The problem did not clear up. So next he replaced the alternator. Working over a hot engine is difficult in the best of conditions. Our conditions were challenging. I tried to keep the boat as level as possible. The moon had not yet risen so the night sky gave little clue as to when a 10-foot rolling wave would send us rocking. Good thing Pete was able to get the replacement alternator installed and working without getting burned by the hot engine. Then we ran the engine to charge the batteries. All the while no one was getting any sleep. So this would turn out to be a long tiring night. To make matters worse, we also set our clocks back one hour because of our westerly progress. So the night was one hour longer than normal.

### April 16, Day 17

As if the night was not long enough, dawn brought with it a storm. This day ended up being a short day for both of us since we ended up taking turns sleeping through most of it. *La Boatique*'s sail area was kept lower than normal. Our progress was slow, but safe.

### April 17, Day 18

We got off to a fast start and kept the pace for the whole 24 hours. The wind blew 12 to 22 knots out of the east-southeast giving us a broad reach run. We used a partial jib, full mainsail and the mizzen sail. The ride was more comfortable than expected considering we had 9-foot waves with a few big 12 to 15 foot waves. We were traveling along fast with the waves.

In the afternoon I got out the flour, sugar, cocoa, eggs and so on and baked a chocolate cake with a cream cheese frosting. When I was trying to pour the cake batter in the pan some of the batter went on the stove and the floor. Since the oven is gimbaled, the batter stayed in the cake pan once it got there. Our cake baked while the oven swung back and forth with the waves.

April 17th ended up being a record-breaking day. We made 162 miles in 24 hours. Over the 24 hours we averaged 6.75 VMG knots per hour. We did have about a 1-knot current helping us.

### April 18, Day 19

We sailed wing-and-wing downwind. We reefed the mainsail to the double reef point and set it on the starboard side. The jib was set to the port side and held in place by our whisker pole. We reefed the jib to the same size as the mainsail. As we sailed with the wind from the stern the air flowed from the main into the jib. This sail combination was easier on us than flying the spinnaker since the boom and the pole held the sails in place. They did not have to be monitored closely like the spinnaker. Also the wind and seas were a little heavy for the spinnaker.

At dusk we caught a blue fin tuna. The colors of the fish were beautiful shades of blue. I expected the meat to be a light color but the meat was as dark and red as fresh beef. Pete cut the fish into steaks and then I filleted the steaks to remove the skin and bones.

We did not get much sleep because during the night Pete decided to reinstall the alternator he thought was broken. It was not broken after all and worked fine.

### April 19, Day 20

The wing-and-wing sail combination allows us to keep a good course but poor Harvey & Joyce, the autopilot, must work very hard and use possibly double the normal power. We listened to the autopilot groaning and straining as the boat rocked from side to side. The ride was not very comfortable. Even so I was able to make my Mom's recipe for whole wheat bread. I think her bread comes out better than mine but she uses an electric mixer where I have to try to stir while holding on to keep my balance.

### April 20, Day 21

The end would be only days away. Our talk on the SSB to *Cherokee, Calypso,* and *Lady Katherine* was mainly about when to arrive and where to arrive. *Lady Katherine* had decided to head quickly and directly to the island with the best medical services. We did not want to arrive at night so we were purposely slowing the boat down. We were taking it easy and taking naps. We were not looking to set any more records. I felt like the game was in the fourth quarter with less than 2 minutes remaining and we had a comfortable lead. Now all we needed to do was play it safe and stay healthy.

### April 21, Day 22

We were having a rolly ride and would have liked the trip to be over. I studied the charts and cruising guides in anticipation of our arrival on Monday morning in only 2 days. As I looked at the charts I thought about all the boats heading to the Marquesas. Some started out from Panama while others started out from California or Mexico. It seemed as if we were all on cross-country interstate highways moving west day and night through any kind of weather. We had our single side band radios to keep in touch and get weather information. Listening to the SSB, the highway seemed crowded but rarely did we see another boat.

**April 22, Day 23**

This was our last full day out at sea. We sailed under the jib alone to keep the boat slow so that we did not arrive at night. We would have only one more night of 3-hour watches.

**April 23, Day 24**

Dawn brought with it the sight of a small island, Fatu Hiva. The steep slopes and jagged peaks of the island made it look like a cathedral. A few hours past dawn our anchor was down, the journey completed.

---

**Statistics of the Longest Passage**

- 23 Days at Sea
- 2898 Total Nautical Miles
- Averaged 126 Nautical Miles Per Day
- Ran the Motor 143.4 Hours
- 34 Knots Highest Gust of Wind
- April 17 Most Nautical Miles Traveled 162, Averaged 6.75 Knots Per Hour
- March 31 Least Nautical Miles Traveled 87

---

# Polynesia

## Marquesas Islands

The Marquesas islands are in about the middle of the Pacific Ocean. They are far away from everything. Yet, they are part of French Polynesia. They are high volcanically formed islands with steep cliff walls. From the ocean they look like black boxes topped by clouds. The cannibalistic Marquesas tribes numbered 60,000 in the eighteenth century. Today the population is only about 6,000 and cannibalism is no longer practiced. The population was decimated not by cannibalism but by diseases introduced by western contact. The women wore fresh flowers in their thick black hair every day. The men had ornate tattoos. They spoke French and their own Polynesian language.

*La Boatique* anchors at Fatu Hiva after 23 days at sea.

We visited three islands in the Marquesas group: Fatu Hiva, Hiva Oa and Tahu Ata. While in the Marquesas we met up with the cruising boats we knew from the Caribbean: *Cherokee, Argonauta, Maritime Express, Ladybug, Aldebaran,* and so on. We were joined by a new group of cruising boats. These boats began their crossing to the Marquesas from Southern California and northern Mexico. The majority seemed to be from Seattle. In general they were a younger crowd and traveling for months instead of years.

Fatu Hiva was our fist anchorage and we spent the most time ashore there. Only 200 people live in the village we visited and about 100 of them seemed to be children. There was no bank so we could not exchange money. There was only one tiny store about 15 feet square with mostly empty shelves. So there was not much to buy even though the shopkeeper did take dollars. There was a bread maker but he would go days without making bread. When he did make bread he sold out quickly. There were wild chickens under foot but no eggs for sale. Eggs were hard to come by since the wild chickens hid their eggs. I saw no vegetables except for breadfruit trees. Some tropical fruits like bananas and citrus fruits were plentiful. Coconuts abounded. Produce was available only from backyard gardens. The villagers would trade their produce not for money but for things. We fixed a fax machine and got a stalk of bananas. We traded cologne for pamplemoussse (similar to large grapefruit). Pete fixed a flashlight at the small grocery store for cheese that does not need refrigeration.

We walked the village streets. We took a scenic walk through the rain forest in mountainous terrain to a spectacularly high waterfall. Above us tropicbirds with long white streamers for tails enjoyed riding the mountain thermals. The pool at the base of the cascading water invited us in for a refreshing fresh water swim.

Even though there were no restaurants 17 of us cruisers enjoyed a Polynesian feast. The feast was arranged at the home of Rosa for about $8 a person. Many villagers contributed food for our feast. It was like a potluck of exotic foods that we did not prepare. We sat squeezed together in a large living room in her house on plastic chairs and benches. The feast included baked bananas, bread, rice and baked sweetened manioc. The breadfruit had been cooked over a wood fire. The raw barracuda was "cooked" by the acid in a limejuice marinade and then it was served in a coconut sauce. Small pieces of chicken with sweet papaya were served in a coconut milk sauce. The beverage was a tropical fruit punch. Dessert was cake and donuts.

Our next stop was Hiva Oa where we checked into French Polynesia. Most of the boats completing the check-in procedures ahead of us were from the European Union. The Europeans do not have to purchase an $850 bond. Each person aboard a U.S. boat normally must purchase the bond before his or her passports are stamped. The bond is to cover the price of a plane ticket to the U.S. Our passports were stamped but we were never asked to pay the bond. Carol, a German, from Calypso interpreted the French language for us. We thought that the officials might have included us with the Europeans.

Hiva Oa has a population of about 2000. There was a bank with an ATM, Internet access, and grocery stores with eggs, bread and frozen meat. A lady sold fresh vegetables from the back of her pickup truck.

At Hiva Oa we saw paintings from the famous painter Paul Gauguin. Gauguin lived and was buried on this island.

After Hiva Oa was Tahu Ata where we anchored in an uninhabited bay with a soft sandy beach. The creamy sand was very inviting but our fellow cruisers who lingered on the beach received nasty itching no-see-um bites. They did not feel the effect of the bites until hours after leaving the beach. I walked the beach but I did not linger. Pete played it safe and stayed off the beach. Tahu Ata was a meeting place where we visited with friends we met in the Caribbean.

## Tuamotus Atolls

While many of our friends headed off to the beauty of the northern Marquesas we decided to head to what is known as the dangerous archipelago, the Toamotus.

The northern Marquesas are exotically beautiful but they were beastly to our friends. Colleen from *Bow Bells* was severely bitten by no-see-ums and had to take elephantiasis pills to ward off this dreaded disease that makes your legs swell up like an elephant's. Sally from *Argonauta* was bruised when *Some Day is Here's* dinghy was rolled as they tried to land through big surf. Henry from *Maritime Express* broke his wrist while on a waterfall hike. The severe break required an operation and pins.

On the other hand, our trip to the dangerous archipelago of the Tuamotus was a superb 3½-day sail. *La Boatique* and *Cherokee* sped along in 15-knot wind under jib, main and mizzen sails on a broad reach day and night.

Our destination was a Pacific atoll called Manihi in the northwestern part of the Tuamotus. The Tuamotus archipelago covers an area of 1000 miles. The southeastern portion is now uninhabited due to French nuclear testing. The area is highly radioactive. The testing ended in 1996.

There are 78 islands in the Tuamotus, all but two being atolls. An atoll is a sunken volcano with a build up of coral around its rim. Atolls are low-lying and not visible from far off. The coral forms an oval shape many miles in diameter. Inside the oval of coral topped by palm trees is a lagoon that looked to me like a large salt-water lake. Usually there are breaks in the coral where seawater can flow through. At some atolls there are passes to the inside lagoon big enough for a sailboat to enter.

Navigating the narrow passes must be properly timed to avoid up to nine-knot currents. When the strong current flows out of the atoll it causes steep short seas. These seas roll down the passes into or out of the lagoon. The best time to go through the pass is when the tidal current is slow, about one to two hours after high or low tide.

Manihi was not what we expected. The pass looked like white water rapids. From a distance the white water looked as if it were flowing over rocks. But the center of the pass was deep enough for *La Boatique*. We were surprised when we got inside the atoll that we could not even see the other side. The ocean swell was gone. The water was calm. I had to keep a sharp lookout on the bow so that we avoided the numerous coral heads. The water was clear and we could see very far down.

Pearl farm on the Pacific Atoll of Manihi

Manihi is known for its production of black pearls. There are at least 50 pearl farms on the atoll. We bought some pearls and traded for others. We visited the small village on the atoll and found very limited supplies.

After a night of motoring along in calm wind, the second Tuamotu we visited was Rangiroa. We entered Rangiroa on May 18th with a 4-knot current against us even though we had timed our entrance for low tide. At nearly full throttle *La Boatique* inched along over close chop and turbulent water through the pass. Rangiroa is the second largest atoll in the world. Its circumference is over 100 miles. The entire island of Tahiti could fit inside it. It was much more populated than Manihi. But it only had one pearl farm. We anchored off the high-priced Kia Ora Hotel. Each room at this hotel is a beautiful cabin made from woven palm fronds. Some of the cabins are on stilts over the light blue water.

While at Rangiroa we joined five California cruisers who decided to drift snorkel the pass. The day was bright and sunny with only a whisper of a breeze. We had perfect conditions for snorkeling. The Californians had timed the snorkel trip so that the tide would sweep us quickly along from outside the lagoon through the pass into the lagoon. Pete and I thought we would be snorkeling near slack tide. But we did not check the tide schedule. Instead we would be snorkeling when the current was near its maximum velocity. We entered the ocean near the pass. Pete and I stayed close together.

Soon the current swept us along at much to quickly a pace. We found we could not swim against the current. The pass was full of interesting fish. But we were drifting much faster than expected. Before I realized it we were through the pass and being swept into the lagoon. We had planned to go ashore before the end of the pass.

Pete was ahead of me and tried to swim to shore, but the current was taking him out faster than he could swim. Since I was behind him I was in even faster current. I looked up to see a small coral island ahead of us. I decided that since I could not make the shore, I thought I could at least make the island. In seconds the sharp coral seemed to rise to the surface. The current was dragging me over the sharp coral. I tried to keep my feet in front of me and use my flippers to protect my body from cuts. After bouncing along the coral I found a spot in knee-deep water where I could brace myself with hand holds in the coral and my flippers wedged in grooves. Ocean swells coming down the pass washed over me.

I held on in this spot for a half-hour. There was no sign of Pete. I saw three of the other snorkelers drift to the other end of the tiny coral island. They did not seem to be in trouble. If I could just get out of the shallow coral garden I was in and get back to deep water I could probably swim back to the island where the current was not so strong. But I had about 30 feet of shallow coral to get through. Ocean swells continued to roll through the pass and over the shallow water. My knee and one finger were already cut. I planned to head to deep water where there were lots of sharks and the fast current. Where I had braced myself, the current pulsed through. Waves crashed against the coral shore. If I jumped off when the current was light and swam hard away from the island through the deepest water I could find I figured I might not get dragged against sharp coral. I hoped that the sharks were not hungry.

It was a gamble. I jumped. I swam trying not to touch the coral in the fast moving shallow water. I made it to the deep water. I looked up to see the island sweeping by. I did not look down at the sharks below. I headed back toward the island. The water got calm. There were colorful fish everywhere. I could make it to shore. As soon as I stood on the coral island Pete called out to me. He had been swept along the other side of the island and was safe in calm water along with the three snorkelers I had seen. I walked across the tiny coral island and joined them. The remaining two snorkelers had kept closer to shore than the rest of us. They had been able to climb out ashore and walk to the dinghy. Then they picked us up and took us back against the strong current to our boats.

We saw lots of fish while snorkeling but looking down from *La Boatique* we saw nearly as many. The surface of the lagoon was often calm enough to be like a windowpane. Through the window were all sorts of fish. We often fed them table scraps. Pete caught a few with his fishing pole but we threw them back. Lagoon fish could be poisonous with ciguatera.

Our weather since the Marquesas had been unbelievably great. The wind at Rangiroa calmed down to nothing. The air was too still. Bad weather had to be brewing. If the wind blew out of the southeast, south, or southwest it had 17 miles of open water available for the build up of ugly waves. As long as the wind was out of a northerly direction we had protection from the shoreline of the atoll.

The bad weather came on May 21st and stayed for two days. The wind gusted over 30 knots and switched from the northwest to the south. Big short waves built quickly. *La Boatique* yanked hard on the anchor. As we came off the backside of one wave our bowsprit buried down into the next wave. This is a rare occurrence at sea, let alone at anchor. Pete and I had to secure everything as if we were at sea. At least the big waves that buried our bowsprit only lasted an hour. The boats circled their anchors as the wind clocked around. The second day of bad weather brought with it an entire day of rain. I used the rainwater to wash clothes. The clothes got plenty of rinsing as they hung on the line waiting for dry weather.

On the afternoon of May 26th we left the atoll of Rangiroa for Tahiti. *Cherokee* and *Aldebaran* followed us out the pass. The atoll pass was calm. We timed our exit perfectly. We were out only a half-hour before we had a fish on our lure. As we sailed along we fought the fish. We caught a mahi-mahi 58 inches long. It would provide us with many great meals.

We had pleasant sailing conditions for the first half of the trip. Then the wind died away and we ended up motoring to Tahiti.

Marina Tiana on the island of Tahiti — not as nice as we expected

# Tahiti

We arrived in Tahiti the morning of May 28th. Tahiti is the largest of 118 islands and atolls in French Polynesia. It has a large airport and is the center for commercial activity for thousands of miles. The lush vegetation and angular mountains rising over 7000 feet add to the exotic beauty of the island. But there are also detractions. The main detraction is smoke from open burning on the ground. Smoke from one fire often drifts around and mixes with smoke from the next fire. The smell is annoying. Instead of clean air, there is smog.

We enjoyed our anchorage in Tahiti because we were in clean and calm protected water. We had nice views of the islands of Moorea and Tahiti. Shopping was close to the dinghy dock. Bugs did not bother us.

Tahiti has good and inexpensive public transportation called Le Truck. We used Le Truck often to get around the capital city of Papeete and to sight see. We took Le Truck to the other side of the island and then walked to three nearby waterfalls with John and Colleen from *Bow Bells*. We took Le Truck the other direction and visited an industrial section of the island.

One of our stops in the industrial section was at the Ariki Micro Brewery. Ariki was tiny with only 2% of the Tahitian beverage market. The company was run by an ex-New Yorker named Mark. We toured his facilities and tasted his various products from candy to cookies to sodas to beer to liquors. Friday hamburger lunches at the brewery became the norm for many cruisers. The price was right: about U.S. $2 for a beer or soda and a cheeseburger grilled over an open fire with lettuce and tomatoes. Even McDonalds here in Tahiti was double that price. For less than $4 Ariki served a grilled dinner.

Our stay in Tahiti was long (over a month) partly because we sent and received various mail and packages. We always tried to send and receive packages with people we found that were traveling between Tahiti and the U.S. Fred Botta from *Aldebaran* brought us mail and a camera. We waited for another cruiser named Lee Moore to bring parts for our digital camera, airplane tickets and a repaired GPS.

While in Tahiti we did our usual boat maintenance jobs. We also added one new item to *La Boatique*. We added a Harken batten traveler system, known as battcars. This system allowed us to raise and lower our mainsail with ease. The batten travelers attach to the mainsail at the batten locations. The travelers glide on ball bearings on a track we installed on our mast. The battcar system resulted in greatly reduced friction between the sail and the mast. Therefore the sail goes up and down with ease instead of a struggle.

The Heiva Parade

We had plenty of time for fun. We enjoyed the traditional Polynesian culture at the Heiva festival. The Heiva festival took place from June 22$^{nd}$ to July 22$^{nd}$. It began with a parade, fireworks and concerts. Then it continued with Polynesian style dance contests, singing, out rigger canoe races, javelin throwing, coconut husking and many other contests. We watched the parade, the fireworks, the concerts, a canoe race and the javelin throw.

Our stay in Tahiti lasted a month and a half. This was the longest we had stayed in one place since we left Trinidad in October. In the seven months getting to Tahiti we had traveled 6,586 miles. It felt good to stay in one place for a while. As far as Pete was concerned Tahiti was his ultimate destination. He had achieved his dream and in so seemed to have lost his purpose for sailing. I did not feel that way at all. As far as I was concerned we were still near the beginning of our South Pacific adventures. We discussed where to head next. A few boats were heading north to Hawaii and then on to North America. Most cruisers were heading west toward New Zealand. We decided to head west with the majority of our fellow cruisers.

Javelin throw at Heiva Festival

## Moorea

On July 9<sup>th</sup> we set sail for a 20-mile trip to Moorea. We departed at 6:30 a.m. For the first few miles we followed the channel markers north between the island of Tahiti and the reef that nearly surrounds the island. At the capital city of Papeete we followed the channel markers leading out to the ocean. Pete raised the mainsail and unfurled the jib. A gentle wind from just abaft the beam filled the sails. The ocean was peaceful. The ride was easy and enjoyable.

We dropped anchor near the entrance to Cooks Bay, Moorea. Cooks Bay is renowned for being one of the most beautiful bays in the South Pacific. Flowers abound in the valley surrounded by abrupt mountains with many spikes. When we went ashore we tied off our dinghy at the Club Bali Hai in Cooks Bay.

One evening we watched local islanders dance for the tourists at Club Bali Hai. We enjoyed Polynesian dancing and went out of our way to attend performances. At this performance both Pete and I were pulled on stage to dance with the men and women in grass skirts. We had a great time.

On July 15<sup>th</sup> Julie (from *Cherokee*) and I dinghied over to the next bay, Bay De Opunohu. This bay was even more beautiful than Cooks Bay. I regretted that we spent so much time at Cooks Bay instead of moving *La Boatique* over to Opunohu Bay. But we had been already delaying our departure for days and the weather was calm. It was time to leave picturesque Moorea. Our departure was timed for late afternoon. Huahine, the next island, was 88 miles from Moorea, too long of a sail for daylight hours.

On passages longer than a day sail we enjoyed the company of another boat. We thought we would be out on the open ocean with the reassuring masthead light of *Cherokee* nearby. Instead we seemed to be in a traffic jam. At one point during my shift at night I used radar to help me monitor the surrounding boats. There were two sailboats less than a mile away, *Cherokee* and a French boat. There was a freighter 8 miles off our starboard bow heading toward us. There was a Renaissance Cruise Ship with rows of bright lights lighting every deck. With all the lights the cruise ship looked very close but was five miles away. And if that wasn't enough traffic, five other sailboats were within eight miles. Everyone uses GPS to set their course so all the boats tend to be in a line from one island to the next. The wind was light so sailing was difficult. Motors were providing most of the propulsion. The waves were tiny but the ocean rollers were huge.

# Huahine

While I slept before the light of dawn Pete made out lights from the south end of Huahine. In the light of dawn we sailed along the west side of the 28 square mile island. A coral reef surrounding the island ran up to a mile offshore. Huge ocean rollers roared as they crashed apart in the reef. Between the reef and the island was a calm lagoon with clear turquoise water with one beautiful bay following another. We entered the lagoon through a pass at the northwest end of the island. For the next two hours we crept south through calm water inside the reef. Only 5400 people live on the sparsely inhabited island. Lush tropical forests and patches of white sand surrounded many uninhabited bays. Our destination was the southern end of the island.

On July 17th Barry, Julie and I went exploring Huahine on foot. As we walked the two streets of a tiny village we heard the familiar sound of Polynesian drums. We followed the sound to a sandy backyard filled with singers, dancers, and drummers. We quietly watched as young men practiced their athletic dance steps. When the music let up the dance coordinator voiced his instructions in English.

In English?

No one speaks English here. Here they speak Polynesian, a language full of vowels. Was this some kind of English lesson? The instructor was telling them to look at their surroundings and dance from their hearts. He said that they would not be dancing for Americans tonight. Tonight they would be dancing for rural Polynesian islanders. The practice session was soon over.

Barry asked the instructor, "How come you are speaking English?"

Arthur, the instructor, said because he is from Sacramento California. All the dancers, singers, and drummers were also from California. But they all looked to be Polynesian to me. Arthur explained that his ancestors were from the Philippines. We found out later that the other dance organizer was born on Huahine, danced in Tahiti at the Beach Comber Resort Hotel, and now lives in California. His name was Joel. The dancers may all have been Americans, but they descended from people from various Pacific islands.

Here we were on a remote Polynesian island watching Americans performing traditional island dances for native Polynesians.

We found out that the show started at 7:30 p.m. We would be there.

At 7:15 as we arrived, the night sky was already very dark. We paid in Polynesian currency the equivalent of $2.30 to see the show. The dance floor was sandy dirt. Our bench seats were made from two narrow logs. The stage was unevenly lit by a few bare light bulbs. The remaining benches filled with islanders. Children sat in front on a blue tarp. An island woman began the show with a Polynesian prayer.

Women swaying their hips in conservative traditional attire to a soothing Polynesian song followed her. A few drops of rain fell. The next dancers were young men and women in grass skirts. The beat of the drums quickened. The drops of rain increased. The dance was athletic. One dance performed by women was a surprise in that the song was in English about a white sandy beach in Hawaii. The rain continued. The next dance was a war dance performed by men with white clubs. As they danced a choreographed battle the rain intensified. The heavy drops of water soaked through my white blouse to my skin. The audience began to disperse. Soon everyone was trying to find cover under overhanging corrugated metal roofs. Lightning and thunder filled the sky. The rain turned into a tropical downpour. The show had to be postponed until 3 p.m. the next day.

I appreciated the daylight show because I was able to take better pictures than at night.

The following day, July 19th, we motored north between the barrier reef and the island. The channel was very well marked. We anchored at the north end of the island where we purchased some groceries.

# Raiatea and Tahaa

On July 20th we set sail for a 20-mile trip west to Raiatea and Tahaa. Once again the wind was light. The wind switched from one side of the stern to the other. We used only the mainsail with a preventer to stop the sail from jibing.

Raiatea and Tahaa are two islands a few miles apart. They are both surrounded by a common coral reef with many passes. Both islands have many bays and fjords. We headed south from the main pass through the coral reef. Then we anchored in a palm-fringed bay off the southern island of Raiatea. The boats Some Day is Here and Stella joined us. The day was hot and sunny as usual. Barrette from the boat *Some Day is Here* and I kayaked up a small shallow stream under the shade of tall trees. When rocks and rapid water stopped me I wedged the kayak between the rocks and took a dip in the cool clear fresh water. Barrette came paddling around a bend and saw me splashing in the water.

He said, "I wouldn't get in that water. Just a short way back I saw something big go in. I thought it was a person but it never surfaced."

That was all I needed to know to cut my fresh water enjoyment short. During our return trip back to the boats we spotted a five-foot long eel in only about 3 feet of water.

We anchored deep in a fjord on the east side of Tahaa on July 21st. We could not see the ocean or hear the crashing surf. Instead we heard songbirds and crowing chickens. The sensation was like anchoring in a pond surrounded by hills and mountains. Pete and I both enjoyed an evening kayak trip.

Sue kayaks in front of a motu.

On July 23$^{rd}$ we left our cozy bay and motored 3 miles to the protecting barrier reef. There I kayaked to a motu (a tiny sandy palm island). Later we watched windsurfers race by *La Boatique* and finish the race at the motu. I would have liked to have been windsurfing with them. Later in the day we went snorkeling with "domesticated" rays in a pen. The rays had their stingers at the end of the tails cut off. The rays are used to being fed so as soon as I got in the pen with them they climbed all over me. They were very soft but I did not like them coming up from behind. (We should have brought the camera but we didn't want it getting wet on the trip there.) We got in another pen with sea turtles and could hold onto the sea turtles and swim with them.

Tahaa looked like a great place for wind surfing.

Tahaa was one of my favorite islands. The anchorages were well protected by the outside reef. There were many deep bays. The Polynesians love to dance and we often watched the local people dance and sing. The vegetation was lush and filled with songbirds. The farmers grew vanilla and tropical fruits. Short distances from the island within the calm water were plenty of tiny island motus with soft white sand and palm trees.

But then, the weather turned windy and rainy for days. One gust reached 47 knots in our protected anchorage. Tahaa was a pleasant place to be stranded by bad weather. We surely were glad we were not out in the ocean.

The Bora Bora Hotel

# Bora Bora

On July 31$^{st}$ we sailed 25 miles from our protected bay in Tahaa to a mooring ball at the Bora Bora Yacht Club. The seas were finally calming down from the windy rainy weather. We could have used more wind but we were able to sail along a little slower than we would have preferred with the jib, mainsail and mizzen.

The famous author, James Michener, is credited with describing Bora Bora as the world's most beautiful island. We made sure to watch South Pacific a few times. Bora Bora is Bali Hai in the movie. The pictures I took did not do justice to the beauty around us. Green tropical plants framed the gray vertical cliff walls of the tallest mountain. At the base of the island was a large lagoon surrounded by small white sandy islands with tall coconut palms. The lagoon water was neon blue. Where the water was over 100 feet deep the neon shade of blue was dark. Where the water was only a few feet deep the color was neon yellow-green. Most of the lagoon water was a bright blinding turquoise. The air was warm with a refreshing breeze.

The economy of the island seemed to be based on honeymooners. Bora Bora seemed to be the destination of choice for after the wedding when cost was no object. A cruise ship visited every other day or so. There were many places to anchor so the sailboats were scattered throughout the turquoise water.

While on the island we stopped at the Bora Bora Yacht Club. We ate lunch at the famous restaurant called Bloody Mary's. We had a drink at the Bora Bora Hotel where we met Jim and Lynda Kosiur from Grand Rapids, Michigan, on their honeymoon. Jim and Lynda were married in Hawaii and came to Bora Bora for their honeymoon.

Bora Bora concluded our stay of over three months in French Polynesia. It would have been nice to stay even longer, but cyclones hit this area so we needed to move while the weather was good.

## Bora Bora to Aitutaki

When we thought the time had come to leave Bora Bora, the weather would not cooperate. The seas became big and the wind blew to 35 knots. We waited for a few days until the weather looked better. When we finally did take off on August 15<sup>th</sup> the seas were still bigger than I would have liked. The wind blew nearly from our stern. We sailed an uncomfortable ride with the jib held out by the whisker pole. Sailing with us for this trip were the boats *Orplid* (from Germany), *Aldebaran* (from Ireland), *Maritime Express* (from Canada), *Argonauta* (from New York) and *Cherokee* (from Texas). We kept in touch by VHF radio and single side band radio. At one time we were spread out over about 80 miles. Poor *La Boatique* rocked back and forth in the waves so violently that even with 20 knots of wind to fill the sail without the pole holding the sail in place the sail would have slapped back and forth against the rigging. I did not like the ride at all. I was beginning to feel very lethargic, an early indication of seasickness.

A few hours out we had our first fish strike our lure and it was a big fish. We continued to sail on course with the poled out jib while Pete played tug of war with the fish. The fish was a long slender mahi-mahi. From tip to the end of its big tail it measured 74 inches. This was the longest fish we had ever caught so far. Soon after we got the fish on board I got that hot sweaty feeling with a headache. I thought about trying to help clean the huge fish but I couldn't seem to lift the knife. I couldn't think clearly. I needed to lie down. Pete would have to clean the fish by himself on the bow of *La Boatique*. Hand over hand I inched my way back along the rolling boat to the cockpit. I checked our course. Harvey & Joyce, our autopilot, were steering an accurate course. I laid flat on my back with my eyes closed. I dreamily pictured myself on top of an elephant. I was lying on a mattress inside one of those gilded canopied cages that they put on top of an elephant where the royalty ride. Except I was not having a royal ride. My elephant could not keep my mattress steady. He kept stepping in holes with one leg and then on big boulders with another leg. Often I would have to grab the sidewall to hang on. As my dreamy elephant ride continued, Pete separated fish flesh from skin and bones. By staying very still I eventually began to feel somewhat better.

As the day wore on, the wind and the seas calmed.

On our second day out my seasickness abated but so did the wind. Tropicbirds with long white steaming tails along with the larger but plainer boobies kept us company. The boobies seemed especially curious as they circled the boat and watched the lure. In the afternoon the wind became so light that our speed dropped below four knots. We ran the engine until the wind picked up again after dark.

Dawn brought with it a busy morning on August 17th. At 7 a.m. we listened to the Rag of the Air Net on the SSB for the weather and sailing conditions reported by other boats. At 7:10 I took a warm shower. About 7:20 we switched SSB frequencies to our own net of boats traveling in our area where we all reported our locations and sailing conditions. At 8 a.m. we tuned in yet another net where we got the weather again and heard from different boats. We reported our position on this net also. While I was reporting our information, a fish struck our lure. Landing this 46-inch long mahi-mahi and cleaning it took up most of the remainder of the morning. So much for my shower since the fish got tiny scales and fish gook over my arms and legs. Cleaning a big fish on a rolling boat is not an easy task. The remainder of the day was a pleasant beam reach sail.

On August 18th the wind backed around from the east to northeast to north to northwest. Then during the night with squalls the wind radically switched from various directions ending up continuing its circle to the west, southwest and then south. It then stayed out of the south for the next week.

A south wind would make the Aitutaki anchorage very uncomfortable. For this reason *Aldebaran* and *Cherokee* decided to continue sailing on past Aitutaki.

210

Henery and Pete on the motorcycles in Aitutaki

## Aitutaki

We arrived at the Aitutaki anchorage at 10:30 August 19th tired and hungry. The wind was still out of the south. *La Boatique* rolled in the waves. I made an omelet but most of it ended up on the floor when my plate slid across the cockpit and fell. While we tried to balance our breakfast plates green turtles four feet in diameter surfaced nearby. Out a little further a family of whales spouted and surfaced. Later the whales came into our anchorage between our boats.

We were never able to get much sleep in this anchorage because the boat rolled in the ocean swell and worse yet our anchor chain kept getting caught on coral. The chain made a terrible racket that often sounded like the whole boat was being dragged over the coral.

The following morning we went to shore. The weather was cool and comfortable during our entire stay. The islanders spoke English.

We much preferred that to the French in French Polynesia. We rented a small motorcycle for only $8 a day. Henry and Gail from *Maritime Express* also rented one, so we toured the island with them. There were few cars and trucks on the island. Most people got around on small motorcycles. The lush tropical island scenery was magnificent, more beautiful than Bora Bora. At Aitutaki there was only one rather small cliff wall, not like the awesome cliffs at Bora Bora. On our motorcycles we cruised by small vegetable and fruit farms. The small plots of tomatoes, lettuce, bananas, arrowroot and taro were arranged in beautiful gardens. There were no dogs on the island and very few cats. Goats and pigs were always tethered. Colorful chickens were plentiful and ran free. Only 1500 people lived on the sparsely inhabited island. Restaurant food was excellent and inexpensive. We ate regularly at the Blue Nun. The Polynesian dances performed by the Titiaitonga Cultural Dance Group were the best we had seen. This group was to represent the Cook Islands in China later in the year. The island had loads of churches. Missionaries must love this place as long as they don't mind having few people to preach to.

Into our second day of motorcycle riding we had traversed every paved road twice and most of the dirt trails. One steep trail that led up to the cliff we had avoided so far, but no longer. We already knew that on this trail Fred from *Aldebaran* (Milwaukee) had wiped out a week ago. Pete started climbing the hill with me holding on behind him. The motorcycle hit a rut and swerved.

"Maybe I should get off and walk," I said.

Pete replied, "No, it's all right."

We hit another rut. The motorcycle was going too slowly. It did not have enough power. The ruts took control. Our balance was gone. The motorcycle fell over with Pete's leg underneath it. Pete's shoulder landed hard on the ground breaking his fall. I landed clear of the motorcycle in weeds. I was fine, not even a scratch. Pete got a foot long scrape on his leg and a bruised shoulder. We walked the rest of the way up this trail.

Aitutaki is in the Cook Islands. Aitutaki is nearly surrounded by a coral reef. It has sandy beaches, a calm turquoise lagoon, and small palm-fringed motus out on the reef. We were very frustrated with the fact that we could not get through the reef into the calm lagoon. But the island government has plans to dredge the shallow cut through the lagoon and set up a place for cruising boats inside the lagoon. Since we were forced to anchor outside the reef with no protection from bad weather, our stay had to be brief.

## Aitutaki to Nuie

On August 23$^{rd}$ at 11:30 a.m. we set out from Aitutaki to Palmerston in the company of *Maritime Express* and *Argonauta*. Our sail was fast and we were making much better time than expected. We had expected to be at sea two nights. But with the fast sailing conditions we could almost make Palmerston by dark. However, we needed to arrive during daylight.

As time went on we realized that *Maritime Express* and *La Boatique* were not fast enough boats to arrive before dark. *Argonauta* could make it. As *Argonauta* sped off to Palmerston, *Maritime Express* reduced sail and slowed down to an uncomfortably rolly ride. We chose a third option. We decided to bypass Palmerston and set sail for Nuie. The sailing conditions were great. Our ride was very fast. If we could keep our speed up we could arrive at Nuie in four more days.

As the days dragged on the wind and sea calmed. The light wind turned from the south to the east and gently pushed us along. We could have sailed the entire way but Pete did not want to spend additional nights at sea. And I could not complain about that. So with the aid of sails and the motor we kept our speed at about 6 knots. Every day we found dead flying fish on deck. We threw them overboard. We fished each day and caught one four-foot long mahi-mahi. On our last day out we brought one mahi-mahi right up to the boat. I decided to snap a picture. As soon as the fish got its picture taken it spit the hook and swam away.

The low-lying island of Nuie rose above the horizon at 10:30 on August 27$^{th}$. By 3 p.m. we were tied to a mooring ball.

## Nuie

Nuie is known as the rock of Polynesia. The oval shaped island has no protected lagoon for a boat to find calm water. Upraised coral forms the island. The entire coastline is composed of limestone cliff walls 150 feet high. The island's protective reef is quite close to the rugged coastline. Along the coastline are caves, arches, chasms, small swimming holes, reflective pools and tiny secluded beaches. Nuie has no rivers and not much soil. Rainwater filters through the limestone. The water for snorkeling around the island was amazingly clear. Surprisingly forests cover much of Nuie. Somehow the huge trees grow around and through the limestone coral. With all the sharp coral, gardening and farming looked difficult. About the only crop I saw under cultivation was taro. Nuie did not have the variety of fruits and vegetables that I saw on Aitutaki.

Sue stands in front of a natural arch along the Nuie coastline

A small indentation in the oval island was about all the protection we got from the ocean. When the wind was out of the east the island offered good protection. However, when the wind came from any other direction, the ocean waves and swell came right into the area where the cruising yachts were moored. All boats tie on to mooring balls instead of anchoring. Attached to the mooring ball *La Boatique* often rolled horribly. I often had to use handholds in the cabin to stop from flying around. Getting anything accomplished on the boat was nearly impossible. So I stayed on board as little as possible. Sleeping was difficult because the ocean waves tossed us in every direction.

Because of the ocean swell, going to shore was challenging. Dinghies were not beached or tied to a dock; they were lifted up a cement pier. Local fishing boats as well as our dinghies were hoisted up the cement pier through the use of an electric crane. All the dinghies were then lined up near the crane. The larger local fishing boats were set on their trailers and taken home.

I got to see a lot of the island while Pete saw very little of it. During our entire stay, Pete sniffled with a cold and did not feel up to sight seeing. While Pete nursed his cold I went on Misa's Nature Tour the first day. The second day Barry and Julie (*Cherokee*), Mike (*Renaitre*) and I rented a car. We visited caves, chasms and arches along the coastline. During our second day with the car we had a flat tire on a bush road with no traffic. We needed a screwdriver to remove the tire from the trunk but we did not have a screwdriver. Julie found a broken nail file and the guys were able to improvise with that.

The stairs near the shore lead Sue to a tiny beach surrounded by vertical cliff walls.

I rented a bike and went on three long bike rides with Mike (*Renaitre*). Our bike ride destinations were along the shoreline where we found caves that lead to the sea and protected pools of clear water. When we snorkeled in the pools the water often seemed to shimmer. The shimmering water was caused by clear fresh water that had filtered through limestone rocks mixing with salt water from the ocean. Poisonous black and yellow sea snakes were present and abundant everywhere near shore.

During one extra long bike ride of about 30 miles Mike and I got lost on poorly marked trails in the bush. While deep in the bush we harvested wild papayas. Our backpacks were heavy with the fruit making our ride over the rutted terrain all the more fatiguing. Mike never seemed to run out of energy. I ran out of water and was very thirsty. Mike had juice to spare and shared it with me.

While I was out on the bike ride, Henry from *Maritime Express* called Pete on the VHF. *Maritime Express* was minutes from arriving. Gail was in pain, disoriented, and had a rash on her neck and back. She needed medical attention. Pete came to her aid with our dinghy as soon as Henry was able to hook onto a mooring. The ambulance was already waiting. However, once Gail got to shore the local islanders nearly decided to send her back to sea because they certainly did not want a new disease introduced to their island paradise. Reluctantly the ambulance driver hauled her off to the hospital. At the hospital the doctors suspected a case of shingles but they were unsure of their diagnosis. All the while poor Gail's symptoms worsened. The hospital could not do much for her so Pete helped Henry get her back to *Maritime Express*.

After one week of Nuie we were more than ready to move on since life on the tossed about *La Boatique* was annoying. We sailed to Tonga with *Cherokee*, *Maritime Express* and *Renaitre*. Gail could not hold her normal watches because she was too dizzy. *Maritime Express* stayed close to *La Boatique* so that we could keep a lookout for them. The conditions were pleasant with wind at our back. The wind was either just right or too light. Off and on we ran the motor to assist the sails. During the trip we crossed the International Date Line so September 6$^{th}$ never happened. Instead of being 7 hours behind Ohio time we were 19 hours ahead of Ohio time. That meant that our date was always one day ahead of the date in the U.S.

Anchorage Number 1 in the Vavau group of Tonga

Dinghies moored at Ana's Waterfront Cafe in Tonga. Ana's was the place to meet other yachties.

# Tonga

Tonga, like Tahiti, was another meeting place where the cruising yachts gathered. The anchorages were many and well protected from the ocean swells. We enjoyed the calm restful nights.

Left, Catholic church in the town of Neiafu, Right, Free Church of Tonga in the small village of Tefisi.

September 12$^{th}$ (now known as 911 in the U.S) found us anchored in a calm clear uninhabited bay off a tiny island in the Kingdom of Tonga. Henry and Gail were anchored a few miles away. Gail was beginning to show signs of recovering from the shingles. Gail woke up about 4:30 a.m. She did not feel like going back to bed so she turned on the SSB radio for company. The words she heard in the early morning darkness seemed to be from a science fiction radio melodrama. But no, this was real. She woke up Henry. Henry announced on the VHF radio for all U.S. boats to turn on their SSB radios to the Voice of America or the BBC. We scrambled out of bed at 5:20 a.m. Pete turned the dials on our SSB radio and was able to pick up the BBC broadcast. The voice was often distorted and difficult to follow. We sat stunned in the early morning darkness listening for news of the airplane crashes that had occurred only 4 hours ago in New York. For the next three hours we listened to the broadcasts from the BBC and Voice of America. The SSB radio does not work well during the daylight hours, so we turned it off after the sun rose high in the sky. My thoughts were of New York. I remembered our evening anchored next to the Stature of Liberty with the twin towers standing above the New York skyline. We spent the rest of the day quietly walking ashore discussing the terrorists' attacks with the other cruisers in our anchorage. The boats were from the U.S., South Africa and Germany. As the days went by we continued to listen to the SSB radio for news. A few days later we took *La*

*Boatique* to the town of Neiafu where we were able to watch the BBC World News on a television in the bar at a hotel. The television was the only one with satellite coverage available for hundreds of miles.

Tongan boys dance a raucous warlike dance with clubs.

While in Tonga we had lots of time for sight seeing. Sometimes Pete and I went together on trips and sometimes we split up. We went snorkeling, dinghy exploring, hiking, biking and kayaking. Nearly every Friday Pete raced in the Tonga Friday Fun Race on a cruising boat named *Aurora.* On Friday, September 28th, the crew of *Aurora* dressed up in coconut shell bras and bandanna hats. Their teamwork was perfect and they won the race in a fleet of 15 yachts.

Tonga is known for its large population of whales and from *La Boatique* we often saw humpback whales with their babies. We saw a lot more of the babies since they needed to surface often for air. Many of our friends were lucky enough to be able to swim with the whales.

Pete had wanted to learn to scuba dive for years. He finally took the PADI Open Water Diver course while in Tonga. Tonga was a perfect spot for the course. The water was warm and clear. The cost was inexpensive. The views of fish and coral were spectacular.

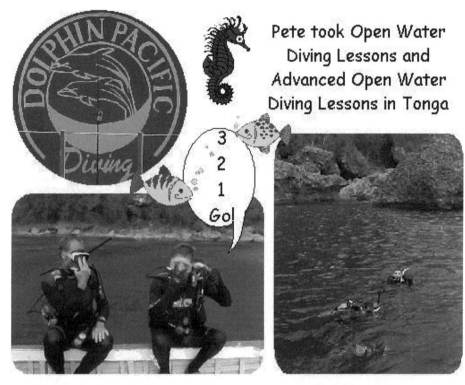

Pete took Open Water
Diving Lessons and
Advanced Open Water
Diving Lessons in Tonga

3
2
1
Go!

The story behind Pete learning to scuba dive began with a simple good deed.

Over the VHF radio one morning came a request for contact lens cleaner. There was no response. Pete began digging deep through a few drawers and found what he was looking for. Pete put a response out on the VHF radio and declared that he had contact lens cleaner. He no longer used contact lenses since he had LASIK eye surgery in Venezuela. A few hours later a powerboat from Dolphin Diving pulled along side us. The crew aboard requested the contact lens solution. Pete asked if Dolphin Diving gave scuba lessons. They sure did.

A few days later Pete dropped in to the Dolphin Diving office. The cost for the PADI open water diving course was only $150, less than half the cost charged elsewhere. Pete signed up.

Pete spent a week carefully studying the course material. He watched the PADI video over and over. By the first day of the course he was more than ready. He ended up being the only student. His instructor was a beautiful tall slender woman named Aroha. Because of all his previous studying Pete was able to breeze through the printed material and tests. He was ready for diving his first day.

The first day he did two dives and was in the water 124 minutes. The second day he did two more dives, completed the course, and passed the final exam. Two days later he did three dives from a boat that included the film crew from a popular magazine. Pete saw giant clams with a length of 2 feet. He also saw green and yellow sea horses 6-inches long. Pete enjoyed the open water diving course so much that he decided to sign up for the advanced diving course. During the advanced course he dove down to 100 feet. He dove through tunnels and into caves. Swirling sea slugs called Spanish Dancers with bright yellow and red "skirts" entertained him during his night dive. During one dive he heard the endangered humpback whales conversing and singing. Then from the depths of the ocean a whale approached and swam by.

John and Colleen from Bow Bells enter Swallows Cave near anchorage number 7.

If that wasn't enough excitement, on September 28th a new volcanic island over a mile long was born in the Pacific Ocean only 25 miles from our anchorage in Tonga. By the next day it had doubled in size to two miles long.

From Tonga to Fiji islands appear and disappear at an alarming rate. The two-mile long island that rose from the depths of the ocean on September 28$^{th}$ sank back into the ocean and disappeared in less than a month. It left behind a boiling hot turbulent area in the sea.

Our sail through the 170 small islands that made up the Kingdom of Tonga covered about 200 miles. The islands of Tonga are in three main groups. Less than 100,000 people live in all of Tonga. The Vavau group is to the north. This group was one of the main destinations for cruising yachts in the South Pacific. We spent over a month in Vavau and really enjoyed ourselves. There were so many anchorages in Vavau that they were given numbers beginning with 1 and ending with 42. Anchorages 1 and 7 were our favorites. Anchorage 1 was off the town of Neiafu and was a good place for restocking, restaurants, bike riding and laundry. Anchorage 7 was in an uninhabited bay with a big sandy beach. Anchorage 7 was close to Swallows Cave. Anchorage 7 was a great place for snorkeling, diving, kayaking, swimming, wilderness walks, and beach barbeques.

The middle group of islands is called the Ha'apai group. These islands did not offer the protection from bad weather offered by the Vavau group. Many dangerous reefs hid just below the ocean's surface. The reefs were not well charted. The islands were a difficult cruising ground and were often bypassed by cruising yachts. We had to keep a close eye on the weather during our stay in the Ha'apai group. If the wind turned to the west we would have to leave immediately and head out to sea directly into the weather.

Our 68-mile sail south to the Ha'apai group from the Vavau group began on October 15$^{th}$ at 5 p.m. We had to sail during the night so that we would have plenty of daylight to cover the final 15 miles of reef-strewn water. Traveling with us were the yachts *Mirage, Bow Bells* and *Renaitre*. For the first time in a long time we had to sail to weather. Sailing close to the wind pounding through the seas certainly was not as nice as gliding along with the wind and waves from our stern.

About the time the water became shallow we landed two mahi-mahis and *Bow Bells* landed one barracuda. We were about to approach the Ha'apai group.

Our destination was Ha'afeva, one of the western most of the anchorages in the Ha'apai group. The island of Ha'afeva offered better weather protection and less travel through reefs than most of the islands in the group. By 10:30 a.m. on October 16$^{th}$ we had the anchor down. Ha'afeva had a superb new cement landing dock for our dinghies. However, there was no habitation within sight of the anchorage or the dock. Surf, breaking reefs and a sandy beach rimmed the oval shaped island. We saw no business, no industry and only subsistence gardening. The largest buildings on the island were the five churches. The largest of the five tiny stores was about 8 feet by 15 feet. About the only food Pete saw to purchase were pieces of hard candy. Pete enjoyed handing out the candy to the children on the island.

Since we had plenty of fish for all the yachts with the 2 mahi-mahis that we caught, John and Colleen from *Bow Bells* decided to give their fish to islanders. The present of the fish to a family foraging along the shoreline began our relationship with an island family. The family composed of a mother, father and two children. The grandparents and other relatives lived in nearby homes. The "homes" were composed of small one-room buildings. One building was for cooking and eating. Cooking was done over a wood fire. I saw no electricity and no refrigeration in the cooking building. One building

Mike on *Renaitre* with a mahi-mahi.

223

was for sleeping. One building seemed to be for storage. Pigs, chickens and dogs wandered around the yard. A large multi-family garden was way back behind the buildings. Coconuts seemed to be the preferred food for the people, the pigs, the chickens, and even the dogs. People walked or rode horses. We saw no cars and no gas stations in the Ha'apai islands.

On October 19th we sailed from Ha'afeva to Numuka Iki. Iki must mean tiny since we anchored off a tiny island near Numuka. The tiny island was called Numuka Iki. We did this trip with *Mirage, Bow Bells, Renaitre* and a large Nordhaven motor yacht called *Rover*. Only a few motor yachts crossed the Pacific Ocean during the season that we crossed. The motor yachts were all Nordhavens and all needed to carry thousands of gallons of diesel fuel. *Mirage* and *Renaitre* landed mahi-mahis during the sail. No one lives on the island of Numuka Iki. We walked completely around the island but did not travel far from shore. We harvested wild papayas and had a fire on the beach. We dinghied a half mile to Numuka where we visited with the inhabitants. Pete passed out candy to the children. We saw a number of people on horseback. Just off the beach we noticed a water desalinization plant. However, the diesel motor running the desalinization unit had stopped working. The expensive unit sat idle since no one knew how to fix it. There were plenty of churches but only one tiny store about 6 feet by 10 feet selling a few canned items. We were hoping to find bread and eggs, but no luck. Pete snorkeled with most of the others and found the snorkeling the best he had seen. The coral was lively and the fish and sharks were large and many. There were a few too many 6 foot sharks for comfort but Pete figured with all the fish around the sharks were not hungry.

We had a fun day of sailing on October 22nd. We had a 56-mile day sail with *Bow Bells, Silver Heels* and *Renaitre*. The easy breeze was just aft of abeam. The breeze filled the jib, mainsail and mizzen sails. The ocean swell was nil. It was one of those great days of a nice dream where the sailing is on calm water past small palm-fringed sandy islands. Boobies and petrels soared and dove for fish. John and Colleen on *Bow Bells* landed two large fish. Then we landed two mahi-mahis. Finally Mike on *Renaitre* also landed two fish. Joan and Andy on *Silver Heels* don't fish. With all the fish we would not need to purchase any meat for our trip south to New Zealand.

We arrived at Nuku'alofa, the capital city of Tonga in the late afternoon. The wind was beginning to build and the sky was filling

224

with clouds. The good weather along with our sail was coming to an end. Nuku'alofa has a yacht basin well protected from the ocean. However, only about 25 to 30 yachts can fit in the basin. Luckily, there was room for us. We dropped our anchor in the center of the channel and then ran lines from our stern to the wharf ashore. All the yachts, both large and small formed a line along the wharf. When the weather turned bad, as is did for the next few days, we were safe and snug. We did not have time for sight seeing while in Nuku'alofa since we spent our time getting ready to sail for 8 to 10 days to New Zealand.

## Tonga to New Zealand

Cyclone season begins in the South Pacific in November. We needed to head to cold ocean water to get out of the cyclone belt. According to the book, <u>The Pacific Crossing Guide</u>, the 1100-mile passage from Tonga to New Zealand is more demanding than any other across the Pacific. We were apprehensive. This would be our second longest passage. It seemed to me that most of our time in Nuku'alofa, Tonga was spent discussing strategies for the trip to New Zealand and the weather. Every day we would listen to our single side band radio. The radio was tuned to Des from Russell Radio broadcasting from New Zealand. Des would predict the weather for each boat heading south to New Zealand. Before our trip and every day during our trip he gave us weather forecasts and helped us to decide our course of action. He did an excellent job and helped us to avoid nasty weather.

**October 27, Day 1**

We departed Nuku'alofa at 8:30 a.m. With us were *Bow Bells, Silver Heels,* and *Renaitre. Cherokee* and *PJ's Dream* had left the day before. The sky was blue. The Pacific showed us its peaceful side. The wind was a pleasant 12 knots. We decided not to fish since we had plenty of fish in the freezer.

We spotted a large group of pilot whales, at least 20 in total. About an hour later we saw the back of a humpback whale off our starboard bow. The whale was at least as long as *La Boatique.* It looked like it might go directly in front of us. Colleen from *Bow Bells* also saw it and called us on the VHF to make sure that we had spotted it. I was quite concerned that the huge whale would collide with the bow of our boat.

Pete said, "No, we will be fine."

Since we were motor sailing, I had my hand on the throttle ready to put the boat in neutral. The whale passed ten feet off the bow and then went below the surface and we never saw it again.

One of the many humpback whales we saw while in Tonga

### October 28, Day 2

We left knowing that there was a weak high-pressure system covering a very large area. The average wind was about 9 knots from the east. That put the wind on the beam, good for us. Also with only 9 knots of wind the ocean was pleasant, no big swell or waves. We ran the engine for all but about 4 hours during the first two days in order to keep our speed up. This is a notoriously difficult passage, so the quicker we got through it the less chance we would have to get hit by bad weather. So far the trip had been extremely easy. The weather forecast from Des was for continued light wind.

We were eating well, getting plenty of rest and even getting hot showers.

*Renaitre* had fallen way behind because he did not have enough fuel to motor for long. *Silver Heels* and *Bow Bells* were still within sight.

### October 29, Day 3

The conditions were so easy that I enjoyed reading a book. I read The Sea Wolf by Jack London. This is a classic book written in 1904 about hunting seals in the North Pacific. I enjoyed reading sea tales while at sea and making the comparisons between the conditions on *La Boatique* and the conditions described in the books. The conditions in the books were always worse. So that made me appreciate the weather we were getting even more.

By 7 p.m. the ocean was flat calm. There was not even the usual ocean swell. But the motor was running all the time using up our supply of fuel.

### October 30, Day 4

There was scarcely a breath of a breeze. The engine continued to run. The sails provided only a little assistance to the motor. We were beginning to worry about having enough fuel. We were burning 0.7 gallons per hour. We had 96 gallons left. And we had a little over 700 miles to go. We were making 5.2 knots. We hoped for favorable wind soon. We needed to keep fuel reserves. We could not afford to continue to burn fuel at this rate.

Finally, at 5 p.m. the wind arrived and we sailed along at 5 to 6 knots. But during the night the wind dropped off and the motor was started again.

### October 31, Day 5

Fuel consumption continued to be disconcerting. Pete tried raising the spinnaker. But we had so little wind that it collapsed and would not billow out over the bow of the boat.

We reached the halfway point. *Bow Bells* offered to supply us with some of their fuel. Pete took them up on the offer. Just when we decided to catch up with *Bow Bells*, we hooked a mahi-mahi. We brought it aboard and cleaned it.

At about 6 p.m. we rendezvoused with *Bow Bells*. They passed us two 6-gallon jerry cans of fuel. We passed them fresh fish for dinner.

Minutes later the wind picked up and we were sailing along. During the Halloween night under a full moon we were flying along at 7 knots. The moon was so bright that I could see few stars. I missed watching the stars at night.

### November 1, Day 6

The great wind conditions and fast sailing continued. We saw our first ship, a huge bulk carrier too big to fit through the Panama Canal.

Pete rested most of the morning while I rested most of the afternoon. Then at night we went on our usual three-hour shifts. I started the first shift at 7 p.m. Pete began the second shift at 10 p.m. I returned on watch for the third shift at 1 a.m. Pete began the last shift at 4 a.m.

### November 2, Day 7

We had a 0.7 knot current against us. The going was slow. The sky was clear blue and the weather was fine. In fact, we had unbelievably calm and pleasant weather. But bad weather was on the way.

### November 3, Day 8

I suspected that my birthday would be our last full day and night at sea for a long, long time and I was right. I tried to savor every bit of the day and night even though the weather was not kind. Pete was ready for the long overnight passages to end. He was not tired of living on the boat but he was tired of the rigors involved with the cruising lifestyle. I hoped that after a long break in New Zealand he would be ready to cruise again.

# The Sue's Birthday Storm

Our easy traveling conditions ended on my birthday. The forecast was for bad weather. This day would prove to be a very eventful day. It would be our last full day of our last long passage in the South Pacific. The South Pacific decided to be a spurned lover giving us a spiteful goodbye. After being so gentle with us, the Pacific threw at us the biggest seas and highest winds we had ever received during our entire time sailing out on this ocean.

At 1 a.m. on November 3<sup>rd</sup> with calm seas, a gentle breeze on our beam filled our sails. By 4 a.m. the wind built to 20 knots and moved to our stern. The morning was hot and muggy. By 8 a.m. the seas had built to 8 feet and the warm north wind was sucking us south into the path of the storms. We altered course to a more westerly set in anticipation of southwest winds. With our more westerly course we also hoped to avoid the worst of the weather.

At 11 a.m. the weather ahead of us looked worrisome. Dark cumulonimbus storm clouds towered ahead of us. And yet, 23 knots of wind and 9 foot seas pushed us on toward the storm. We were ready with only a tiny amount of sail raised. Our mainsail was set with a triple reef. Boats ahead of us like *PJ's Dream* and *Cherokee* reported 40 knots of wind for sustained periods. The storm raced along to the east-northeast as we moved to the west-southwest.

The first squall hit us at noon with a blast of cold air. There would be no lunch on this day.

The wind held at 30 knots and gusted to 35. Big seas hit *La Boatique* and threw spray in the air.

Splat!

The thick salt spray buffeted the dodger, side curtains and bimini top over my head. Pete installed the hatch boards so that if water got in the cockpit it would not then flow down into our cabin. The gusts blasted at us from the north, west and south. But the storm was moving so fast to the east that the worst of it blew by in front of us.

Additional squalls blew upon us, but they were nowhere near as intense as the first one.

The wind changed to the southwest at 20 to 30 knots. A current pushed us east. With the sails up and the motor running we could not hold our desired course. New Zealand was only 70 miles away, but on our course we would miss the island.

**November 4, Day 9**

Astonishingly during the night the current reversed itself. We could easily hold our course. Our speed increased to 7 knots. As far as I was concerned my birthday present was being bypassed by the worst of the storm and having the current unexpectedly change in our favor.

The green hills of New Zealand presented themselves in front of us at dawn. The seas calmed. The sky cleared. The bright sun warmed the cool air. Our 9-day passage to Opua, in northern New Zealand was soon concluded. By 10 a.m. we were tied to the customs dock.

# New Zealand

We arrived in New Zealand on one of the few warm sunny days. We saw very few days of sunshine and many days of gale force wind. We spent our first week in New Zealand tied to a mooring ball in a beautiful bay off Opua. On November 13th we moved from the mooring ball to the comforts of a dock at the Opua Marina. The Opua Marina was only one year old and was first class. We had not seen such a nice marina since we stayed at Anchorage Marina in Baltimore, Maryland. The two marinas may have a lot of similarities but the surroundings could not be more different. Anchorage marina was in the heart of a very big city. Opua Marina was in the heart of scenic green countryside. We could walk to a large assortment of restaurants from Anchorage marina while no place served food most days in Opua.

Our home for the cyclone season, Opua Marina

Since our plan was to stay for the cyclone season and beyond we splurged on some comforts. Pete got a great deal on a car, a Suzuki Swift for only US $350. We adapted *La Boatique* to handle the New Zealand power of 240 volts. Since we could not run our old appliances on 240 volts we bought a small heater, a television, a toaster, and a heating element for our hot water tank. With all the rainy days, those items made life more livable.

We were becoming part of the local community. Pete and I often took turns speaking on the morning net on Tuesdays and Fridays. Running the net was like being a radio talk show host for a 20-minute program with no commercials.

New Zealand does not celebrate Thanksgiving Day as we do in the U.S. However, traditionally a big turkey dinner was served at the Opua Cruising Club. A lot of cruisers from the U.S. were in Opua during late November. Julius (from *Argonauta*) and I helped a few local club members carve the turkeys. For about U.S. $3 the club provided the turkeys, dressing, gravy, potatoes and cranberry sauce. Each family brought a side dish or a dessert. About 150 people showed up, a much larger crowd than I expected.

After Thanksgiving Day most of the cruisers headed south toward the Auckland area. We decided to stay based in the far northern area of New Zealand. Northern New Zealand was sparsely inhabited, had magnificent scenery, but still offered most services that cruising boats needed. From our investigations we found the Opua Marina to be the nicest in New Zealand. However, this cruising area was not the least expensive. So, there were the usual trade-offs.

The place to hang out in Opua was the Opua Cruising Club. The club was open all day and served free water, coffee and tea during the day. It was open on Sunday, Wednesday and Friday evenings for dinner with a limited menu. Usually on those days sailboat races began and ended at the club. The cruising boats rarely raced. The boats that did race were designed for racing. I was able to race once in December before the spring racing season ended. I liked racing so much that I thought I would try to race again once the summer season began in January.

# The Chain Gang

One day after dinner at the Opua Cruising Club Terry, from the boat *Stella,* asked Pete if we would be interested in having our anchor and chain re-galvanized. After a year of anchoring over rocks and coral nearly everyone's anchors and chain had seen a lot of wear. Yes, we needed re-galvanizing work done. Avon Industries would do the work, but they wanted chain from a few boats before they geared up their equipment. We asked around and then put the word out on the morning net. We were expecting anchors and chain from maybe 6 to 10 boats. Unexpectedly, 28 cruisers brought us their anchors and chain. Most cruisers brought more than one anchor. With that many boats involved, we had a real coordination effort at hand. Terry, his wife Arial, Pete and I spent hours trying to keep track of money and orders. The total came to about $10,000 New Zealand dollars, a very large order for Avon Industries. Pete and Terry made many phone calls and hour-long trips to Avon Industries to check on the progress. Avon Industries was overwhelmed with all the anchors and chain we had delivered. So was the trucking company. But it all worked out for the best. When the anchors and chain were delivered a week later, they were all bright silver colored and all looked better than new.

Most of the cruising boats that sailed across the Pacific with us were settled for cyclone season on the north island of New Zealand. With us in Opua were *Argonauta, Calypso, Renaitre* and *Auror*a. About an hour's car drive south in Whangarei were *Bow Bells* and *Silver Heels*. Further south yet near Auckland at Gulf Harbour Marina was *Cherokee*. Then furthest away at Tauranga Bridge Marina were *Aldebaran, Maritime Express*, and *Some Day is Here*.

# Tiny Biting Flies

Before we got to New Zealand, no one warned us of the terrible little black sand flies. They hung around near the water and especially by the boats. They were not fast but they sure did bite. The bite itched at first and then the itching stopped until night and then it itched like crazy. Then the next day the bite area became swollen and made a red circle about an inch around. Then it itched nearly all the time. The swelling went away after a day or so but the itching continued on and off for a week or more. Then we were left with a red dot that lasted for weeks. We wore long pants and long sleeves when it was cold but when it was hot I wore shorts and took my chances. I got lots of bites. Pete continued to wear long pants. We kept screens up to try to keep the pesky flies out of the boat.

# Work, Work, Work for Pete

Once we got to New Zealand it did not take Pete long to get to work.

Pete got busy working on *La Boatique* and many other boats. Pete's reputation for fixing things preceded him. So cruising boats with engine problems were lined up waiting for Pete's expertise. Pete did not mind the work since he enjoyed being the local expert. Pete went from being a man without a purpose to a man enjoying life with goals once again. He went from working on our fellow cruising boats to working on New Zealand sailing yachts, sport fishing boats and ferryboats. He was becoming renowned in the area for his mechanical skills.

Our refrigerator had worked fine until we got to New Zealand. About the time we got to New Zealand the refrigerator started running more and more often. As time went by it no longer kept our food cold. We suspected that we had a small leak in the line containing the refrigerant. But we could not find the leak. Pete decided to replace the evaporator and the refrigerant lines. The evaporator is the cold box inside of the refrigerator. When we pulled out the old evaporator and lines Pete found a tiny leak where an old nail had rubbed against the line. We got rid of that nail. We snaked new lines under the cabin sole from the refrigerator to the compressor. Then we had a man come and add refrigerant and test the system. Pete changed the oil and filters in the engine and then changed the oil in the transmission. He rebuilt the hydraulic steering cylinder. He worked on replacing the worn out exhaust system. The exhaust system was a challenge since the parts Pete wanted were not available. Pete had to improvise with what he could find and have made. Pete thought that New Zealand was a nice place to relax and fairly inexpensive.

On December 23rd Pete painted inside the galley lockers. The boat smelled of paint and all the stuff in the lockers was lying around. To stay out of the mess I went kayaking up the river. The river wound its way through surrounding landscape that was hilly and many shades of green. I saw black and white birds that looked like cormorants hanging their wings out to dry while they perched on a large overhanging tree branch. I stopped paddling long enough to watch a white-faced blue heron wade out from shore and catch a fish. Then as I paddled around a bend in the center of the now shallow river, right in front of me I caught sight of a swan — a majestic black swan with its long graceful neck. There were many lovely bays within paddling distance of the marina and I often went exploring on the kayak. Pete and I both spotted penguins. A little blue penguin even spent time in the marina.

The shoreline near the marina was bordered with hiking trails that often poked through the surrounding rain forest covered hills. I took a walk on a trail nearly every day. I often walked with other cruisers like Frank and Teresa (*Dannsa De Marra*, Scotland) or Barry and Lynne (*Sunrise*, California). The aromas from fragrant flowers and the pine scent of tea trees made each breath a pleasure. By the water were the peaceful sounds of gentle lapping waves and sea birds. In places in the forest we had to shout to be heard over the buzzing of the cicadas. On rare days bright colored parrots could be heard conversing in the treetops.

Sometimes I felt sorry for Pete missing out on the kayak trips and the hiking trails. But he enjoyed tinkering and got real satisfaction out of fixing things. He preferred getting an engine running smoothly to tramping through the forest. Opua was a place where Pete could work on engines while I could explore forests and streams.

# 2001 Down the Drain

The year of 2001 ended with long and beautiful summer days sunny and warm. Sally and Julius (*Argonauta*) invited me to ride along with them for a drive north to Kerikeri and Kawakawa. While in Kawakawa I took a few pictures. Sally and I smiled for the camera at Kawakawa's tourist destination, the public toilets. The public toilets in Kawakawa were a work of eclectic art. The door to the ladies' room had a propeller, a horseshoe, and an assortment of tools welded in the grate. Empty bottles were molded into the brick wall behind us as we stood in front of the building. Kawakawa was inland from Opua and lay in a valley. The tiny town did not have the majestic views most other towns had so it relied on its toilets to draw tourists. We visited the Kawakawa toilets on the last day of 2001. In other words, we flushed 2001 down the drain at Kawakawa.

# 2002

Tall Ships Race

## Tall Ships Race

On January 6th both Pete and I raced on *Aurora* in the Tall Ships Race. The race began a few miles from Opua in the Bay of Islands outside of the small town of Russell. Only boats with more than one mast or boats over 30 years old can enter this race. Rob, the skipper told us that there were about 100 boats racing. All the boats started at the same time. With all the congestion we did not get a good start. We ended up placing 27th in our division of classic yachts over 30 years old. We dealt with fog, rain, light wind, no wind, a tiny bit of sunshine and strong wind all in less than four hours. We enjoyed watching the assortment of sailing yachts and the rugged coastline scenery.

## Small Ships Race

In January I began racing often. I was having so much fun racing that I raced every chance that I could get. That meant racing every Wednesday and Friday. There was a practice on a Thursday. And then there was one race on a Saturday and twice I raced on a

Sunday. At the beginning of the year I would stand around near race time in my racing attire and hope that someone would need crew. Then as the month went by I had my choice of boats. Lots of skippers began requesting that I race with them. I raced on boats from 40 feet down to 15 feet long. Tony Atkinson asked me if I would be his crew on his 15 foot long Flying Fifteen sailboat in the Little Ships Race. I was glad he asked. Sure, I would race on his boat named *Firebird*.

The prestigious Tall Ships Race from Russell, New Zealand, drew about 100 boats. Two weeks later the Small Ships Race also began in Russell. The race was small, all right; only about 10 boats showed up for the starting gun. To qualify for this race, the racing sailboats had to be less than 31 feet in length. The course was about 15 miles long, a long course for a small boat. Added to the mileage of the race, we had to sail about 2 miles to the starting line and then back toward Opua. We ended up being out on the water for about 6 hours in an open boat with only a bucket for a toilet.

I raced on all three of these boats, Titan (top left), California Kiwi (top right) and Fforte (bottom left).

The weather was unkind. As we headed out away from land a squall line approached. I quickly put on my bright yellow foul weather jacket. I would have liked to have slipped on my foul weather pants, but that task appeared too difficult on the heeling, bouncing boat. The wind gusted from 20 to 30 knots and built up three-foot waves. In the small boat we were only a foot from the water. We leaned back as far over the windward edge of the heeling boat as we could. Our tummy muscles were getting a great workout. The waves smashed against the gunwale lifting the boat. The spray from the crashing waves drenched me with salt water. Then the rain pelted down upon us. Cold water was finding its way inside my yellow jacket while below my waist I was sopping wet. I was beginning to get cold. But we had to concentrate on sailing through the gusts and wind shifts. In the strong wind the Flying 15 was living up to its name and we seemed to often fly above the waves. This small keelboat can actually get up on a plane and then its waterline length does not limit its speed. A few minutes later I saw a glimpse of blue sky on the horizon.

The squall ended. The wind stopped. We drifted along for a few minutes until a light breeze returned. Bright sunshine warmed and dried my cold wet skin. The boat was level and the ride was gentle. We took turns eating sandwiches and drinking plenty of water. We were now on a new leg of the course and could raise the spinnaker. I decided that this was my best chance to make use of the bucket toilet. Trying to steer a straight course with the tiller while pulling my pants down and back on was difficult. While I was balancing this task Tony looked forward and manned the spinnaker. We circled an island out in the bay and headed for the finish line. We ended up placing third. The two boats that finished in front of us were twice our length. Considering our size, we had a great finish.

## The Awful Smell

I had a few sore muscles and bruises after the Small Ships Race. A warm Jacuzzi would have been nice. The next day when Lynne and Barry suggested searching for hot springs hidden in a mangrove forest with their dinghy I was ready. We dinghied to the correct bay. We smelled the telltale sulfur odor. When we put our hands in the water, the water felt quite warm. With the dinghy engine off we grabbed at mangrove branches to claw our way deep into the watery forest. But we could not find any hot bubbling water. We saw a building near the shore with a dock on the other side of the bay so we thought we might ask for directions. We found out that the building was part of an oyster farm. The oyster farmer told us that the hot springs were in the bay in water about four feet deep. There was really nothing to see. If we wanted to soak in some natural hot springs we would have about a

15-mile car drive inland. So we decided we would search out the inland hot springs the next day.

Frank and Theresa decided to join us. The entry fee was $3 NZ ($1.25US) per person. The sulfur odor at the hot springs was quite pungent. All the owners of the Ginn Ngawha Hot Springs needed to do to get hot water was to dig a shallow hole. I decided to test the temperature with my fingers before I stepped in. After all, the ugly brown water looked boiling hot, had a scum on top, and smelled awful. Theresa got right in the hot water followed by Lynne. Barry and Frank soon were also soaking in various pools. We found that the bottom of the pools were sandy. The temperature of the pools varied from way too hot, to just right, to warm, to cool. When we got out of the Hot Springs we had sand all over inside our bathing suits and we smelled like sulfur for days.

Top left, Sue tests the water. Top right, Lynne is on the step. Theresa is in the water.

On February 4th with mixed emotions I flew to the cold winter of Ohio. I had a year and a half's worth of mail and paperwork to sort through. Pete continued to work on all sorts of boats in New Zealand. He also worked on an assortment of boat projects on *La Boatique* including remodeling the front head.

238

# Dream of a Lifetime

Sailing far away to an exotic tropical paradise is a dream for many. But a trip across the Pacific takes a real commitment. We put a lot of thought into our decision to cross the Pacific Ocean.

Pete's health was a major concern. Since we began cruising Pete had gone through operations for both a hernia and kidney stones. His chances of having reoccurring kidney stone problems were high unless he made the correct changes to his diet. He needed to greatly increase his intake of water and reduce his milk intake. Still, a reoccurring kidney stone was a possibility. If something happened to Pete I might have to care for him and sail the boat.

What if we changed our minds and wanted to stop? Sailing with the trade winds for days on end would be no piece of cake, but turning back toward America could only be done by sailing far to the north or south.

*La Boatique* would be an unstable working platform. A task like boiling water for spaghetti could be difficult and dangerous. Slips could occur and bones could be broken while working on a heaving deck reefing the sails or extending the long and heavy whisker pole.

*La Boatique* was built for ocean trade wind sailing. The sails, rigging and engine had been thoroughly checked and repairs and replacements completed. Plenty of tools and spare parts filled many lockers. Purchasing boat parts anywhere in the South Pacific would be nearly impossible and extremely expensive. We carried 70 gallons of fresh water and had a reverse osmosis water maker. But fresh water would be scarce if our water maker broke.

Would *La Boatique* make it intact across the Pacific? We could have a collision with an unseen whale during a dark night. A small mistake in navigation could have our floating home torn apart by crashing surf on a coral reef.

Would the weather be kind to us? Would a severe storm or even a cyclone blow upon us?

How many of our cruising friends would become injured or ill? Would boats be lost at sea?

**Would anyone die?**

We prepared the best we could and then did not dwell on the pessimistic possibilities.

Sally and Julius

The fact was that our trip across the Pacific made a Pacific-crossing look easy. After all, we had no severe storms. A cyclone hit Tonga a month after we departed but by then we were safe in New Zealand. Pete stayed healthy. We had a few colds, a touch of the flu and bouts of travelers' diarrhea. Our illnesses were insignificant. Neither of us got injured. *La Boatique* showed little wear and tear after the long ordeal.

Our cruising friends did not fare as well.

Julius and Sally and even their boat, *Argonauta,* all had their share of problems. *Argonauta's* headstay broke in 25-knot winds and 12-foot seas during the long passage from the Galapagos to the Marquesas. The headstay helps hold up the mast and without it the mast could have come crashing down on top of them. In the rough seas they were greatly challenged getting their roller-furling system down and the mast stabilized. Their troubles were not over when they reached the anchorage. During a dinghy ride to shore though large surf Sally got tossed overboard. She got bruised when she was run over by the dinghy and motor. Julius got a very high fever in the sparsely populated Tuamotus. He did not get malaria but he did get a disease almost as bad, dengue fever.

Henry and Gail on *Maritime Express* also had their share of problems. Henry was concerned about destroying the diesel engine on *Maritime Express* when he found diesel fuel mixed in the engine oil. Henry fell and broke his wrist in the Marquesas. The break was severe and required pins. He could not use his wrist for a long time. Gail was left to sail the boat and care for Henry. About the time

Henry and Gail

Henry finally recovered, Gail got shingles. She was unable to get the proper medical treatment that could have saved her great pain. The shingles spread across her neck and began to move onto her face. Her nervous system was affected. She became dizzy and had trouble standing. Her recovery has been slow.

We probably sailed the most with *Cherokee*. During the voyage Barry and Julie had no more trouble with illness than we did. *Cherokee* had few problems except that the in-boom roller-furling system used on the mainsail broke soon after they entered the Pacific. But they were able to sail along nicely using their spinnaker, jib, staysail and mizzen. Barry and Julie had an especially nice trip. They loved the spectacular scenery of Tahiti, Moorea and Bora Bora. Barry commented, "It doesn't get any better than this."

They, like us, made it all the way to New Zealand without much trouble. From New Zealand they flew to Houston, Texas to visit with friends and family. They must have had wonderful stories to tell of sailing their own boat across the Pacific. From Texas they flew back to their home, their boat, *Cherokee*. But then Julie and Barry decided to put *Cherokee* up for sale in New Zealand.

Pete, Barry, Sue and Julie during happy times in Panama January 2001.

After a pleasant walk on February 9th Barry bent down to take off his shoes. He keeled over from a massive heart attack. It was very sudden and quick and he felt no pain. He didn't even have time to cry out.

Just like that, he was dead. He will never have the chance to cruise again. He was a young 60 years old.

Barry Dobbs got to live his dream. That was not such a bad way to go. Then why was I crying?

I suspect it is not just Barry's death that had me upset. I was concerned that our sailing adventures may have come to an end. The political instability of our likely cruising grounds caused us concern. The monetary costs were magnified since our investments were not performing well. Furthermore, our emotional resoluteness and physical endurance were no longer as strong as before we headed across the Pacific Ocean. I wanted the sailing adventures of *La Boatique* to continue. But they ended on my birthday in the South Pacific with New Zealand just over the horizon.

# Epilogue

## Where do we go from here?

Where do we go from New Zealand? That question has been worrisome for both of us. Pete's dream was to sail to Tahiti. We did more than the dream by cruising all the way to New Zealand. We traveled nearly half way around the world on *La Boatique*. We had high adventure on the high seas and in exotic lands. From our research we realized the second half of a world cruise would involve more danger, many long passages, unfriendly destinations, and tougher ocean conditions.

During our time back in the United States we were able to appreciate so much more what we have in this country. Our mouths gaped in awe when we walked into our local Sears store and saw the abundance of appliances, hardware, and tools. We enjoyed the taste of real peanut butter once again. People in Ohio speak American English so we did not have to strain with a language barrier. I hate to admit it, but I enjoyed watching television once again. Once we left the U.S. we were foreigners in a foreign land. We were given a time limit in each country and then we had to move on. Our home was *La Boatique*, but our neighborhood was always changing. We realized during our travels that people in the United States and in Ohio especially, have a strong work ethic. We rarely saw much of a work ethic outside the U.S. Sure, the lifestyles of the people at our destinations were laid back and less hectic, but just try to get anything accomplished accurately and on time. Even when the people tried to work hard, the tools and supplies were often not available.

In foreign ports we were often told how lucky we were to be U.S. citizens. But we had to leave the U.S. for an extended period to see for ourselves how truly lucky we are. It is as if we went "over the rainbow" and then realized "there is no place like home." While Pete and I were together in Ohio we met the yacht, *Haven*. *La Boatique* is a superb cruising boat, but *Haven* seemed to open up a somewhat different cruising style that we now long for. The story of *Haven* will unfold in the years to come.

The decision to purchase *Haven* has helped us with our decision to sell *La Boatique*. In December 2002 *La Boatique* will be loaded on a ship that has been specifically designed to haul yachts across oceans. This ship, owned by a company called Dockwise Yacht Transport, will carry *La Boatique* from New Zealand to Tahiti, on through the Panama Canal, and end up in Florida in late January 2003.

# Appendix A

## About *La Boatique*

MAKE: TRANS WORLD CO., LTD

MODEL: ISLAND TRADER 41

PLACE BUILT:  TAIPEI TAIWAN, REPUBLIC OF CHINA

YEAR: 1979

HULL # 40

STYLE: Ketch

Designer:  Hardin

COLORS: White and Burgundy

LENGTH: 40'9"

LWL:  33'6"

LOA:   43'

HEIGHT:  52'  Main mast above the water

HEIGHT:  41'  Mizzenmast above the water

BEAM: 12'2"

DRAFT: 6'2"

DEADRISE: 4'

DISP.: 15 tons

BALLAST: 9500 pounds

HOLDING TANK: 20 gallons   fiberglass tank

FUEL:     56 gallons and 47 gallons = 103 gallons (358 liters) poly
tanks

WATER: 2 tanks X 35 gallons = 70 gallons  (259 liters) stainless
steel tanks

CONSTR.: Fiberglass Hull with Aluminum Masts

ENGINE MAKE: Perkins     MODEL: 4.108   50 HP

TRANSMISSION: Borg Warner Velvet Drive AS15-72C

PROP:  3 blade 1.25" Shaft. x 19.68" D x Self Pitching Feathering Autoprop

ELECTRICAL: 12 volt 120 amp alternator 520 amp hours house batteries

12 volt 115 amp starting battery

COOLING: fresh water

# Appendix B

List of Photographic Contributors:
Thank you for your contributions.

Mary Jane Arwine

Gregg Boehlor

Don Wogaman

Dierdre Wogaman

Barbara Albrecht

Marge Scrowcroft

Sally Jenks

Julius Fiorillo

Ken Moore

Brenda Collins

Susan Abel

Mike Fritz

Julie Dobbs

Barry Dobbs

Gail Souccoup

Henry Drew

John Mathie

Carl Cox

*Cherokee* sails past Moorea with Shark Tooth's Mountain in the distance. I can almost hear Barry saying, "It doesn't get any better than this."